MW01635528

A Second Look at Calgary's Public Art

Barbara Kwasny and Elaine Peake

DISCARD

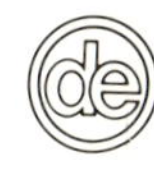

Detselig Enterprises Ltd.
Calgary, Alberta

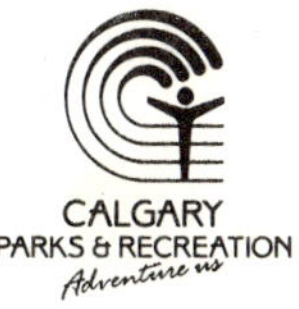

CALGARY PUBLIC LIBRARY

©1992 Barbara Kwasny and Elaine Peake

Canadian Cataloguing in Publication Data

Kwasny, Barbara.
A second look at Calgary's public art

Includes index.
ISBN 1-55059-041-3

1. Art, Municipal—Alberta—Calgary. 2. Public art—Alberta—Calgary. I. Peake, Elaine. II. Title.
N6547.C34K8 1992 7098.7123'38 C92-091194-3

Detselig Enterprises Ltd.
P.O. Box G 399
Calgary, Alberta
T3A 2G3

All rights reserved. No part of this book may be reproduced in any form or by any means without permission in writing from the publisher.

Printed in Canada SAN 115-0324 ISBN 1-55059-041-3

Acknowledgments

The authors acknowledge with thanks the support and encouragement offered by the City of Calgary, Parks and Recreation.

All photos by Barbara Kwasny except: p. 83, *Boundary Waters* - Hollis Williford; p. 144, *Speed Skater* - J.Weaver; p. 148, *Heroic Entrance* - Forbo Industries, Inc; p. 150, *Bas-Relief* - Geological Survey of Canada; p. 162, *Cross Country Skier (Spirit of the Winter Olympics)* - J. Weaver.

front cover: *The Wonderful Energy Machine* (1982) by Richard Prince.

Detselig Enterprises Ltd. appreciates the financial assistance for its1992 publishing program from Canada Council and the Alberta Foundation for the Arts.

Preface

A Second Look at Calgary's Public Art is an attempt to answer the *Five Ws* of some of Calgary's most visible art: Who did it? What does it mean? Where is it? Why was it done? When was it made? The book is not intended to be a critique of the artworks and, where possible, we have used the artist's own words to explain the piece.

Using these guidelines, we have produced what we hope is a handy companion for walking tours of the city, as well as a permanent record of Calgary's fascinating sculptured art.

The works covered are primarily statues, sculptures, carvings and sculptured murals. A few stained glass pieces are included, but only if they are part of a large collection of artworks in a defined space. What we consider to be architectural decoration has been omitted.

We set rather arbitrary limits on what constitutes public art. Our criteria? It must be readily accessible — outdoors, in lobbies or in public areas of a building. It must also be on a permanent site, or as permanent as anything is these days, and in a location that does not charge admission.

The book is an update of a 1977 edition, and we are delighted at the number of new artworks that have appeared in the city in the past fifteen years. Thanks to the 1988 Calgary Olympics, and an increasing awareness of the need to include art in our parks and new buildings, this book has twice the entries of our first, *Look at Calgary's Public Art*.

We hope it brings you pleasure.

Barbara Kwasny and Elaine Peake
1992

Since the early 70s, Calgary Parks and Recreation has had a broad interest and involvement in the placement of artwork in the public domain. As you read *A Second Look at Calgary's Public Art*, you will see how our beautiful parks and open spaces are enhanced with visual representations by local, regional, national and international artists. Calgary Parks and Recreation are pleased to have played a role in the publication of this book.

For more information, advice or assistance in arts or cultural activities — or if you have questions about or problems finding an artwork shown in the book, contact:

The Cultural Resource Centre
268-5207

Joyce Chorny
Supervisor of Cultural Services

Contents

East of Centre Street 7

West of Centre Street 41

City Parks 95

Post-secondary Institutions 113

Northwest 149

Northeast 159

Miscellaneous 165

Artists' Biographies 173

Glossary of Terms 204

Index 205

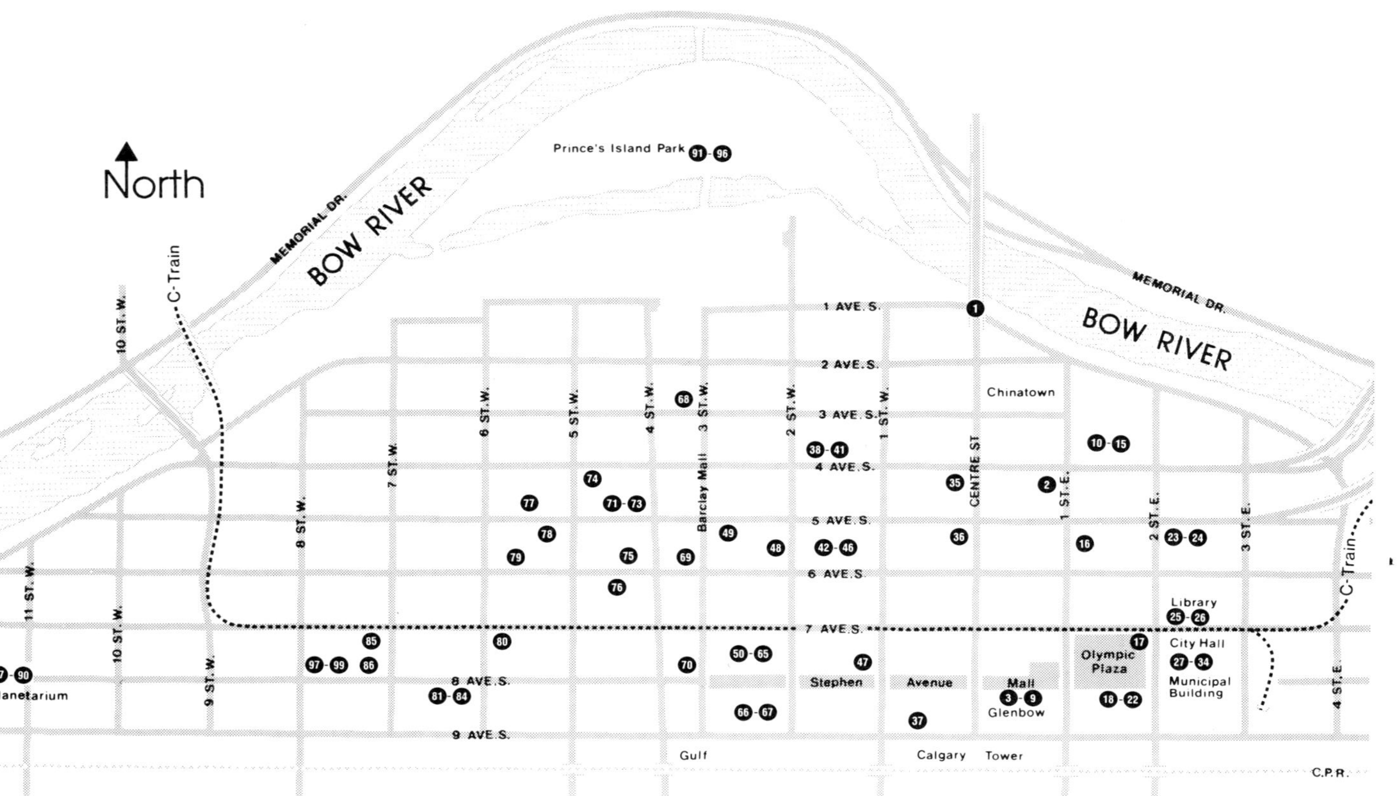
North
BOW RIVER
MEMORIAL DR.
BOW RIVER
MEMORIAL DR.
Prince's Island Park 91-96
C-Train
C-Train
1 AVE. S.
2 AVE. S.
3 AVE. S.
4 AVE. S.
5 AVE. S.
6 AVE. S.
7 AVE. S.
8 AVE. S.
9 AVE. S.
11 ST. W.
10 ST. W.
10 ST. W.
9 ST. W.
8 ST. W.
7 ST. W.
6 ST. W.
5 ST. W.
4 ST. W.
3 ST. W.
Barclay Mall
2 ST. W.
1 ST. W.
CENTRE ST
1 ST. E.
2 ST. E.
3 ST. E.
4 ST. E.
Chinatown
Library
25-26
City Hall
27-34
Municipal Building
Olympic Plaza
Stephen Avenue Mall
Glenbow
Calgary Tower
Gulf
Planetarium
87-90
C.P.R.
1
2
3-9
10-15
16
17
18-22
23-24
35
36
37
38-41
42-46
47
48
49
50-65
66-67
68
69
70
71-73
74
75
76
77
78
79
80
81-84
85
86
97-99

East of Centre Street

1. The Lions

James L. Thomson

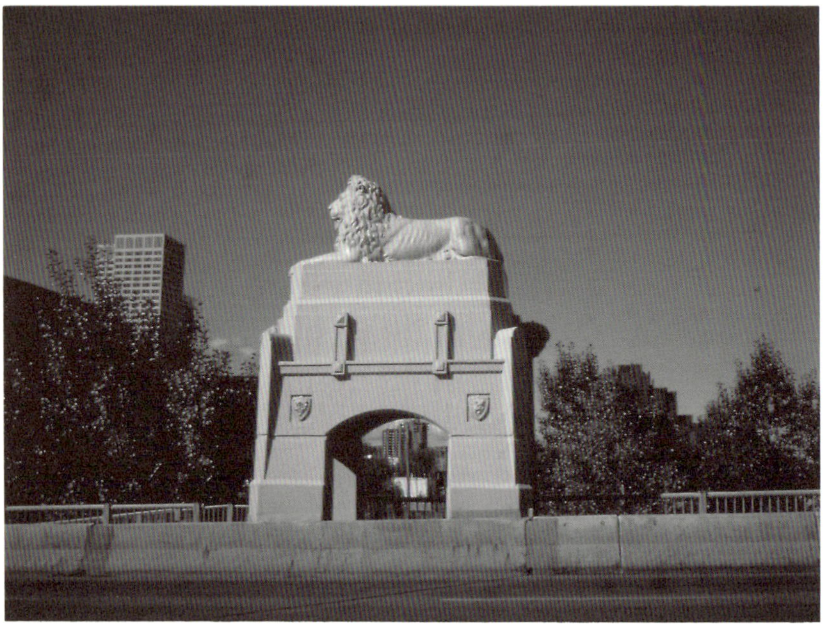

From their vantage points on Centre Street Bridge, four sculptured lions have kept a stony eye on Calgarians and their antics since 1916.

The lions, modelled after the bronze ones at the base of the Nelson column in Trafalgar Square in London, lie on kiosks spanning the pedestrian walks on each corner of the bridge. Other decorations on the kiosks are the rose, shamrock and thistle of Great Britain and the buffalo head and maple leaf of Canada.

When the bridge was under construction, city council felt the finished structure needed to have a statue or two as decoration, but prices quoted for statuary were so high that it was almost decided to settle for a plain, utilitarian bridge.

Luckily, one of the city aldermen recalled having seen a handsome stone lion on a porch in northwest Calgary. They contacted the owner, James Thomson, who had been a stonemason in Scotland, and he agreed to create four larger lions for them.

The fact that he was a laborer for the City simplified the project. A shack was set up on the north bank of the river and Thomson was able to devote all his time to creating his clay models.

The finished lions are of concrete and have suffered from years of damage by weather and urban pollution. In 1983 costly restorations were carried out to stop further disintegration of the popular lions and the other decorative features of the bridge.

Location: Centre Street Bridge across the Bow River
Date: 1916

2. Maple Seeds

Roy Leadbeater

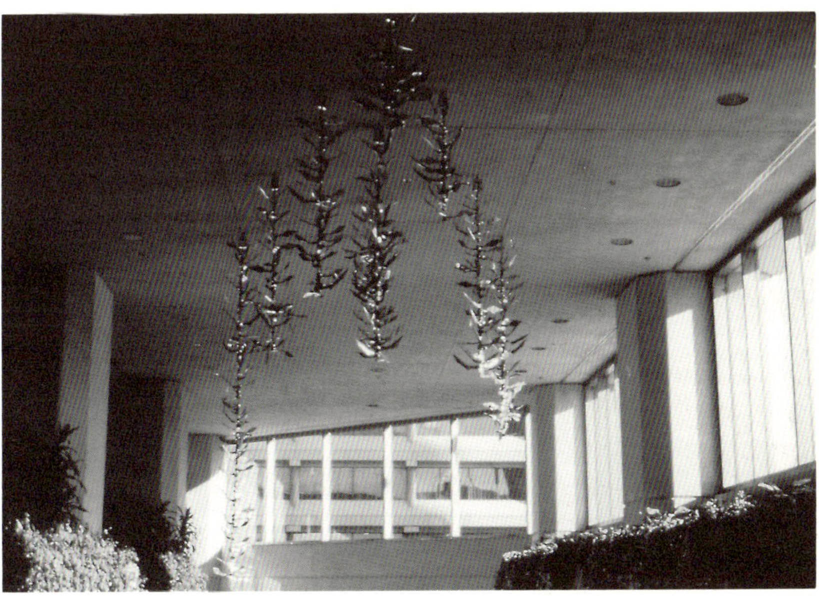

In the high-ceilinged lobby of the Alberta Government Telephones (AGT) Building, burnished bronze maple seeds hang in clusters giving an illusion of fluttering wings.

Although the whimsical sculpture looks light and airy, it weighs well over a tonne, with each lacquer-dipped "wing" weighing 1 kilogram. The wings are fitted onto a number of stainless steel rods, 9 millimetres in diameter. These are fastened to 16-millimetre rods projecting through the ceiling.

The multi-part sculpture was inspired by the artist's memories of his childhood when he had watched the falling seeds of the maple trees. They became exotic insects or fantastic flying machines as he marvelled at their flight.

Location: 411 - 1st Street S.E., AGT Building
Date: 1981

3. Citizen of the Century

Hazel O'Brien

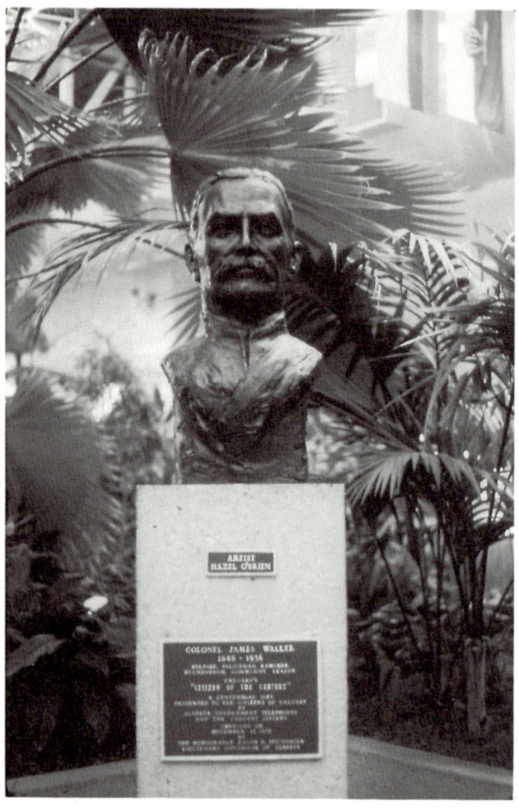

Unveiled on November 17, 1975, this likeness of Colonel James Walker (1848-1936) is a tribute to the person judged to be the most outstanding citizen of Calgary over its first 100 years. It was presented to the City by Alberta Government Telephones and the Calgary Jaycees.

Colonel Walker was a member of the North-West Mounted Police from 1874-1880. Also active in the militia, at his death his was the longest military record in Canada. A pioneer rancher, he was also the first immigration agent, operated the first telephone system, organized the first school, built many of the first buildings, and contributed immeasurably to Calgary's early development.

In the base of the statue is a time capsule containing information pertaining to the *Citizen of the Century* competition; the 10 000 submissions received for the Citizen of the Century; copies of the two daily papers for the day of unveiling; a 1975 telephone directory; and a 1975 silver dollar. The capsule will be opened in 2075.

Location: 120 - 9th Avenue S.E., Calgary Convention Centre
Date: 1975

4. Bronze Spaceflower

Roy Leadbeater

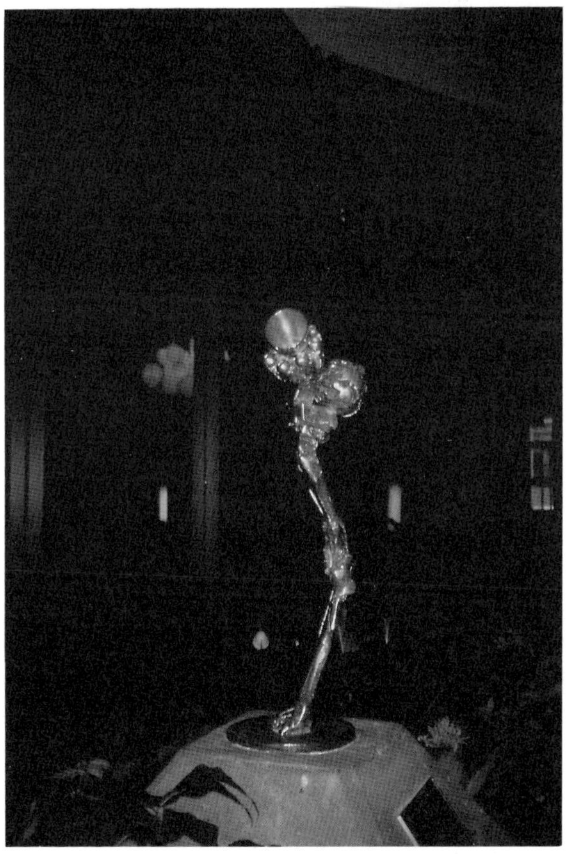

Spaceflower, a small, modernistic bronze, was Leo and Goldie Sheftel's gift to the Convention Centre and the people of Calgary.

Mr. Sheftel was chairman of the board that organized the Convention Centre and, as well, served as a board member for six years.

The sculpture is located along the west wall of the Garden Terrace.

Location: 120 - 9th Avenue S.E., Calgary Convention Centre
Date: 1974

5. The Gargoyles

Mark V. Marshall

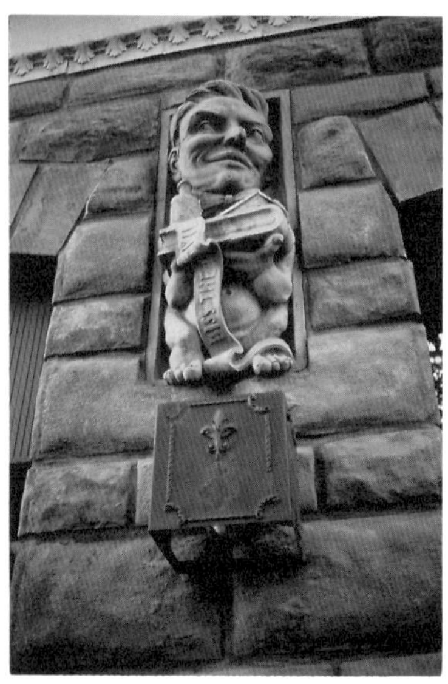

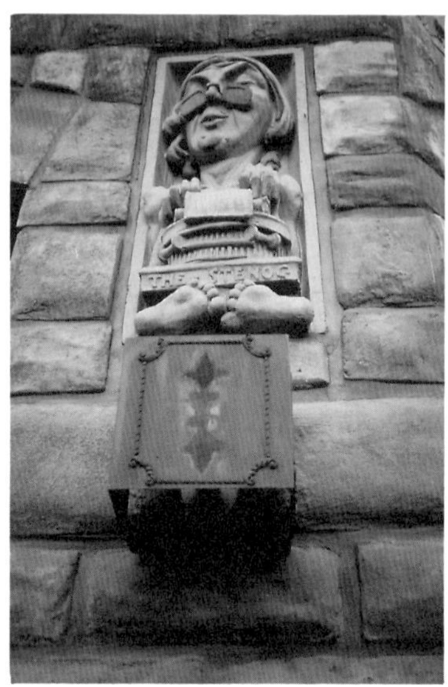

Originally defined as a grotesquely carved figure of an animal with an open mouth that served as a spout to carry rainwater off buildings, today the word *gargoyle* is used to describe any grotesque and usually humorous figure. Calgary's examples, which satirize the newspaper world, were created by Royal Doulton in England and are unique in Canada.

They were commissioned by the Southam family to be installed on the outside of the Herald Building, then located on the northeast corner of Seventh Avenue and First Street S.W. Later known as the Greyhound Building, and finally demolished in 1972, it was for many years a point of interest because of the unusual dwarf-like creatures — sixty in all — which leered down on passersby.

In addition to these figures, Marshall crafted several hundred smaller pieces that were also used to decorate the building.

During renovations in 1966, forty of the sixty large figures were destroyed, causing a public outcry. When AGT decided to build on the site, they located a stonemason who had worked on gargoyles in England. Chipping carefully, he managed to preserve the remaining caricatures and they are now situated in several Calgary locations.

The most impressive display is in the Colonel Walker Mini Park at 114 - 7th Avenue S.W., while others are in the Treasury Branch Building, the University of Calgary, the Greyhound Bus Terminal, the AGT Building, and the Alberta Hotel Building. Two unusual gargoyles with surveying tools, also by Mark Marshall, may be seen on the original Southern Alberta Institute of Technology (SAIT) building.

Location: 120 - 9th Avenue S.E., Calgary Convention Centre, and other locations mentioned above
Date: 1913

6. The Little Mermaid

Edvard Eriksen

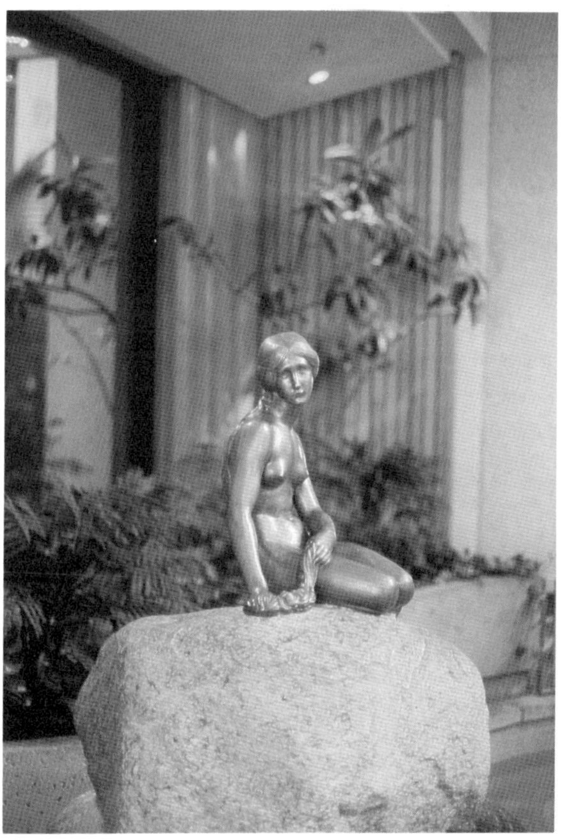

A bronze sculpture of Hans Christian Andersen's delightful fairy-tale heroine has graced the harbor of Copenhagen, Denmark, since 1913. Commissioned by the head of the New Carlsberg Brewery after he was enchanted by the Little Mermaid ballet, the sculpture was created by Danish artist Edvard Eriksen.

He also made three half-size replicas. One of these sits on a rock in the indoor Garden Terrace of the Convention Centre, a gift from the Carlsberg Arts Foundation to the Danish Canadian Club of Calgary. The club, in turn, presented it to the City of Calgary in 1973. Prior to this, it was on display in New York City for many years.

One of the two remaining replicas is in a private collection, while the other is located in Brasilia, Brazil.

Location: 120 - 9th Avenue S.E., Calgary Convention Centre
Date: 1913

7. Aurora Borealis

James Houston

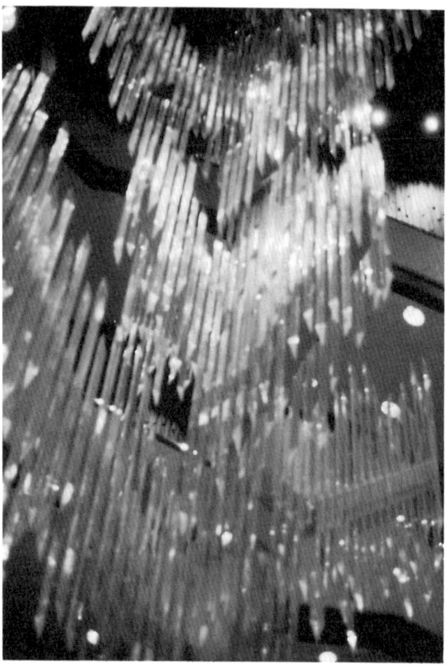

When the artist first saw the area where his sculpture would stand in the foyer of Glenbow Museum, he was overwhelmed. "I had never tackled anything that size, and I was awe-struck," he admits. "The building was still in its early stages and the roof was not yet on. As I lay in my hotel room that night, thinking of this huge space, open to the sky, I remembered the northern lights and the wonderful patterns they create."

Thrusting up four storeys, this acrylic and brushed-aluminum abstraction depicts the aurora borealis and is a focal point on the public floors of the building. Every hour on the hour, a subdued light and sound program brings to life an impression of the ever-changing northern lights. "If you listen closely, you can hear the actual sound recording of the Arctic wind," says the artist.

Each of the more than one thousand acrylic prisms was bolted to the centre core in an undertaking that required a specially constructed swinging platform and the expertise of a high-rig installation worker. Wearing white jeweller's gloves to avoid smudges, the workman followed a master diagram drawn up by the artist. Mirrors on the base and ceiling add to the sensation of space.

Houston says of the work, "It's the first thing I've ever done that has given me such a glow of pleasure. Usually I look at the finished product and wish I had done something different, but this time everything worked."

Location: 130 - 9th Avenue S.E., Glenbow Museum
Date: 1976

8. Eric Harvie (1892-1975)

Bob Scriver

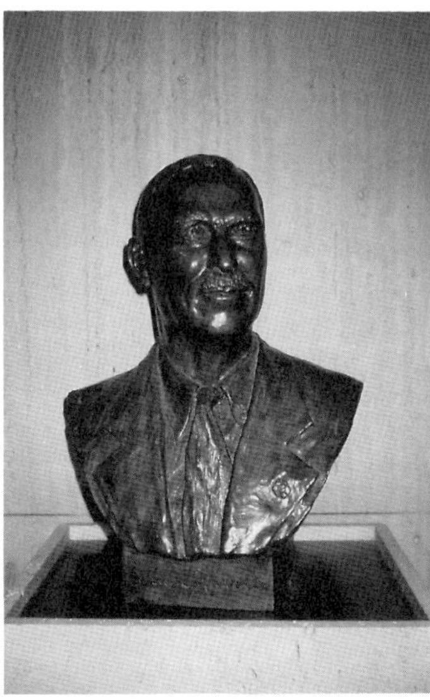

A bronze bust of Eric Lafferty Harvie, OC, CD, QC, LLB, LLD, DUC stands in the foyer of the Glenbow-Alberta Institute. Work on the bust was completed shortly before the dedication of the new Glenbow Museum in 1976.

The artist says of Harvie, "I was much impressed by him and what he was doing for all of us here in the West. A wealthy man, yes, but a very kind man who gave us all the benefit of his wealth."

Glenbow-Alberta Institute stands as a tribute to Harvie and his interest in Calgary. With its art gallery, museum, archives and library, it is a treasury of the art and artifacts that he collected. In 1966 he donated his enormous accumulation of paintings and other collections, along with five million dollars, to establish the institute.

Another large collection of museum artifacts is held by the Devonian Foundation, established by Harvie in 1956. This collection is available for study by qualified individuals and organizations. Many of Calgary's public sculptures have been donated to the City by the Devonian Foundation.

Among his many other gifts to Calgary are statues of General James Wolfe and Robert the Bruce. He also donated River Park and established Heritage Park and the Devonian Gardens for the enjoyment of Calgarians.

Harvie was born in Orillia, Ontario, in 1892. He was admitted to the bar in Alberta in 1915 and practised law in Calgary. He became a multimillionaire through involvement in the Leduc-Redwater areas and died in Calgary in 1975.

Location: 130 - 9th Avenue S.E., Glenbow Museum
Date: 1976

9. Glenbow Exterior Murals

Bob Oldrich

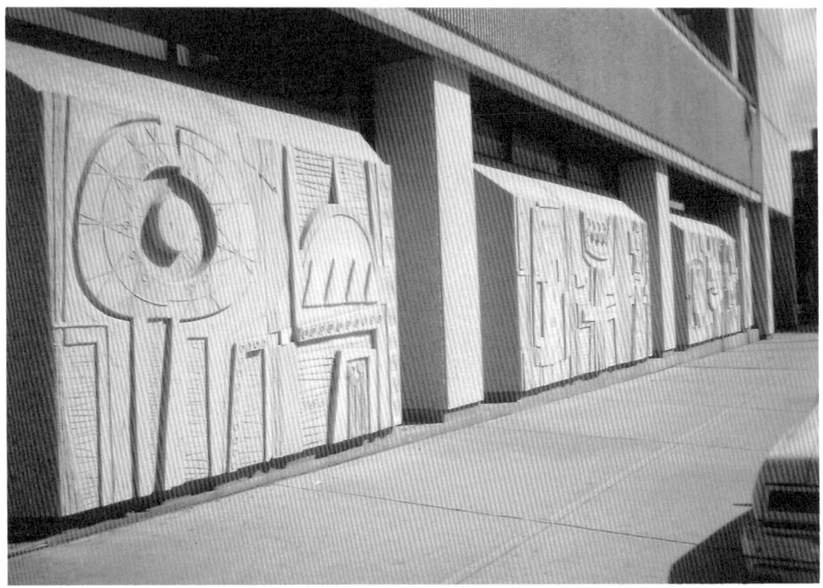

On the south side of the exterior of Glenbow Museum is a large concrete mural. Its three panels are intended to depict three phases of the area's early development.

The first illustrates the early history and the Indians; the second shows the influence of the white man, with development and the accompanying greed; and the third depicts our cultural evolution, with people working together in music and the arts.

Visible above this mural, on the inside wall of the Plus 15 level of the Museum, is another version of the same theme. A painting done in bright colors, it is also the work of Oldrich.

Location: 130 - 8th Avenue S.E., exterior Glenbow Museum on 9th Avenue
Date: 1976

10. Untitled Aluminum

Doug Bentham

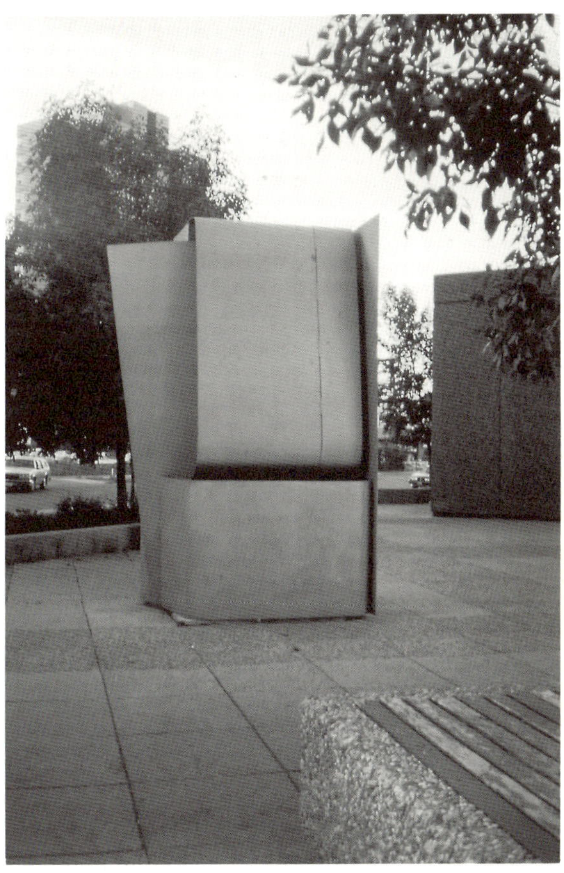

In the artist's own words, "This untitled sculpture in aluminum was designed to create a highly independent statement in contrast to the dominating architecture of the Government of Canada Building."

The artist says of the piece, ". . . light and shadow penetrate the interior spaces to set up a quietly dynamic statement — abstract yet illusively suggestive of something known to us."

The sculpture is of etched aluminum and measures 3.6 by 2.7 by 2.4 metres.

Location: 220 - 4th Avenue S.E., Harry Hays Building
Date: 1981

11. Jacks

Henry Saxe

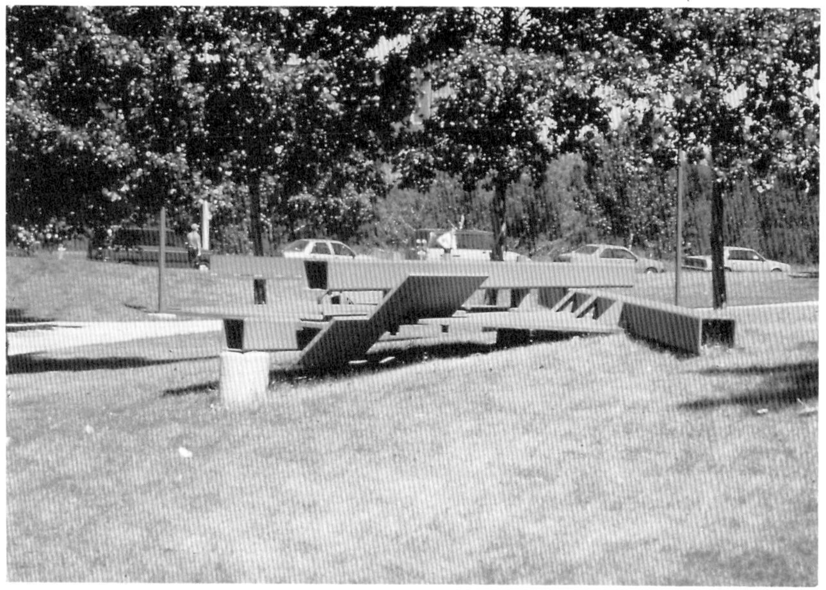

A horizontal piece on the grounds at the northwest corner of Calgary's federal building, *Jacks* was commissioned shortly after Saxe represented Canada at the Venice Bienale International Exhibition.

The large concrete and steel piece, which measures 3.6 metres in length, was built in Kingston, Ontario, from the original half-scale model. The artist supervised every facet of construction, then transported the finished work by truck to Calgary. At the selected site at the main entrance to the building, a crane was waiting to place the work on a special concrete base designed by Saxe to emphasize the sculpture's self-supporting structure. The installation went smoothly and was finished in two hours.

The sculpture has since been moved to its present location on the grounds of the building.

Location: 220 - 4th Avenue S.E., Harry Hays Building
Date: 1978

12. Plate Wall (1979)

Annemarie Schmid Esler

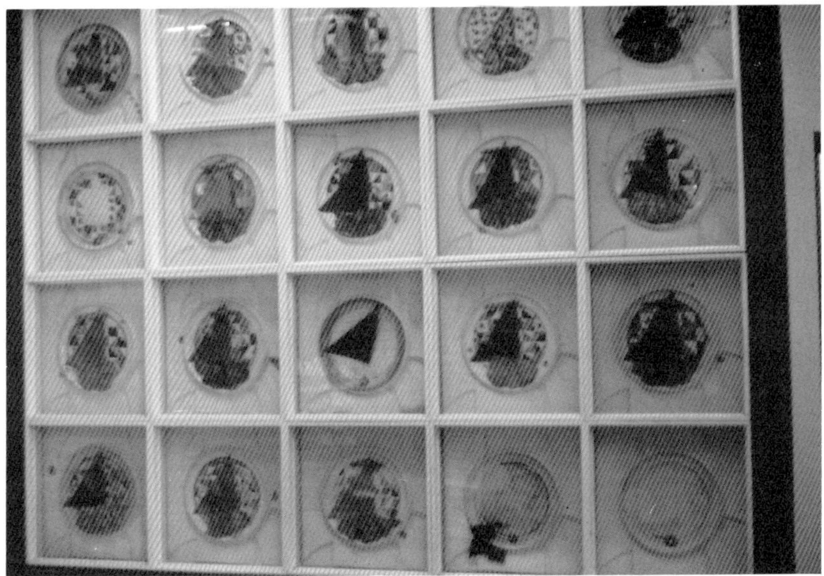

This collection of colorful ceramic plates repeats the theme of an earlier work titled *Something to Do With Sailing*. It is recessed in a wall measuring 2.5 by 2 metres, which was designed for the artwork at the time of the building's construction.

Each plate, embellished with different designs and rich in varied lustres and hues, displays the sail motif either clearly or subliminally. The work is encased in glass to blend with the storefronts of the commercial area in which it stands.

Location: 220 - 4th Avenue S.E., Harry Hays Building
Date: 1979

13. Bread Wall (1979)

David Gilhooly

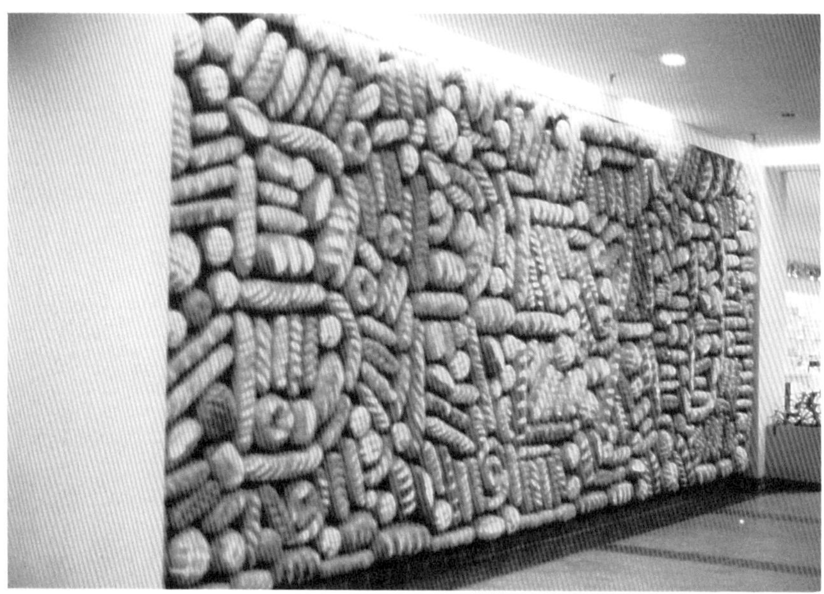

It is difficult to walk by this display without pausing to investigate. The ceramic mural, which measures 3 by 9 metres, is made up of earthenware replicas of fresh-from-the-oven breads and rolls, and tempts passersby to reach out to it, which was the artist's intention.

He chose bread from several Calgary bakeries to make the original molds. "I fired the 400 loaves in my kiln outside the back door and filled up my basement studio with them," says Gilhooly, who adds that he had about fifteen left over, which he gave to the workmen who admired the piece when it was being installed. The loaves are mortared to the concrete-block wall. "It should last until it's ground up for road aggregate," the artist says philosophically.

The word BREAD is spelled out in long loaves. Some of Gilhooly's *Frog World* artifacts (see artist's biography), notably frog currency (cookies), also mingle with the ceramic doughnuts, bagels and seed buns.

Location: 220 - 4th Avenue S.E., Harry Hays Building
Date: 1979

14. & 15. Coat of Arms and Map of Canada

Joe Chomistek

Carved from limestone, these two large stone installations are appropriately located outside the Calgary offices of the federal government.

The Coat of Arms stands over 3 metres high, and the colors are reproduced in acrylic paint. It was completed in 1984. The Map of Canada, with a beaver above, was finished two years later. It is about 4 metres high and is also colored with acrylic paint. They were donated by Chomistek to the Government of Canada.

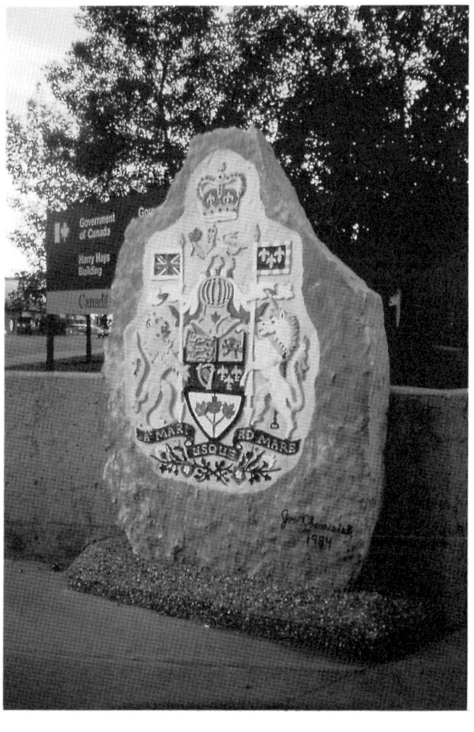

Installation of the permanent display, valued at 11 000 dollars by a local art appraiser, was funded by Agriculture Canada and the Prairie Farm Rehabilitation Administration. The works were unveiled by Harvie Andre, MP, in 1986.

The artist also created an Olympic carving which was purchased by the McDonald's restaurant chain for their location across from Canada Olympic Park on the western outskirts of the city.

Location: 220 - 4th Avenue S.E., Harry Hays Building
Date: 1984, 1986

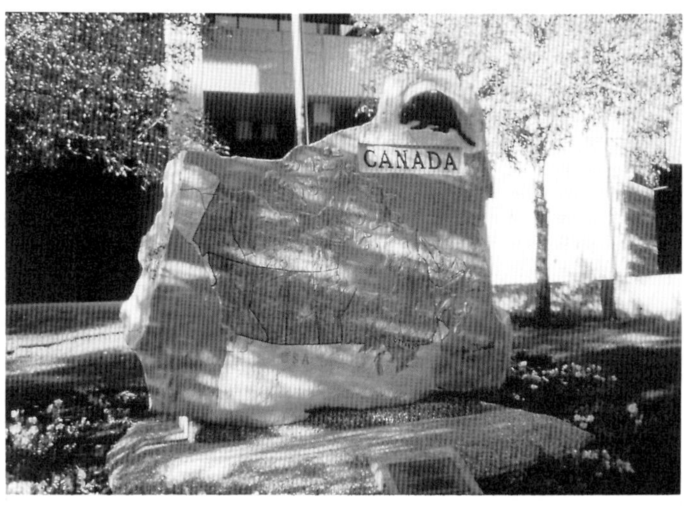

16. Brotherhood of Mankind

Mario Armengol

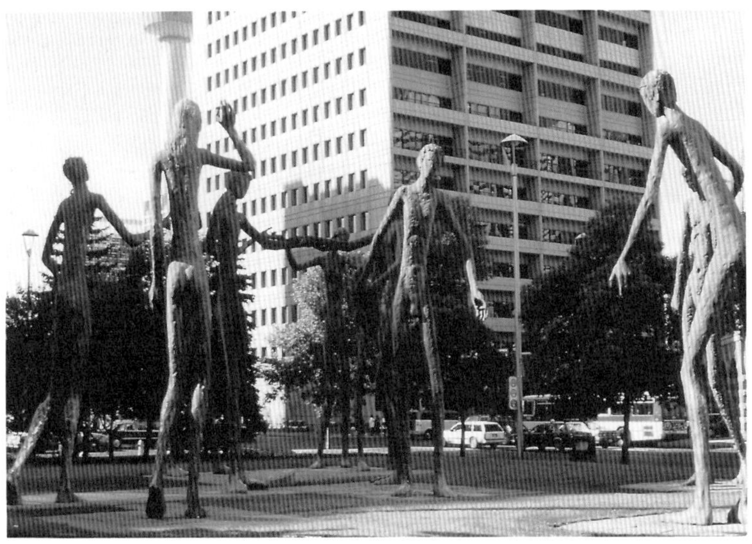

One of Calgary's best-known artworks, this group of ten aluminum figures stands in front of the Calgary Education Centre. The figures reach a height of nearly 6.5 metres and weigh an average of 680 kilograms.

Originally constructed in Great Britain for the United Kingdom Pavilion at Expo '67 in Montreal, the statues were later purchased by Robert M. Cummings on behalf of Maxwell Cummings & Sons. The company had recently completed construction of Calgary Place and the Pacific Petroleum Buildings, and the statues were presented to the people of Calgary as a gesture of goodwill. They were accepted by the Duke of Kent, who was visiting the City on July 8, 1968.

The technique used in this work is complicated. First tabletop-size maquettes were sculpted. These were then executed in plaster and increased to a height of over 2 metres. They were later shipped to France and, through a stretching process, became maquettes for the present statues. Heads and torsos were cast singly and limbs were welded to them when they arrived in Montreal. A patina finish was then applied to the aluminum.

Armengol is a modest artist and said of his unique sculpture, "My attempt at modelling *The Brotherhood of Mankind* was a big undertaking and, as such, beyond my capabilities. A duodenal ulcer — happily now healed — was my reward!"

The figures are arranged in groups of two or three, with hands extended in gestures of friendship.

Location: 515 Macleod Trail S.E., Calgary Board of Education, Education Centre Building
Date: 1967, installed in 1968

17. The Olympic Runner

Artist unknown

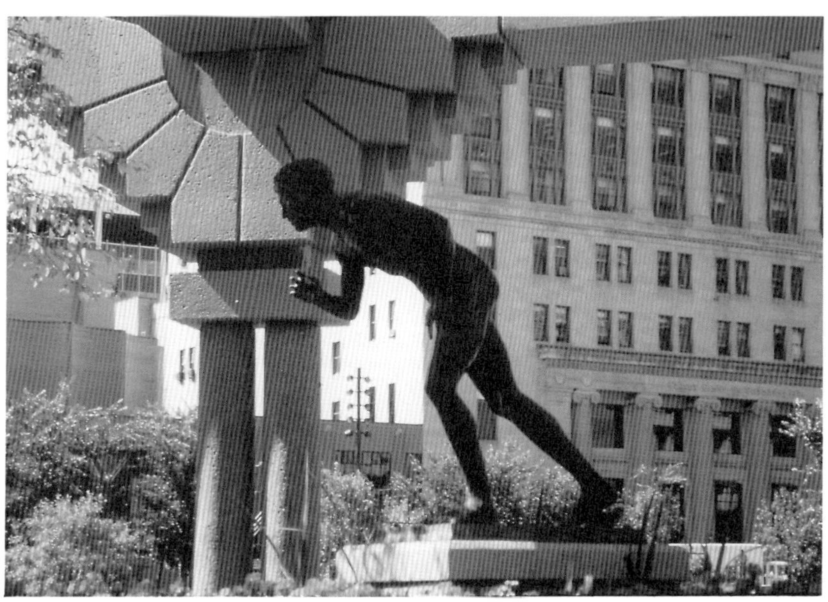

This bronze statue is 114 centimetres high and was cast in Italy early in the 19th century. It is a copy of a Hellenic figure thought to be Coroebus, the first Greek winner of the Olympic Games in 776 B.C. A cook by trade, Coroebus was from Elis, Greece, near Olympia.

The ancient Olympics were held in Olympia every four years without interruption from 776 B.C. to 393 A.D., an amazing 1 069 years. Originally there was only one race, a sprint of 200 metres, and the prize for the winner was a simple wreath of wild laurel. The Games were cancelled in 394 A.D., when the area was in a state of political upheaval.

The work is a gift from the Devonian Foundation, and is found on the northeast corner of the stage.

Location: 8th Avenue and Macleod Trail S.E., Olympic Plaza
Date: installed in 1987

18. Duet

Ray Arnatt

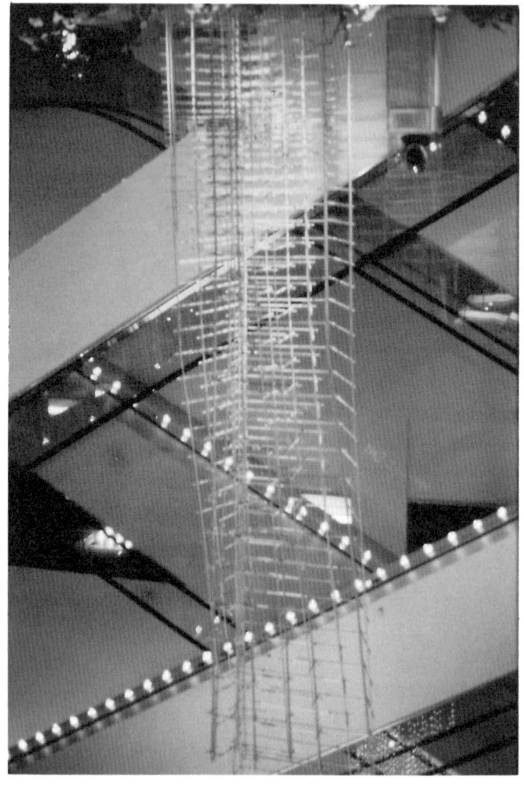

This sculpture was the winner of a competition for placement in the Calgary Centre for Performing Arts. Sponsored by the Alberta Art Foundation, the competition attracted entries from sixty-seven Alberta artists.

The artist describes the 8-metre-high sculpture as "a visual analogy of a musical form." It consists of steel tubes of differing thickness, with the rods representing the notes, and the spaces the musical pauses. The variation in the diameter of the tubing conveys the rhythm.

Color is used to amplify both rhythm and overall cohesiveness by radiating from the core of the work. Hidden within the bands of color is a single twenty-four-carat gold leaf band representing unity within the binary system, a theme that forms the foundation for the sculpture. The ring has an important personal meaning for Arnatt as well. He married sculptor JoAnne Schachtel in the year he completed *Duet*, and the ring was an acknowledgment of Schachtel's "help in making the work."

Location: 225 - 8th Avenue S.E., Calgary Centre for Performing Arts,
Jack Singer Concert Hall Lobby

Date: 1985

19. Gatekeeper

Isla Burns

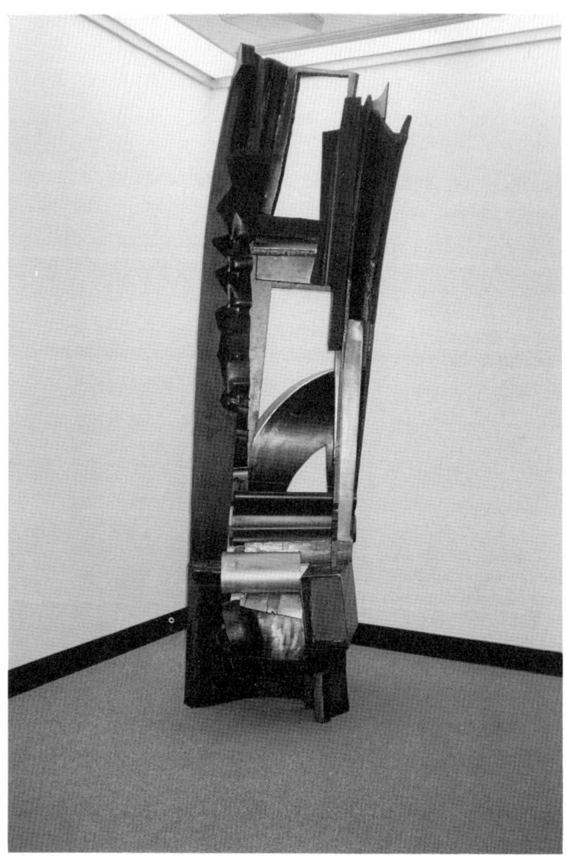

Constructed of mixed metals, this is the largest of a series of pieces created by the artist in 1989. The metals used are steel, bronze and brass plating.

It is located on the Plus 15 level of the Calgary Centre for Performing Arts and stands approximately 2.5 metres high. Says the artist, "most of the shapes within the sculpture I formed myself, using a hydraulic press. The bowl and cylinder shapes were found objects."

The work is on indefinite loan from the Alberta Art Foundation.

Location: 225 - 8th Avenue S.E., Calgary Centre for Performing Arts
Date: 1989

20. Sunbird II

Sorel Etrog

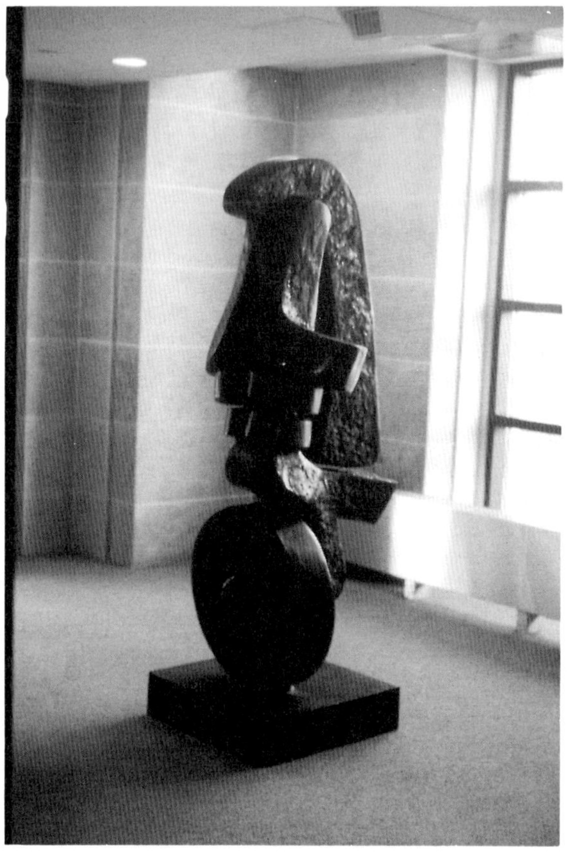

Etrog describes this large, abstract bronze as "a tribute to the Sun, the great partner in life." This is a theme that has inspired many of the artist's works since 1959.

The round base of the sculpture symbolizes the sun, and is surmounted by a bird-like helmet.

It is on indefinite loan from the Art Gallery of Ontario.

Location: 225 - 8th Avenue S.E., Calgary Centre for Performing Arts, Plus 15 level
Date: 1964

21. Endless Totem
Homage to Brancusi (1985)

Michael Hayden

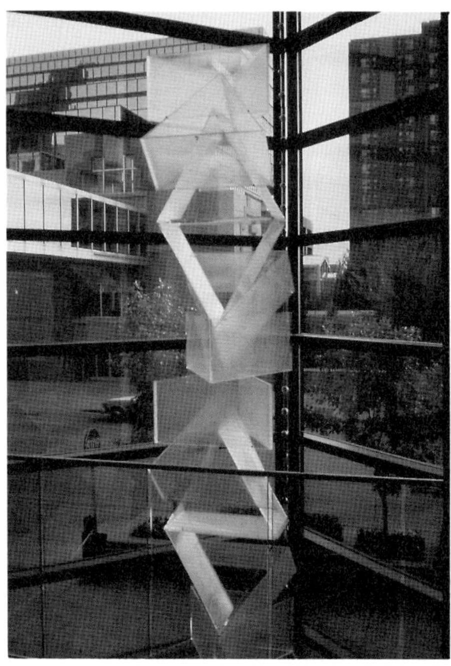

Located in a triangular window and visible from both Macleod Trail and the Max Bell Theatre inside The Centre, this lumetric sculpture stands 3.5 metres high.

It consists of clear acrylic triangles stacked in a column and standing on a 1-metre-high mirrored base. The many angles are captured in light, producing ever-changing color displays that fill the sculpture with rainbows. The piece is influenced by natural light from outdoors and by indoor artificial light provided by rows of incandescent bulbs.

"An observer of the sculpture will witness spectacular displays of brilliant rainbow arrays," explains Hayden in his proposal for the project.

The subtitle, *Homage to Brancusi*, refers to an early modernist sculptor the artist admires and sometimes emulates. The work was commissioned by Comcheq Services Inc., and was installed for the opening of the Max Bell Theatre.

Tucked away in a seldom-used hallway of The Centre is another of Hayden's works. Titled *Dive*, it is a light sculpture of acrylic tubing on loan from the Canada Council Art Bank.

Location: 225 - 8th Avenue S.E., Calgary Centre for Performing Arts
Date: 1985

22. Spectral Arch

Robert Jekyll

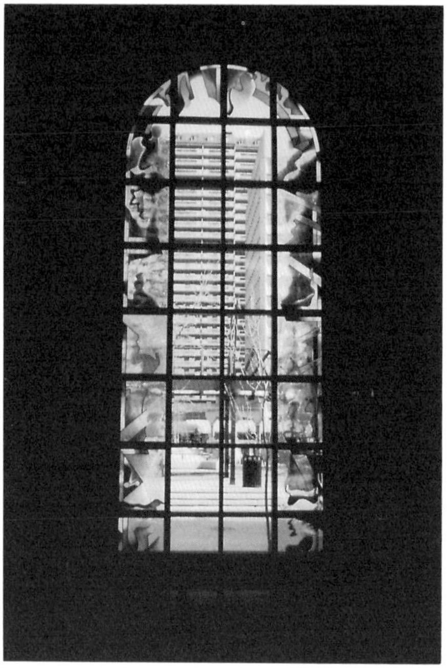

Taking its theme from the seven colors of the spectrum, this stained glass sculpture captures what the artists describes as "a universal symbol of hope — the rainbow." It is located near the main entrance of the Calgary Centre for Performing Arts, east of the Martha Cohen Theatre.

The eighteen perimeter panels of the thirty-six-panel window are blended with the clear glass centre by a delicate use of handmade, laminated glass. This imported European glass is produced by an ancient technique in which an extra layer is applied during the mouth-blowing process.

Jekyll created his sculpture by applying the glass without lead, instead using a clear epoxy to hold the pieces in place. This technique emphasizes the individual panels within the leaded outside "frames," adding another dimension to the work.

In relating *Spectral Arch* to its location, the artist explains, "There is a formal affinity between the seven colors and the notes of a musical scale, and in theatre the allegorical associations of color are everywhere."

Commissioned by his brother, Peter Jekill of Calgary, the piece was a gift to the Centre.

Location: 225 - 8th Avenue S.E., Calgary Centre for Performing Arts
Date: 1985

23. Children's Commemorative Obelisk

10 000 Children

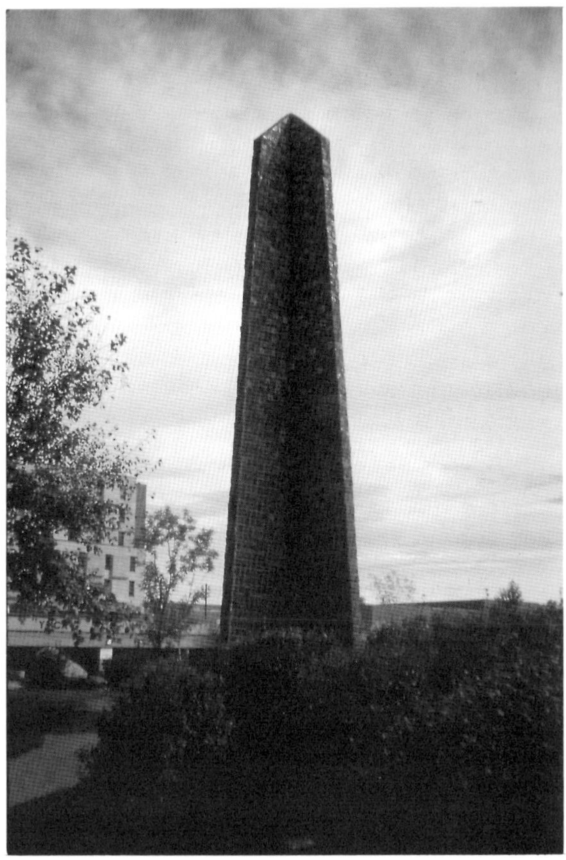

The obelisk was authorized by the board of trustees of the Calgary Catholic Board of Education as a Calgary centennial project. It was unveiled on October 6, 1975.

The unique sculpture is a composite of 10 000 fired-clay tiles, each designed by a child in the Roman Catholic elementary school system at the time. Some of the tiles are also mounted on permanent panels around the terrace of the building. Elisabeth Priegert, who conceived the idea, explains that each one depicts a child's interpretation of Calgary: past, present or future.

The obelisk is a very old art form originating in Egypt, and was chosen in this case because of its symbolic shape — a cross pointing toward heaven.

Because the tiles are virtually indestructible, the students of 1975 can be proud of having created a meaningful artwork that they can share with their children and grandchildren.

Location: 300 - 6th Avenue S.E., Catholic School Centre
Date: 1975

24. Pod

Steven Smalley

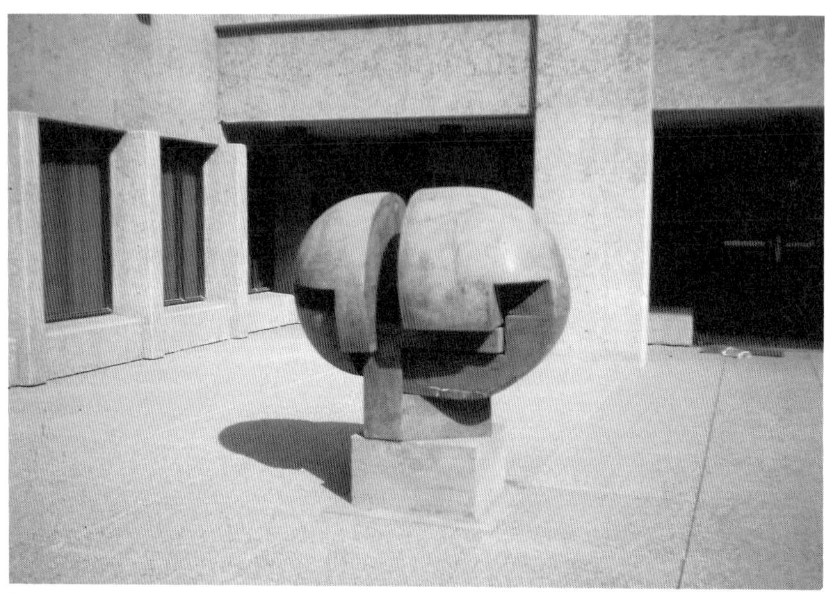

A multisphere, cast-concrete sculpture created to commemorate Calgary's centennial in 1975, this work won the first prize of 2 000 dollars in the post-secondary student category in a Calgary Separate School Board competition.

It consists of four separate pieces of concrete. They were constructed in Kelowna, British Columbia, home of the artist, and transported to Calgary where they were assembled at the present site. *Pod* stands on the plaza at the Catholic School Centre.

Location: 300 - 6th Avenue S.E., Catholic School Centre
Date: 1975

25. Library Frieze

Bob Oldrich

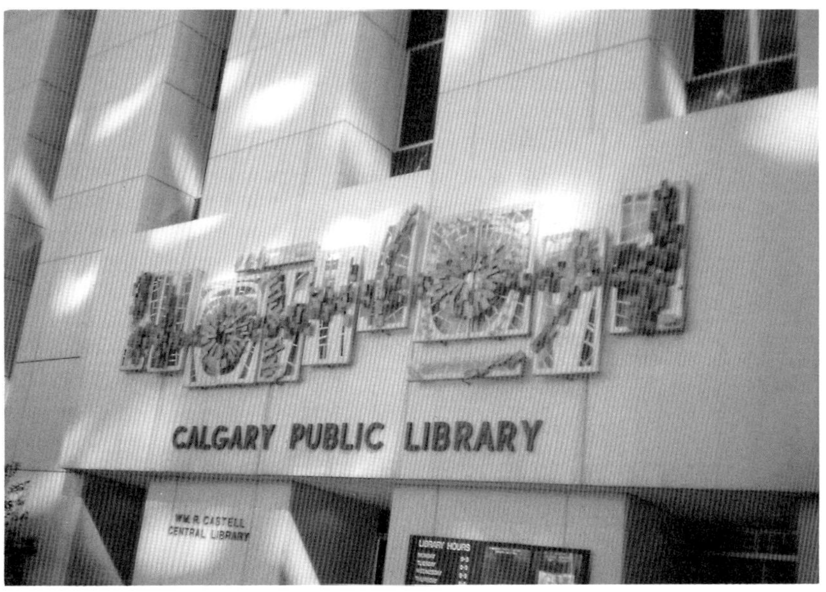

On the west side of the W.R. Castell Central Library is a metal sculpture depicting a variety of learning media.

"Because the building was bland, I felt it needed some color. My intention was that it be intellectual yet a bit playful," says the artist.

It depicts pages of books, stained glass to show age, art (with brush strokes of color), and the feeling of the old and new.

Location: 616 Macleod Trail S.E., W.R. Castell Central Library
Date: 1974

26. The Library Book

Rick Silas

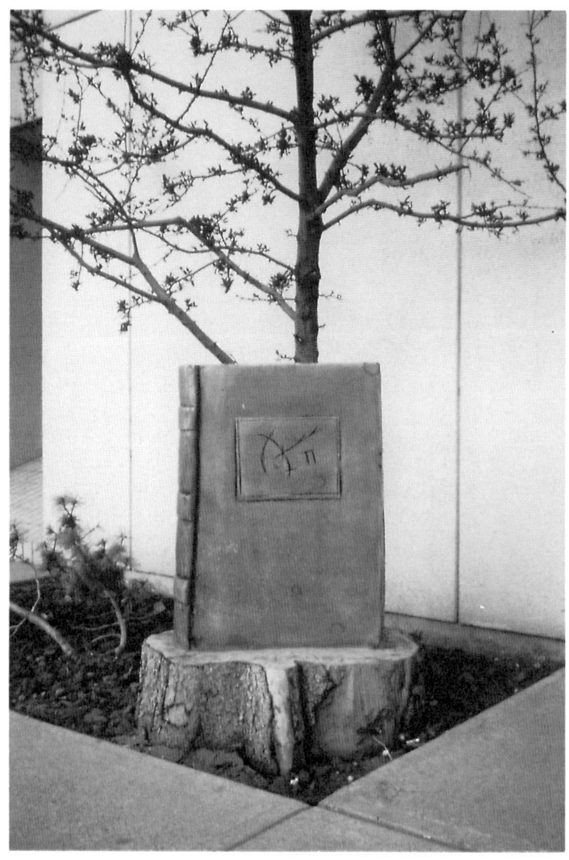

Silas calls this piece "guerilla art" because it was permanently installed without formal permission. Concerned that there was little to call attention to the downtown library, he carved the colorful book and installed it near the main entrance. The bright red tome weighs over 200 kilograms and was produced from a solid piece of spruce.

Location: 616 Macleod Trail S.E., W.R. Castell Central Library
Date: 1989

27. So the Bishop Said to the Actress

J. Seward Johnson, Jr.

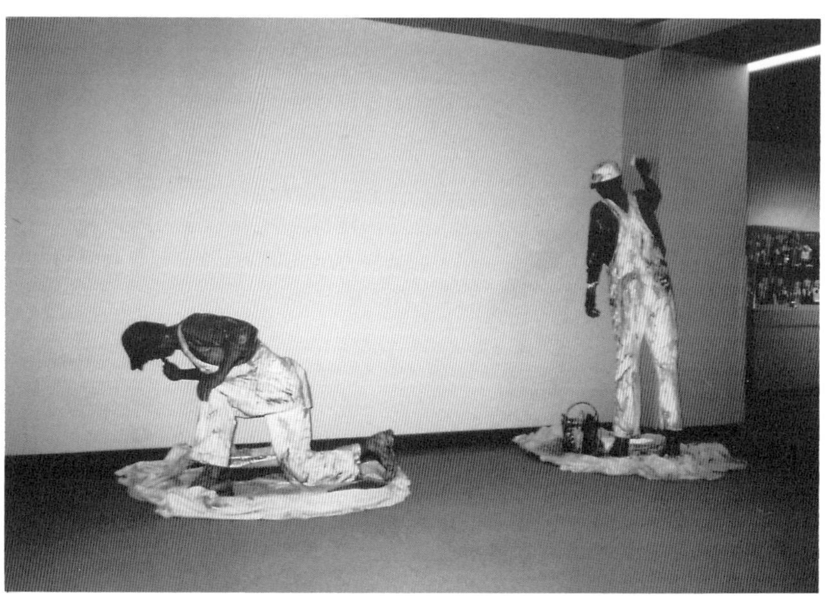

This life-size bronze is not a celebration of the work ethic but, rather, a visual description of the day-to-day relationship established by these two workmen.

Because of their remarkably lifelike appearance and the subtle location of the work, passersby often mistake it for actual workmen. They have been referred to as "the slowest painters in town."

The piece is a gift to the City of Calgary from the Devonian Foundation. A fairly portable sculpture, it has been enjoyed in temporary sites in the Jubilee Auditorium, and in the walkway between City Hall and the Municipal Building.

Location: 800 Macleod Trail S.E., Municipal Building
Date: 1983

28. Joy

Roy Leadbeater

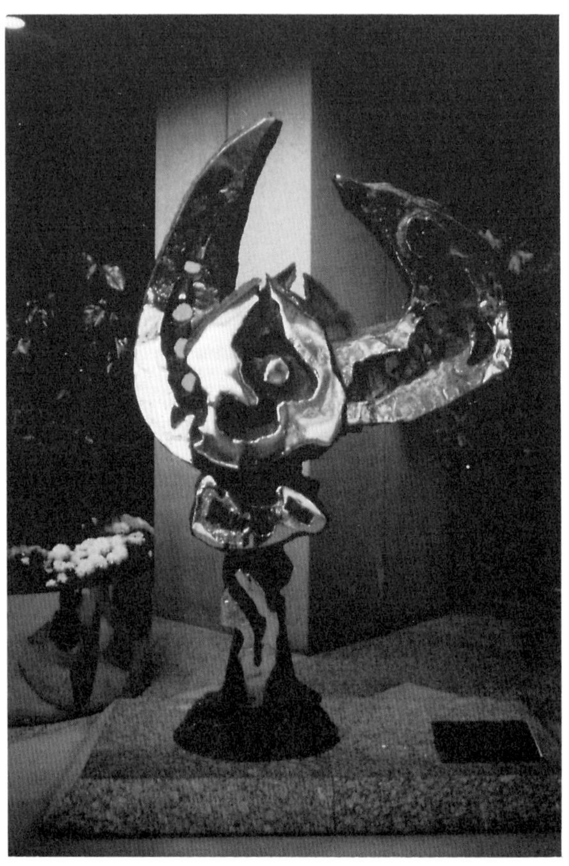

This bronze is the artist's interpretation of joy. Standing 2.5 metres tall and weighing over 900 kilograms, it was crafted in Leadbeater's Edmonton studio and cast in his adjoining foundry.

The sculpture was donated by the Libin and Gurevich families in celebration of Leo and Goldie Sheftel's (their parents) fiftieth wedding anniversary.

Location: 800 Macleod Trail S.E., Municipal Building
Date: 1987

29. Chief David Crowchild Memorial Sculpture

Robert Stowell

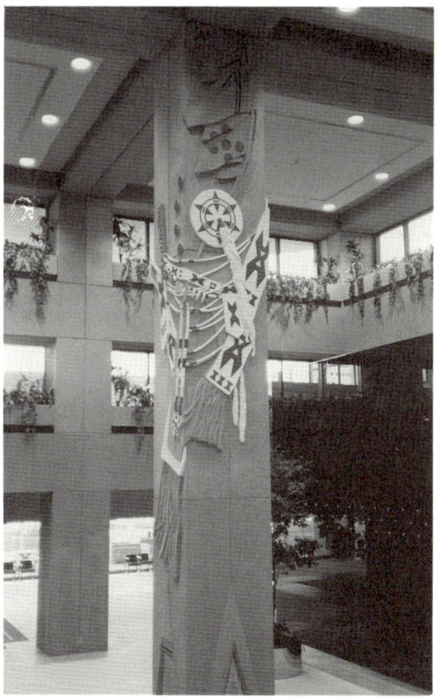

In order to create this unique tribute to one of Alberta's most respected native Indians, the artist created thirty-two separate concrete panels. These were installed on the surface of an existing pillar on the first floor of the Municipal Building by drilling holes and setting pins in a fast-setting resin grout. The design of the panels leaves much of the original surface of the pillar visible so as to incorporate the relief into the architecture of the building.

Stowell began with beadwork designs from Plains Indian artifacts found at the Glenbow Museum and later, after consultation with Victoria Crowchild Aberdeen, daughter of Chief Crowchild, he added the actual beadwork designs worn by the Chief.

There are four teepees in the work; two are plain and symbolize honesty and purity, while the others have Crowchild's own bee design indicating unselfishness and love. All doors on the teepees are open, signifying his love for all people.

Chief Crowchild was an outstanding humanitarian. The beadwork circle on the upper section of the pillar represents the world he travelled to promote peace; the glove means a handshake; at the top is an eagle, recalling the four eagles who circled high in the sky on the day of his death.

This work was selected from three finalists in a City of Calgary competition.

Location: 800 Macleod Trail S.E., Municipal Building
Date: 1988

30. Dancer

Prince Monyo Mihailescu-Nasturel

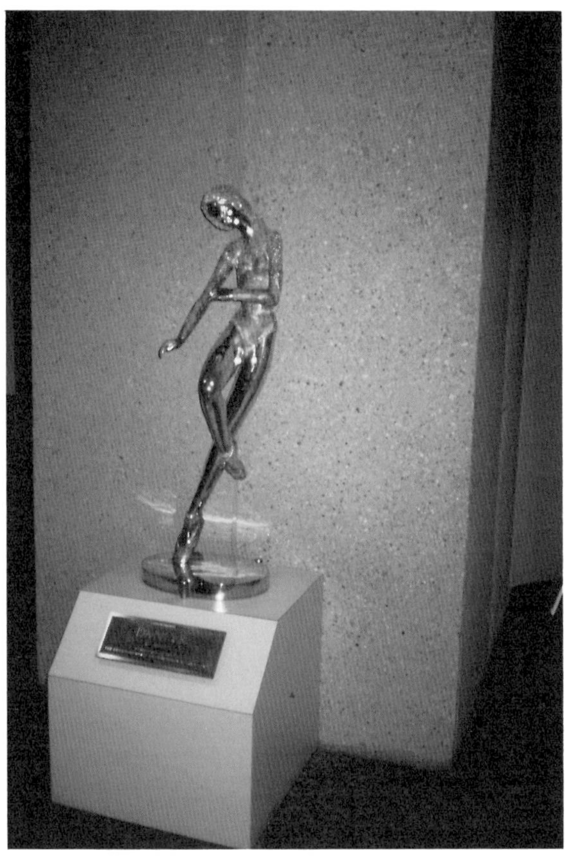

This lively and delicate cast-bronze sculpture was acquired from a Houston, Texas, gallery by the Devonian Foundation of Calgary. The golden dancer is 114 centimetres tall and is found near the elevators on the main floor of the Municipal Building.

Location: 800 Macleod Trail S.E., Municipal Building
Date: acquired by the City in 1982

31. The Bears

Suzanne Sable

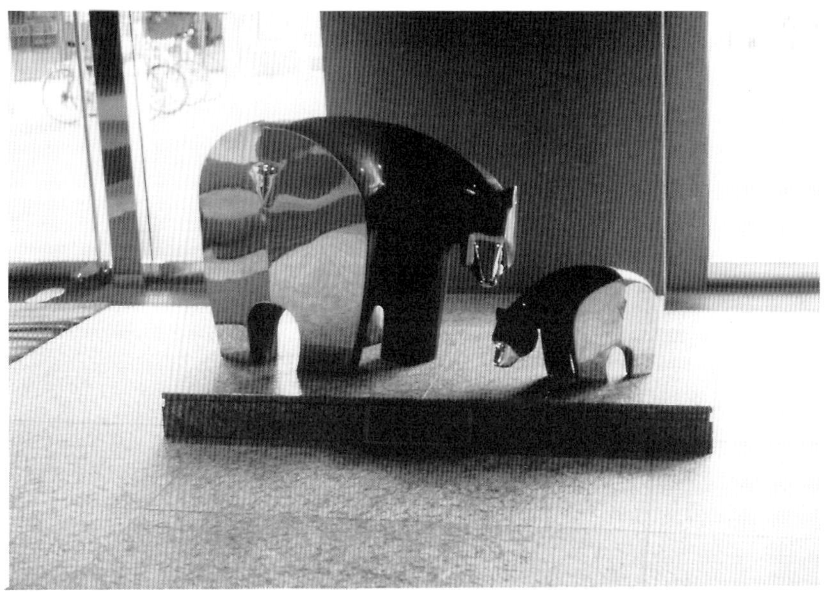

This very visible sculpture of a mother and cub was commissioned by Donald Harvie of the Devonian Group of Charitable Foundations for the new Municipal Building. He was attracted to a smaller version in a gallery in Carmel, California, and invited Sable to visit Calgary before she began the work. She was "amazed to see so much art in public places."

Cast in bronze from a model of Styrofoam and plaster, the sculpture is 91.5 centimetres high and 180 centimetres wide.

The bears are highly polished on their hind parts, providing variation in both color and texture. Lighthearted and very tactile, they are favorites with adults and children alike.

Location: 800 Macleod Trail S.E., Municipal Building
Date: 1983

32. Family of Horses

Harry O'Hanlon

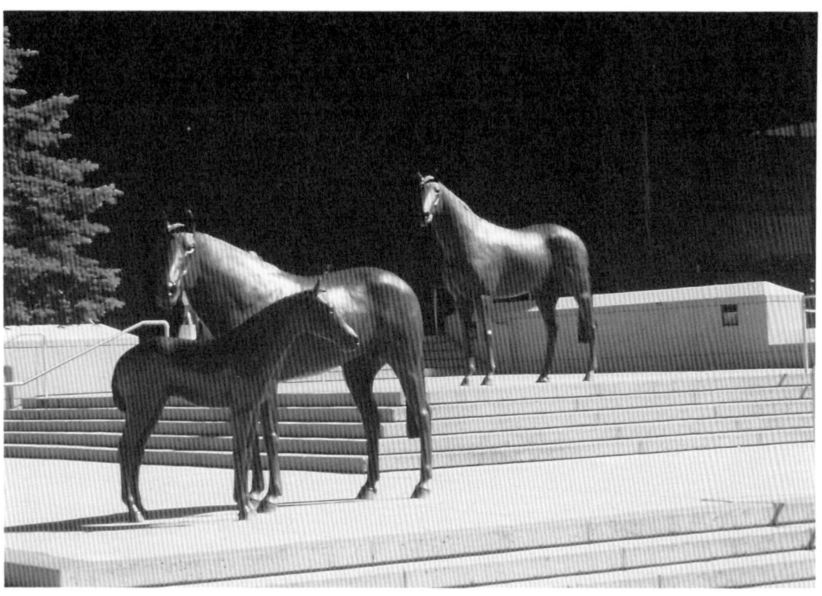

This life-size bronze trio consists of a stallion, mare and foal. Chosen from a selection of maquettes by nine Alberta artists, it was the winner of a civic competition in 1987.

The project was the subject of considerable financial debate in Calgary until 1989. That was when Marg Southern, president and co-chairman of Spruce Meadows, a local, world-famous equestrian centre, agreed to pay the cost of installation as well as meeting a prior commitment of half the cost of the sculpture.

The work was scaled up from maquette to life-size in a combination of wood, clay and Styrofoam. It was then cut into twenty-six pieces for casting and later welded together. Mr. O'Hanlon has high praise for the finished product, which was done in a Montana foundry. "There isn't a sign of the welding job," says an impressed O'Hanlon.

Location: 800 Macleod Trail S.E., Municipal Plaza
Date: 1989

33. Balancing Act

Roy Leadbeater

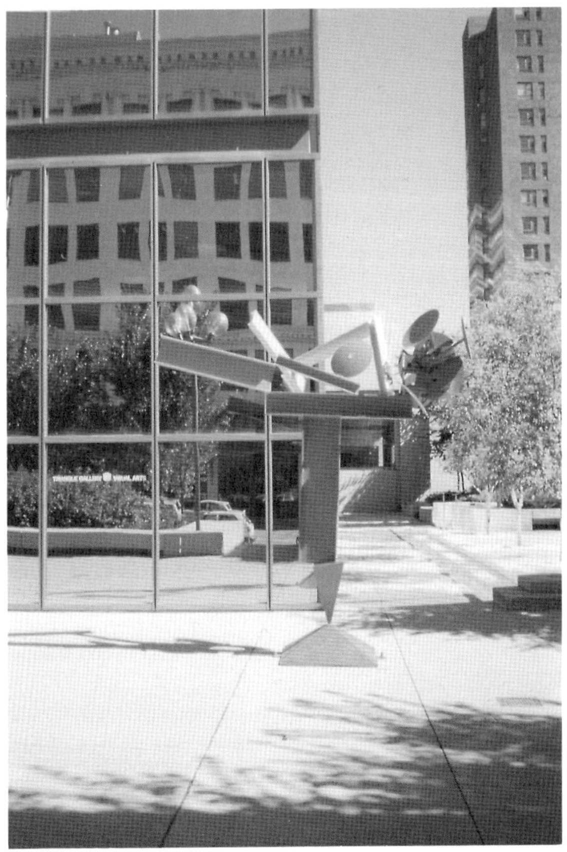

Full of vibrant, primary colors, this welded-steel sculpture is found near the Triangle Gallery at the Municipal Building. The piece is fey and toylike, and intended to bring lighthearted pleasure to passersby.

Location: 800 Macleod Trail S.E., Municipal Plaza
Date: 1989

34. Beaver and Fallen Tree

Don Begg

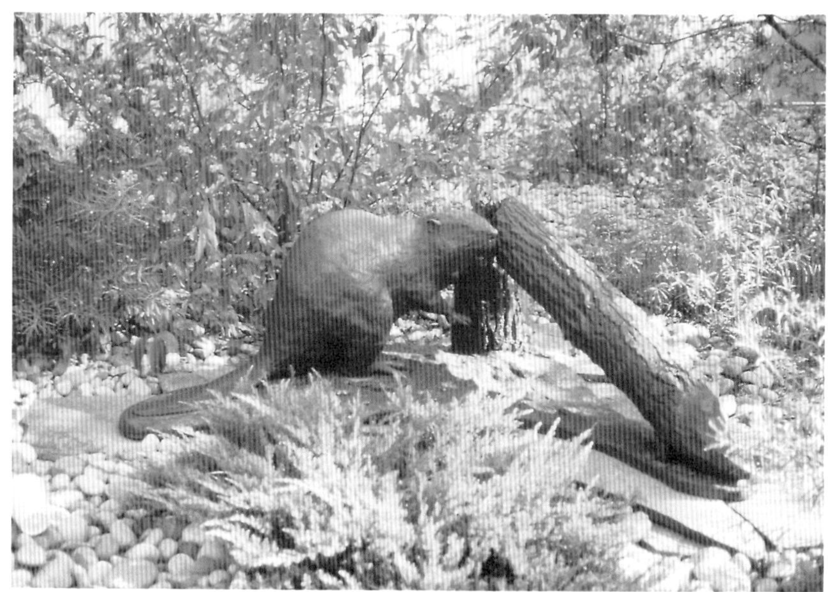

Donated by the Devonian Foundation and set in the City of Calgary's Municipal Plaza Parkade grounds, this realistic piece is meant to convey a sense of what the Blackfoot poet James Welch calls "the world trying to be right."

A symbol of Canada, the beaver evokes thoughts of our past, present and future. Begg's life-size bronze focuses on the texture of aspen bark and wet, silky fur as a subtle counterpoint to the futuristic glass and steel buildings of the civic plaza.

Another *Beaver and Fallen Tree* is situated in the gardens of Rockyview Hospital.

Location: 800 Macleod Trail S.E., Municipal Parkade garden
Date: 1987

West of Centre Street

35. Past, Present and Future

Gernot Kiefer

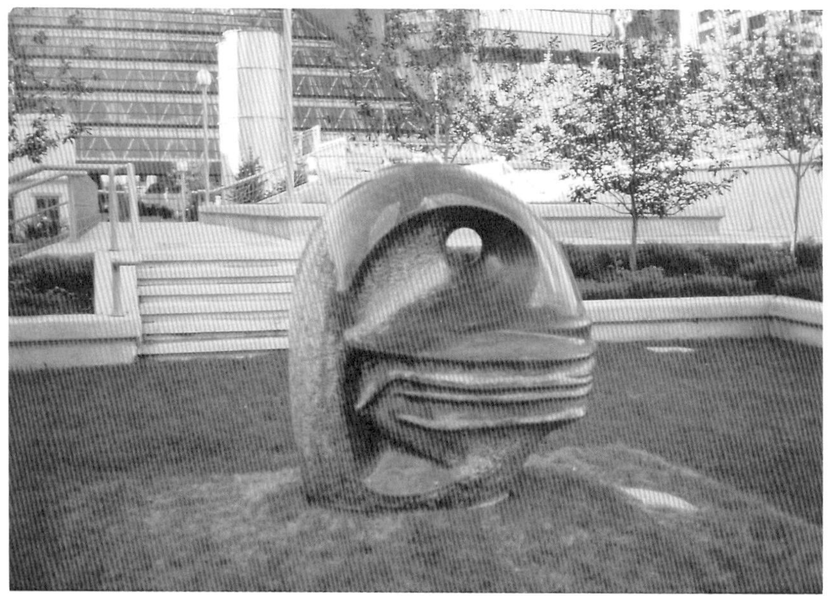

Created from a 5-tonne limestone boulder, this gentle interpretation of evolving life experiences fits the criteria which made it a winner in the 1990 Calgary Downtown Business Revitalization Zone competition.

A "people sculpture" of pedestrian scale, touchable and open to interpretation, it stands approximately 1.5 metres high, 1.3 metres wide and 81 centimetres deep.

Lines at the base depict past cultures; some of these have been lost, others were undeveloped or continue to evolve. The midsection represents the present in a dominant fashion, its high and low undulations typifying individual changes, choices and discoveries. The future, at the top of the sculpture, is smooth and shiny, with a significant opening for individual interpretation.

The artist says his greatest difficulty was resisting the urge to rush to a deadline. The quality of work was vital to him. Small-scale tool marks were deliberately left on the work to show the imperfections we have created that will continue into the future.

Location: Centre Street between 4th and 5th Avenues, James Short Park
Date: 1991

36. Share the Flame

Vilem Zach

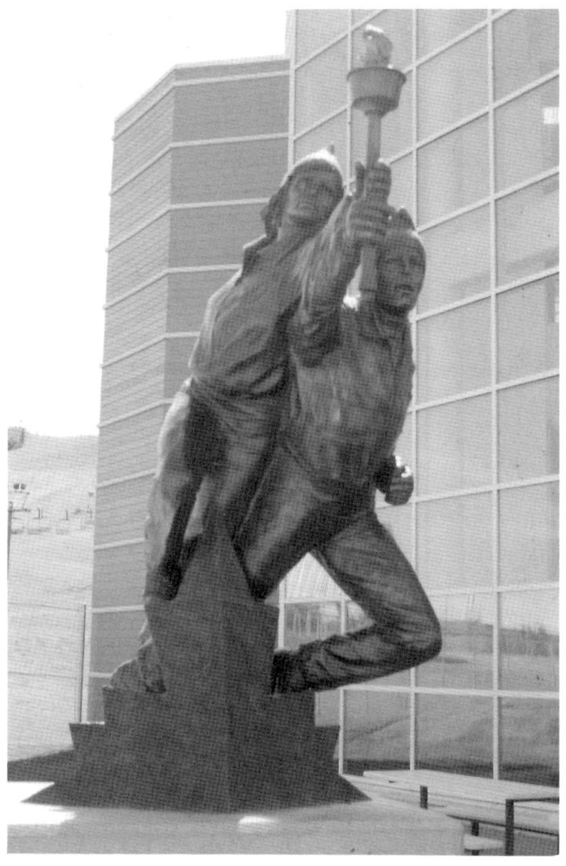

Chosen over entries by sixteen other artists, this heroic sculpture was commissioned by Petro-Canada to commemorate the 1988 Olympic Torch Relay across Canada. Three identical statues were created, with the first unveiled in the lobby of the Petro-Canada Building, near the actual route of the Olympic Torch runners. The second is located at Canada Olympic Park, venue of several Olympic sport competitions, while the third is in the National Sport and Recreation Centre in Ottawa. There were also fifty miniatures cast.

The larger-than-life bronze depicts the relay runners as they pass the torch. The Canadian maple leaf is prominent on the base of the sculptures.

Location: 111 - 5th Avenue S.W., Petro Canada Centre and Canada Olympic Park, Highway #2 west

Date: 1988, 1989

37. Light Rain

Garry Jones

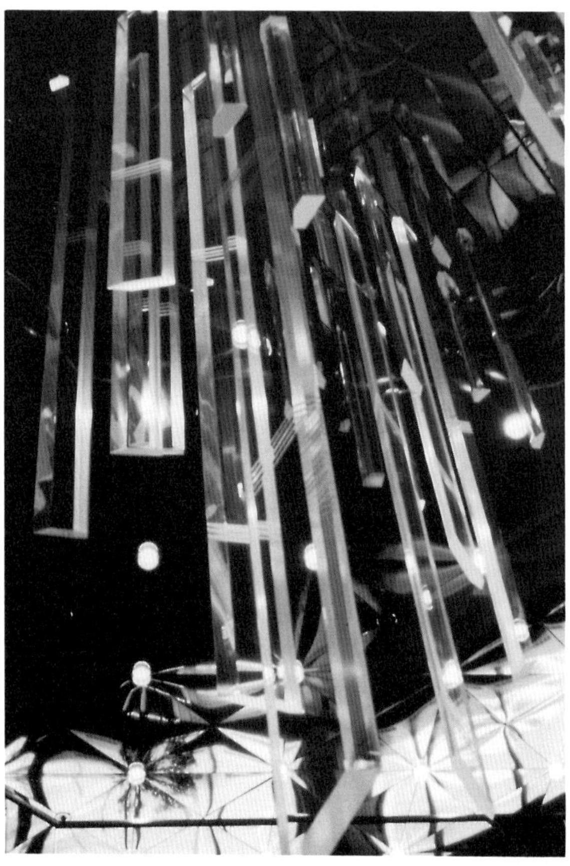

Winner of a competition for Alberta artists, this suspended acrylic sculpture is illuminated by colored ceiling lamps and computerized to display the ever-changing facets of the forty-eight crystal sheets of varying size. The massive light show has also been programmed to music.

Planned as an integral component of the building and commissioned by Marathon Realty, it dominates the ceiling of the main lobby.

Location: 150 - 9th Avenue S.W., PanCanadian Plaza

Date: 1981

38. Flames

Laszlo Szilvassy

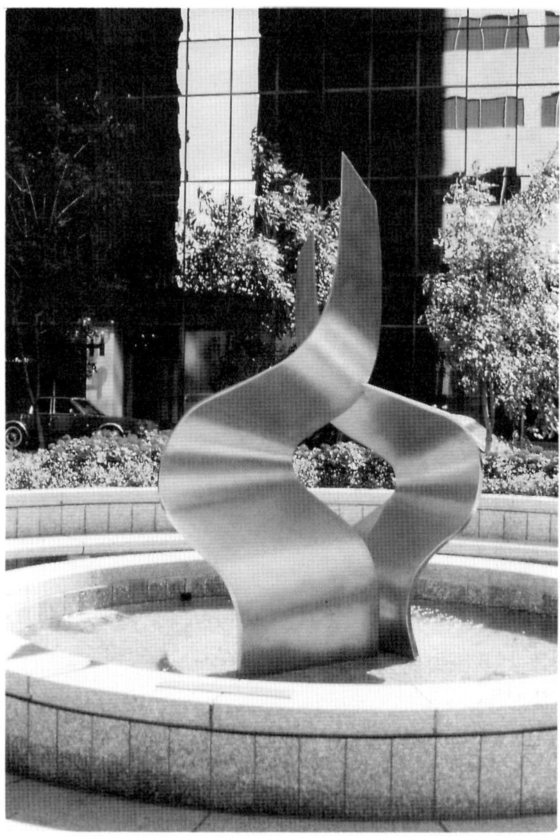

The artist visited Calgary and Alberta several times before he was awarded the commission for an outdoor sculpture at Amoco. When describing his sculpture, Szilvassy commented, "Each time I was there (in Calgary), I felt an upward surge of energy, a burning enthusiasm, the old *joie de vivre*, a certain 'lightness' as opposed to the clumsy dullness of Toronto. So, I am paying homage to this lightness and enthusiasm with my shimmering sculpture."

Flames is constructed of stainless steel, with each flame cut from two separate sheets of metal, then formed, shaped and welded. It is 3 metres high and weighs approximately .5 tonnes.

Location: 240 - 4th Avenue S.W., Amoco Centre
Date: 1990

39. Porte Cochère de Lumière

Michael Hayden

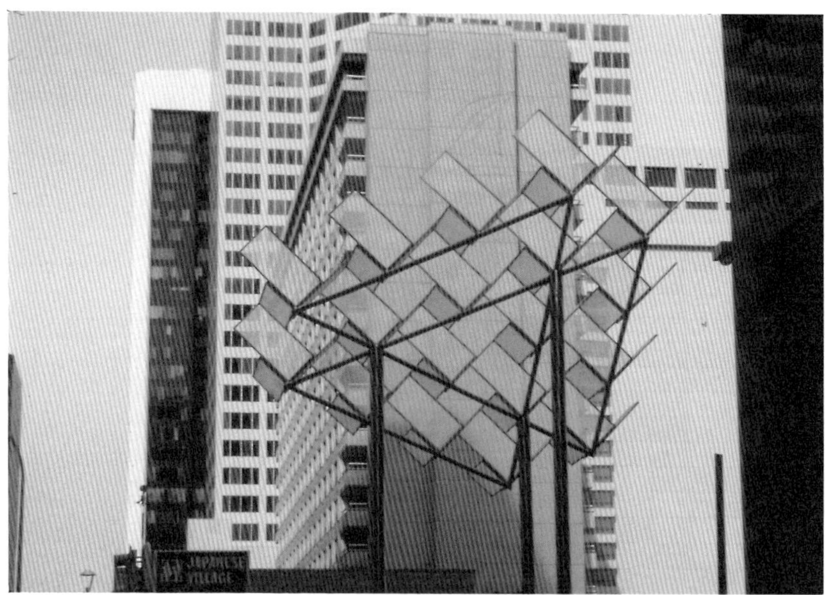

This canopy is made up of many identical acrylic panels held in place by three polished, stainless-steel poles. It is the artist's interpretation of the freestanding structures that once lit the way into buildings for travellers descending from their carriages.

The piece is holographically originated and, as sunlight hits the various angles, a rainbow effect is one of many color changes that occur. The rainbows created by the holograms are projected onto and into the building.

The sculpture stands 10 metres high and was the winner of a national competition co-sponsored by the Alberta Natural Gas Company Ltd. and Olympia and York. Of the 300 artists who entered, only nine, including Hayden, were asked to make models for the final judging of the committee.

Location: 240 - 4th Avenue S.W., Amoco Centre
Date: 1990

40. Killer Whales

Robert Davidson

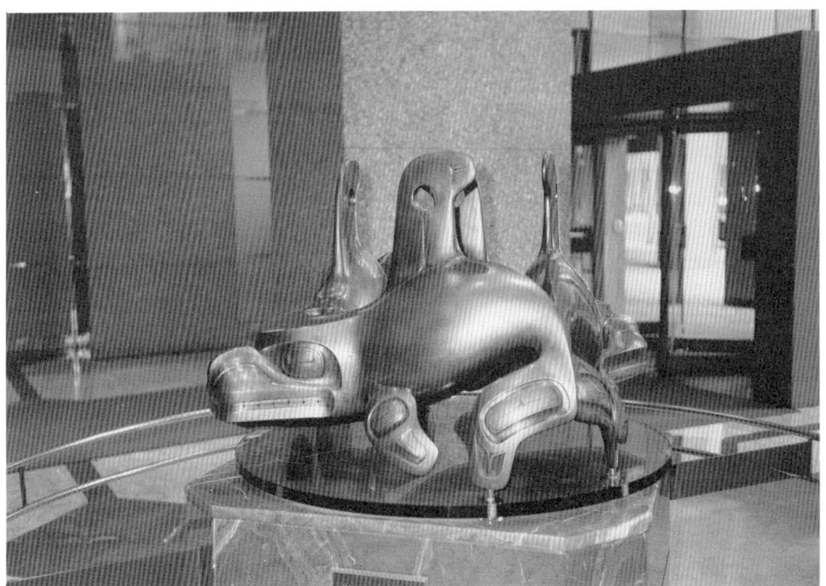

The killer whale is the chief of the underworld in Haida mythology, and Davidson has captured the great animals' power and sleek grace in bronze. The artist says that he "explored new boundaries of sculptural expression . . . and pushed symmetry beyond symmetry" in this split composition of a doubled whale. The intriguing study, decorated with familiar Haida designs, incorporates four identical whales into a ring, with their curving bodies suggesting the free-flowing movement of the magnificent creatures.

The piece, which measures approximately 90 by 65 by 50 centimetres, stands on a 107-centimetre base in the lobby of the Amoco Centre.

Location: 240 - 4th Avenue S.W., Amoco Centre
Date: 1991

41. Memories

Ron Kostyniuk

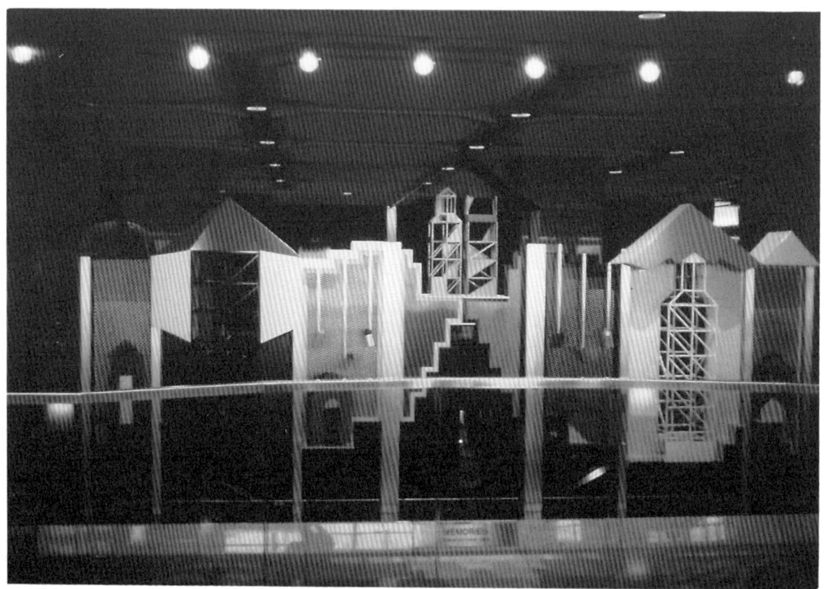

Inspired by recollections of the artist's childhood in Saskatchewan, this large sculpture represents the variations in a typical prairie landscape. It is created in aluminum with a high-lustre enamel finish and stands 2.5 metres high and over 5 metres wide. The blending of angles and textures creates an intriguing variety of visual impressions.

The piece is in the wall of the cafeteria and may be seen from the escalator to the second level as well.

Location: 240 - 4th Avenue S.W., Amoco Centre
Date: 1990

42. & 43. Sadko and Kabuki

Sorel Etrog

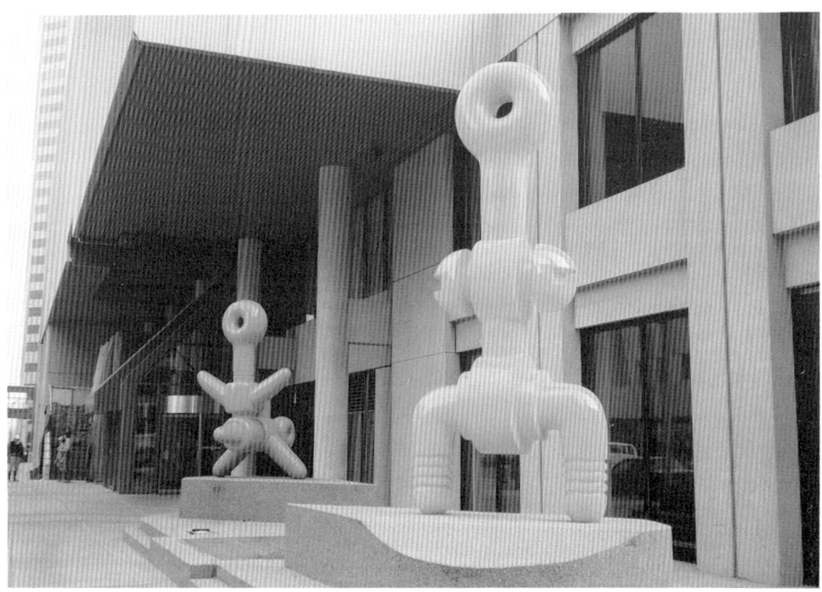

Sadko and Kabuki, two huge, colorful sculptures that illustrate the affinity between the mechanical and organic worlds were unveiled in 1975. They were produced by the lost wax process, then spray painted with automotive paint.

Sadko, the vivid red piece was inspired by a dancer from the Japanese Sadko ballet. The figure is about 4 metres high and weighs approximately 2 tonnes.

Kabuki is the bright yellow figure; it depicts a Japanese Kabuki dancer.

Location: 250 - 6th Avenue S.W., Bow Valley Square
Date: 1975

44. Rushman

Sorel Etrog

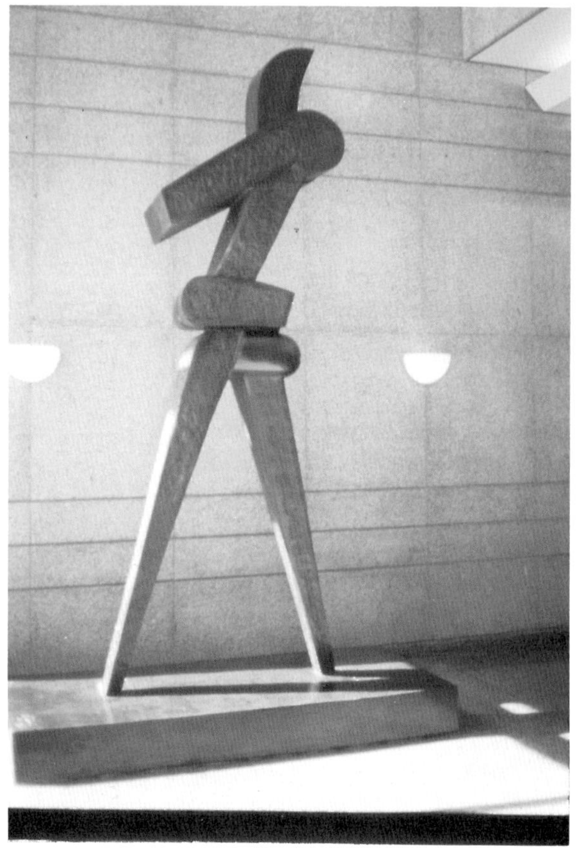

Once again, Etrog depicts man with mechanical qualities. This striding figure seems about to join downtown workers in their rush-hour exodus to the suburbs.

Location: 205 - 5th Avenue S.W., Bow Valley Square
Date: 1976, installed 1980

45. Ritual Head

Sorel Etrog

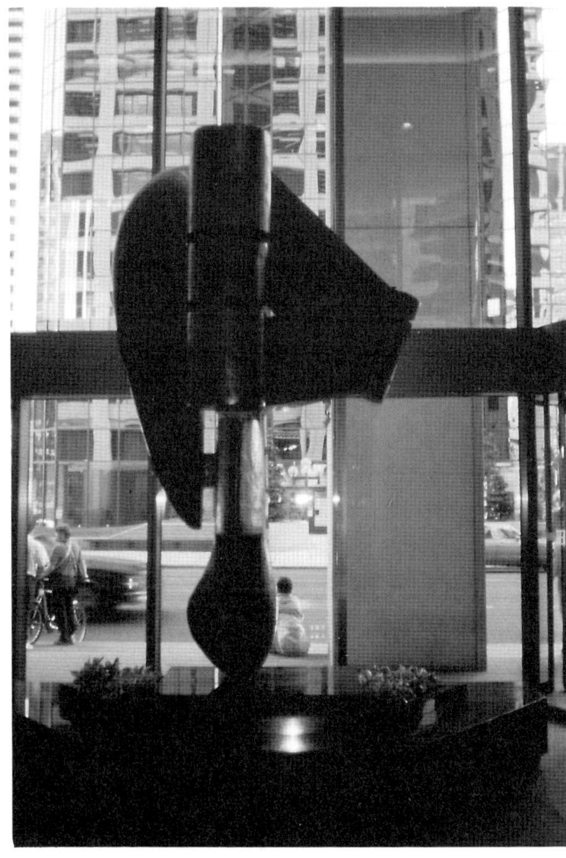

Flat, textured pieces are joined by huge symbolic hinges to create a mechanized version of a human head in this monumental bronze.

Location: 205 - 5th Avenue S.W., Bow Valley Square
Date: 1976, installed 1980

46. Source

Sorel Etrog

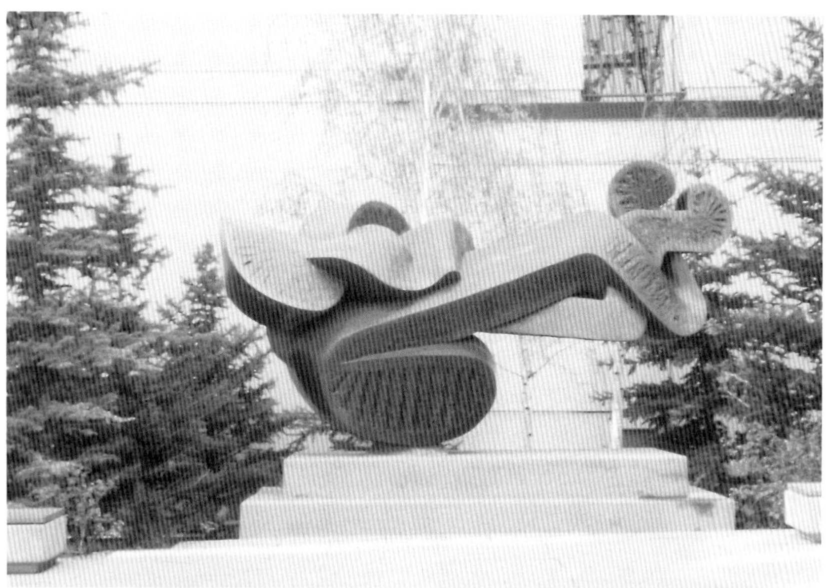

This large bronze stood for many years at the Fifth Avenue entrance of Bow Valley Square. More than 1.5 tonnes of plaster were used to create the plaster mold for *Source*, a sculpture inspired by "the duality of life."

The piece, which is 5 metres long and weighs 2.5 tonnes, is now relocated in the Bow Valley Square gardens where it can be enjoyed by passersby on 6th Avenue S.W.

Location: 205 - 5th Avenue S.W., Bow Valley Square
Date: 1965, installed 1975

47. Conversation

William McElcheran

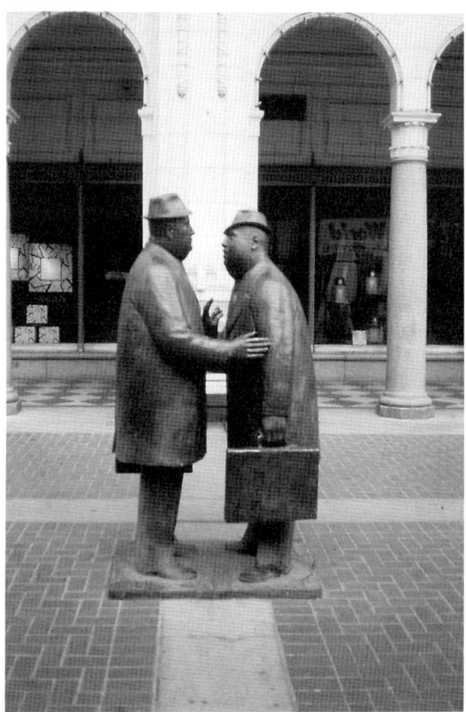

Two bronze businessmen, who obviously have never heard of on-the-job fitness programs, discuss the oil patch on downtown Calgary's Stephen Avenue Mall.

Intent on their wheeling and dealing, they join the lunchtime crowds, slightly out of sync in their bulky top coats and too-small felt hats.

McElcheran says of The Businessman Series of bronze sculptures, "My businessman replaces the classical hero. All the classical artists were dealing with the heroic and how they could find images for this that were larger than life. I, on the other hand, am trying to find my image for the larger-than-life in the non-hero."

Conversation grew in his mind while he watched the "fat cats" discussing their deals on the corner of Bay and King streets in Toronto. He says of their Calgary counterparts, "I guess that Calgarians know about these guys too, and because they're full of Western hospitality, they don't mind a couple of bronze ones having a long conversation in front of the Hudson's Bay Company store."

The satiric sculpture was presented to the City by Norcen Energy Resources, with the location selected by the artist.

Location: Stephen Avenue Mall at 1st Street S.W.
Date: 1980 (acquired by the City in 1981)

48. Cork Mural

Bob Oldrich

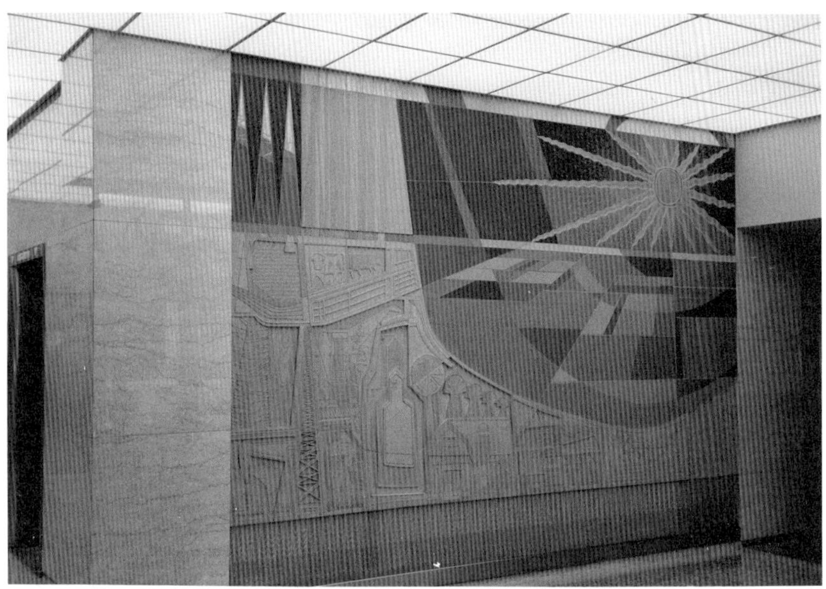

When artist Bob Oldrich was asked to do a mural for the new Alberta Wheat Pool building in 1959, he decided to put in everything he could think of that symbolized Alberta. The result is a scene which completely covers the panel.

Carved from cork, it shows a large sun (for the Sunshine Province), stylized mountains and, of course, Alberta wheat.

The mural, which is surrounded by marble, is located in the main lobby.

Location: 505 - 2nd Street S.W., Alberta Wheat Pool
Date: 1959

49. Flying Dreams

Kevan Leycraft

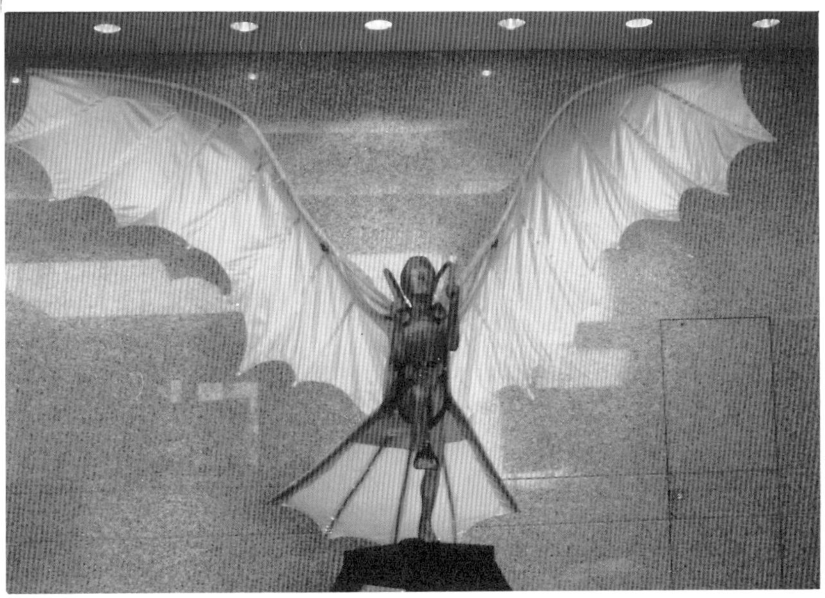

Flying Dreams depicts man and an ornithopter, an aircraft that flaps its wings in order to fly. The "pilot" was created from laminated birch, while the ornithopter was formed from aluminum, steel, carbon fibre and epoxy. The nylon wings have a 6-metre span.

Although his craft is fully functional and capable of sustained flight, Leycraft notes that "few pilots have volunteered to fly it." In conducting ground tests with this ornithopter Leycraft managed to experience lift-off, but self-flight remains the ultimate challenge in human aviation. He is building another, larger ornithopter that he plans to fly.

The piece is a tribute to Leonardo da Vinci, who conceived the strange machine more than 500 years ago. Born in 1452, Leonardo was a true Renaissance man — an accomplished painter, sculptor, philosopher, inventor, scientist and engineer.

Location: 333 - 5th Avenue S.W.
Date: 1990

The Devonian Gardens

The Devonian Gardens, a glass-enclosed space in a city office tower, is an oasis on the Plus 45 level, nearly 14 metres above downtown streets.

The 1-hectare park is a gift to the City from the Devonian Group of Charitable Foundations, and many of the artworks in it have been donated to the City by the Foundation. It is funded from the estate of Calgary philanthropist Eric Harvie, and much of the Garden's art was collected by this enthusiastic and generous world traveller.

Because some of the sculptures were purchased many years ago from galleries and dealers in Europe, information about them and their artists is sketchy. For example, nothing is known about the numerous wildlife bronzes in the area.

50. Natural Harmonics No. 12

Al-Shaikhly
(aka Alan Faith)

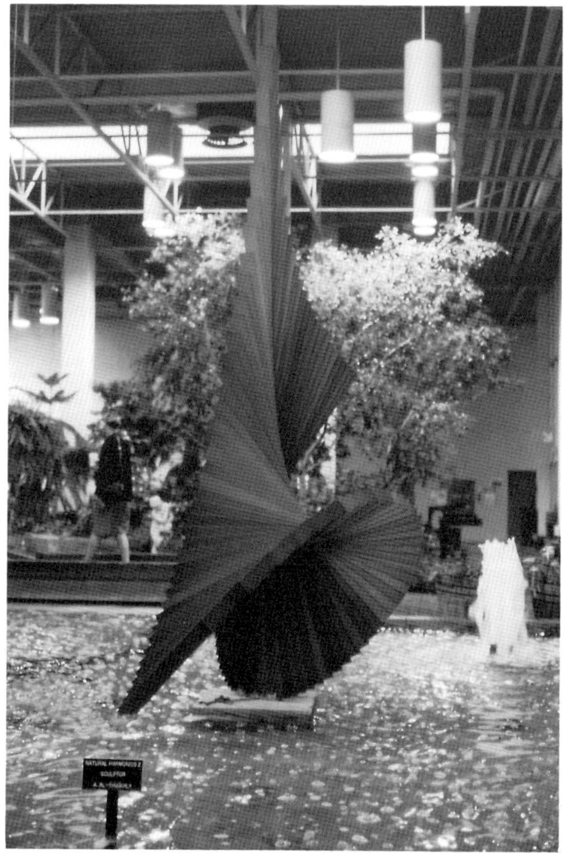

Standing in a large pool in the Gardens is a graceful, pleated and swirled abstract of anodized aluminum alloy. Light and shadow from the glass walls and ceiling of the atrium lend the piece intriguing texture and depth. The artist is hoping to restore the original metallic aluminum finish in order to emphasize the movement of the water and light.

The theme of the soaring, geometrical piece, which is an early sculpture in a series of over a dozen, is "the relationship between physical form and musical structure or concepts."

Location: 317 - 7th Avenue S.W., Devonian Gardens
Date: acquired by the Gardens in 1978

51. Venus at Her Bath

Artist Unknown

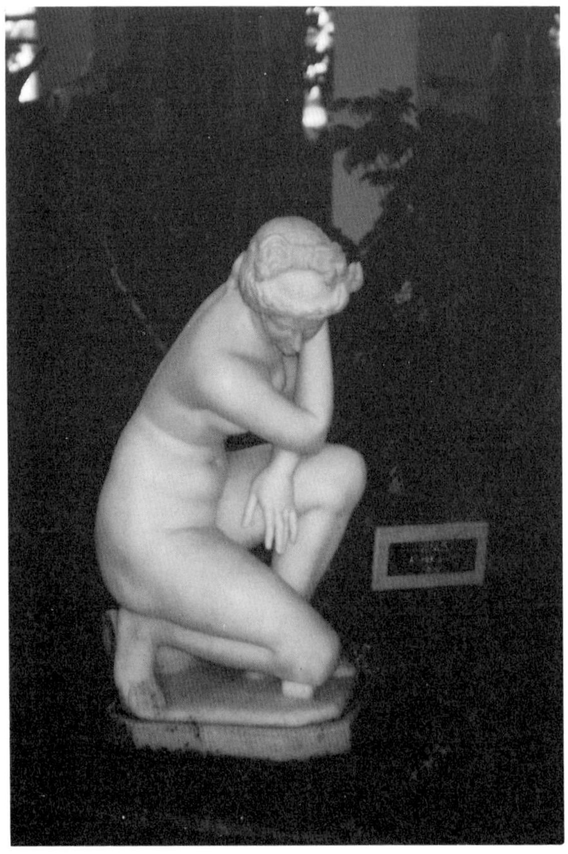

Shielded by shrubbery, a classic marble Venus studies her reflection in one of the Gardens' many pools.

Location: 317 - 7th Avenue S.W., Devonian Gardens
Date: circa 1850, acquired by the Gardens in 1978

52., 53. & 54. Three Bronzes

John Robinson

Three delightful studies of children at play are located at various sites in the Gardens. In *Story on a Summer's Day*, two youngsters listen while a third, who is perched on a rock, reads an engrossing story aloud.

Lost in Flight depicts a child gently holding a captured bird as two others look on in wonder.

The third sculpture, *Boy and Girl Fishing* sits at the back of a pool. It depicts the boy taking a fish off his hook.

Location: 317 - 7th Avenue S.W., Devonian Gardens
Date: placed in the Gardens 1978-1981

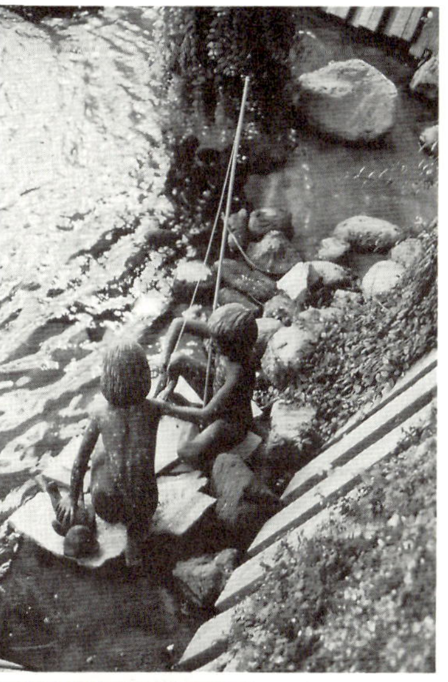

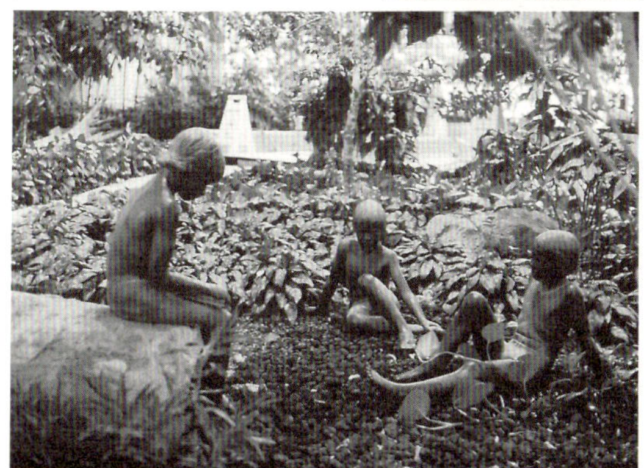

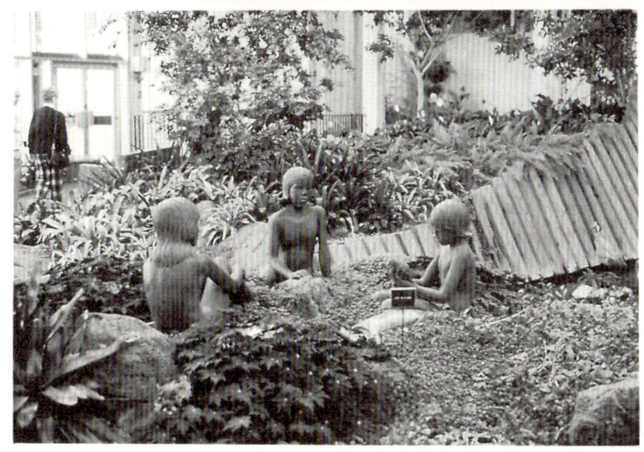

55. Untitled

Jane Charlotte

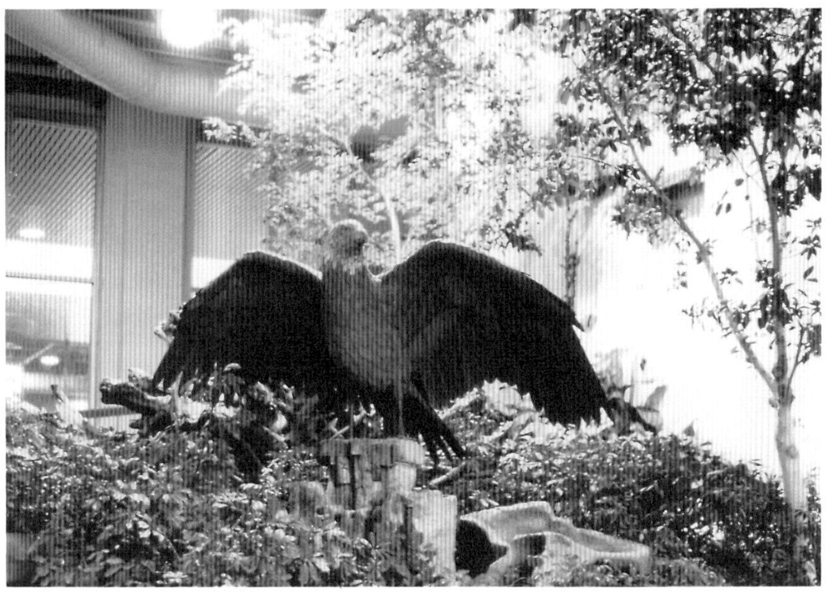

The massive welded-steel eagle sits on a base of wood in a lush green area of the Gardens. It was completed at the University of Calgary sculpture studio during a year of independent study following the artist's BFA degree.

Charlotte says of the piece, "It represents the desire to spread my wings and yet the weight of steel prevents flight. Perhaps I was responding to my youth. The steel bird is an example of material versus subject. Continuing in my work today there is still an underlay of contradiction."

The 2.4-metre bird was loaned to the City of Calgary by the artist.

Location: 317 - 7th Avenue S.W., Devonian Gardens
Date: 1979

56. Wood Carvings

Tom Ward

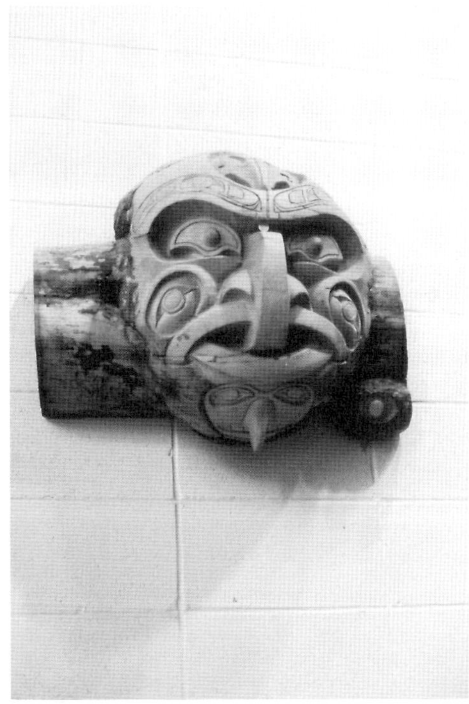

The twenty-nine stylized wooden carvings that decorate the walls of the Devonian Gardens have such intriguing titles as *Kananaskis Weather Woman, Eye Like a Hawk, Kiisehswa Jolly Mr. Sun*, and *Shaganappi Old Rawhide.* They are the work of the late Tom Ward, who was a Calgary artist, and were the first artworks exhibited in the facility.

Carved from burls found on Alberta trees, usually spruce, each is unique because the artist couldn't duplicate his own carvings. As he explained, "the size of the burl and its location on the trunk dictate what the carving will be." Most illustrate Canadian Indian legends, a topic he found endlessly fascinating.

He completed hundreds of such carvings and, when he was a civic employee, the City of Calgary presented a number as official gifts to visiting dignitaries, including HRH Princess Anne and John Diefenbaker.

After his death, the family put this collection on permanent loan to the City for display in Devonian Gardens.

Location: 317 - 7th Avenue S.W., Devonian Gardens
Date: acquired by the Gardens in 1986

57. Bird of Spring

Abraham Etungat

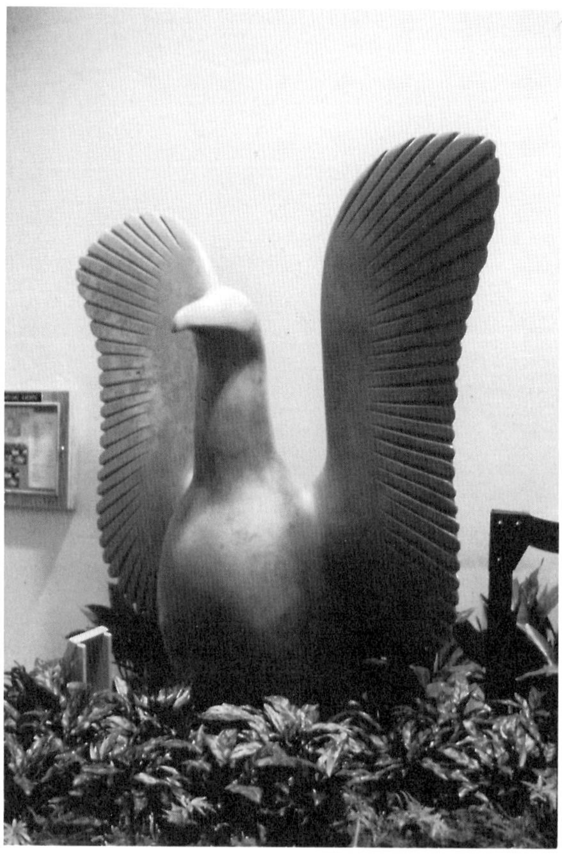

Bird of Spring began life as a 14-centimetre soapstone sculpture. In an experiment by the Devonian Foundation, heroic-sized replicas of this small piece were cast in bronze and fibreglass. The 2.1-metre bronzes were then placed in Ryerson Community Park in Toronto and at the Court House in Vancouver. The Calgary copy is of fiberglass and stood on Stephen Avenue Mall for many years, a focal point for the bustling mall, before its move to the Gardens.

Location: 317 - 7th Avenue S.W., Devonian Gardens
Date: acquired by the Gardens in 1981

58. Guardian

Robin C.H. Bell

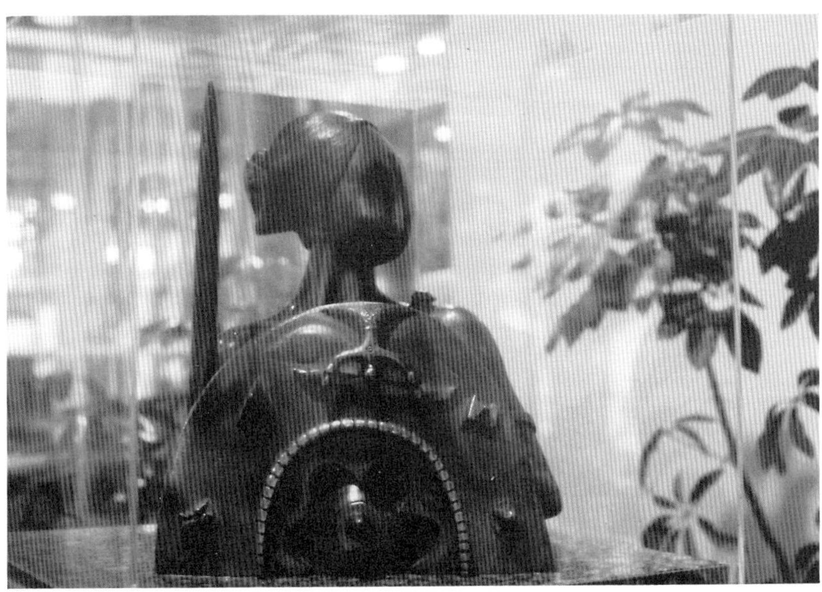

An ancient warrior, portrayed with sword and shield, the bronze is the work of a Canadian artist noted for his talent for giving an antique look to his modern sculptures.

Location: 317 - 7th Avenue S.W., Devonian Gardens
Date: acquired by the Gardens in 1978

59. Frontiersman - Elephant Hunter

Malvina Hoffman

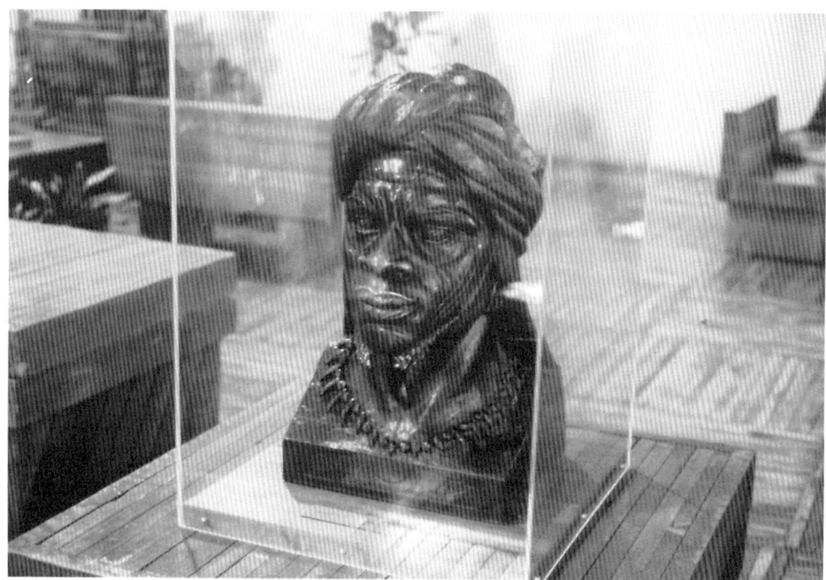

This bronze replica is one of a collection of 101 busts and sculptures depicting peoples of the world.

Hoffman travelled to many parts of the world, creating her works wherever possible and shipping them back to Paris using materials available locally. As a result of careful packaging, only one sculpture received minor damage in transit.

The Glenbow Foundation is fortunate to have bronze replicas of all these sculptures. As a result of negotiations between Hoffman and Eric Harvie, the Field Museum was persuaded to send the original plaster casts back to the foundry to have copies made.

Location: 317 - 7th Avenue S.W., Devonian Gardens
Date: circa 1929 to 1933, acquired by the Gardens in 1979

60. First Jewels

Alice Winant

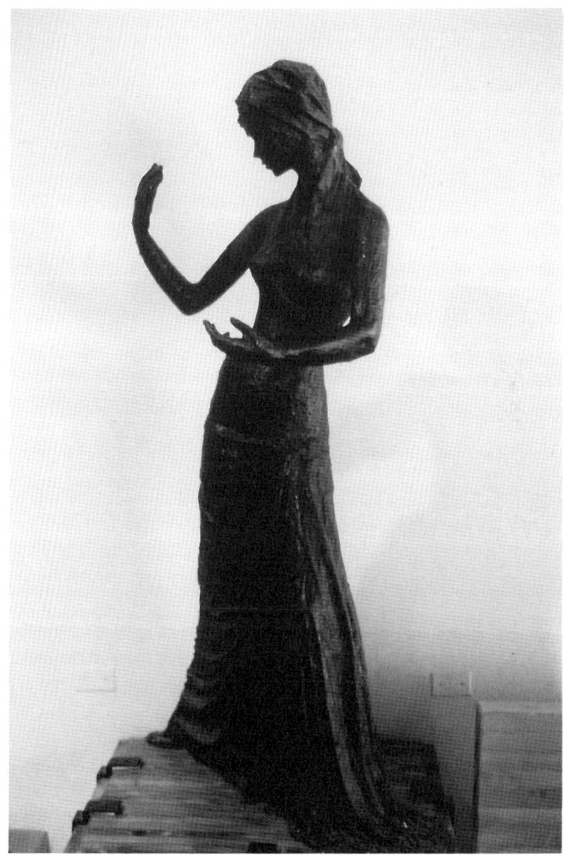

This bronze sculpture depicts the delight of a young woman as she admires a string of beads, her first gift of jewellery. It stands approximately 2 metres high.

The necklace has been missing from the figure for a number of years and probably will not be replaced because it is too easily stolen.

There is one other copy of this work, which was presented to the City of Montreal by the artist's husband after her death in 1989.

Location: 317 - 7th Avenue S.W., Devonian Gardens
Date: acquired by the Gardens in 1978

61. Dogs — Bloodhound and Retriever

Sir Edwin Landseer

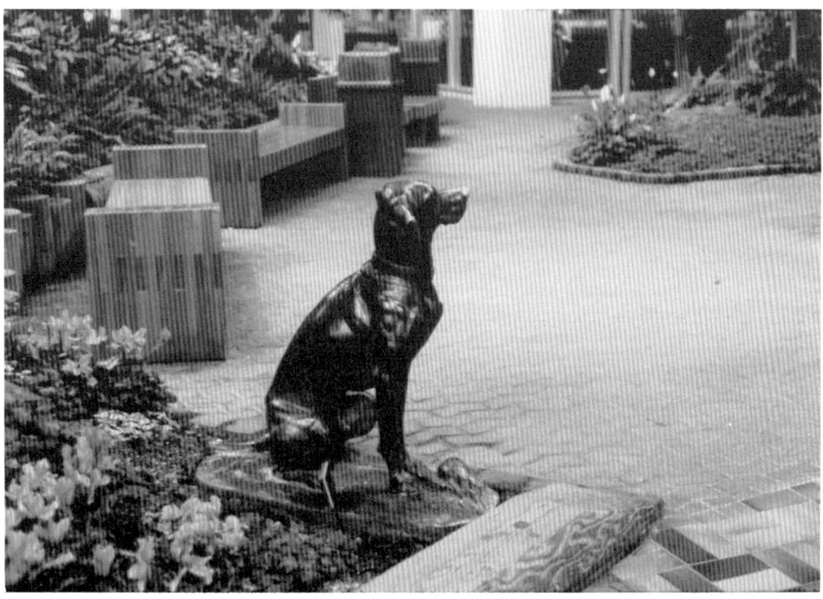

These life-size bronze animals are typical of Landseer's large body of work. Crafted with careful attention to detail, they have a remarkable vitality and grace. They are located by the 7th Avenue elevator.

Location: 317 - 7th Avenue S.W., Devonian Gardens
Date: 1978

62. Inuit Man

Karoo Ashevak

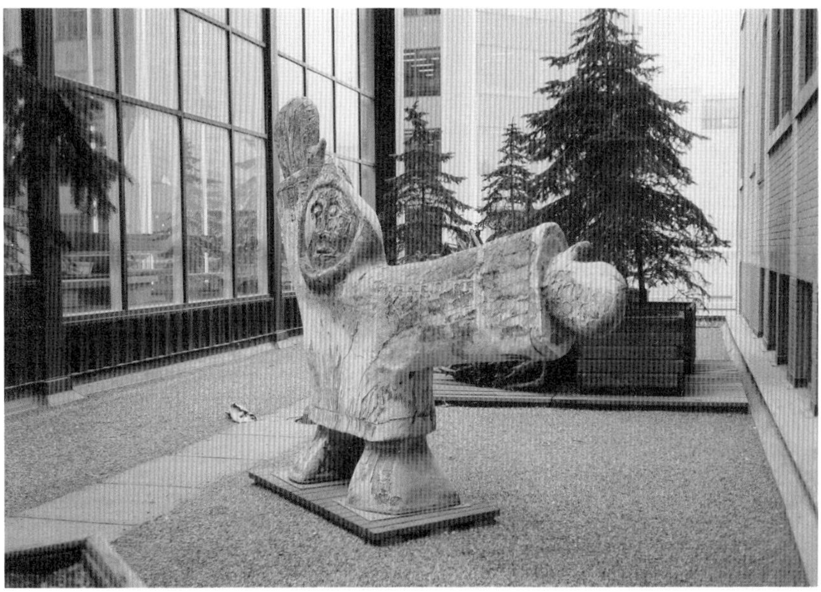

In the 1970s, in an attempt to introduce the Canadian public to the charms of Inuit art, the Devonian Group of Charitable Foundations had a few Inuit carvings enlarged to monumental size. Inuit Man is a copy of an original whalebone carving that was 42 centimetres tall.

Although the copy has been criticized as having lost much of the strength of the original work because of its massive proportions, it has been successful in exposing Calgarians to fine Inuit art.

The 2.5-metre fiberglass sculpture depicts an Inuit man wearing a traditional parka and standing with outstretched arms. It was located on Stephen Avenue Mall for many years before being moved to the outdoor portion of the Devonian Gardens.

Location: 317 - 7th Avenue S.W., Devonian Gardens
Date: circa 1970, acquired by the Gardens in 1981

63. Maiden and Four Toads

Gilbert Bayes

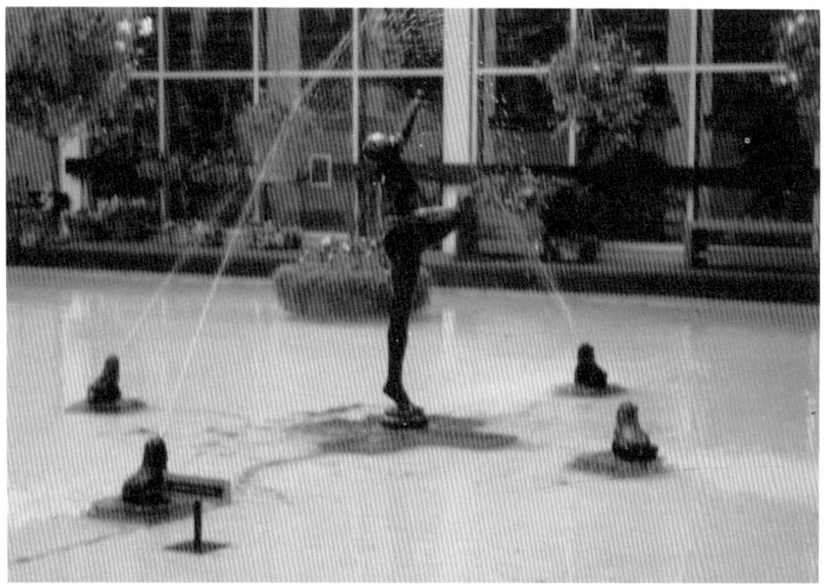

The work of a British sculptor and designer of monuments, this energetic bronze fountain depicts the young woman standing in the midst of four toads. It is located in the outdoor pool.

Location: 317 - 7th Avenue S.W., Devonian Gardens
Date: circa 1920, installed in the Gardens in 1978

64. Boy and Swan

Artist Unknown

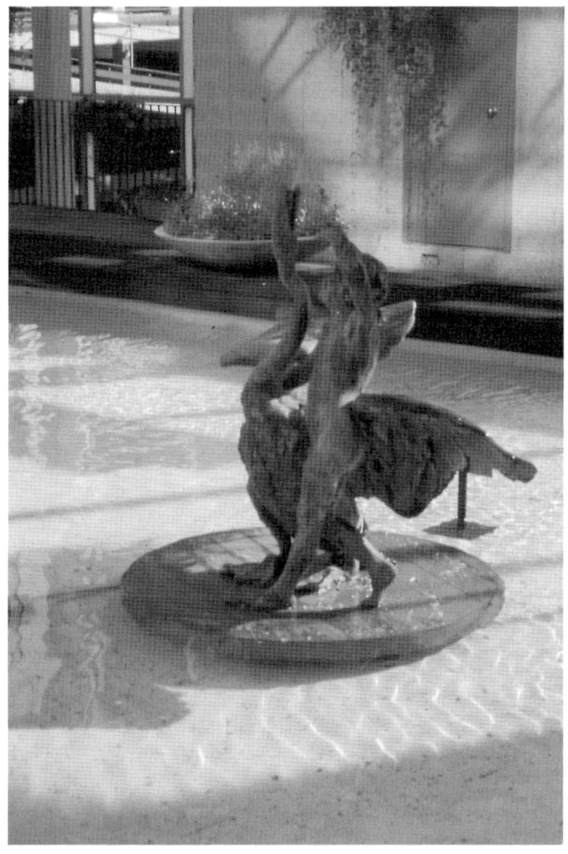

The lead fountain shares the outdoor pool with the *Maiden and Four Toads.*

Location: 317 - 7th Avenue S.W., Devonian Gardens

Date: circa 1870, acquired by the Gardens in 1978

65. Our Land — Our Future
Alberta Farm Family

Vilem Zach

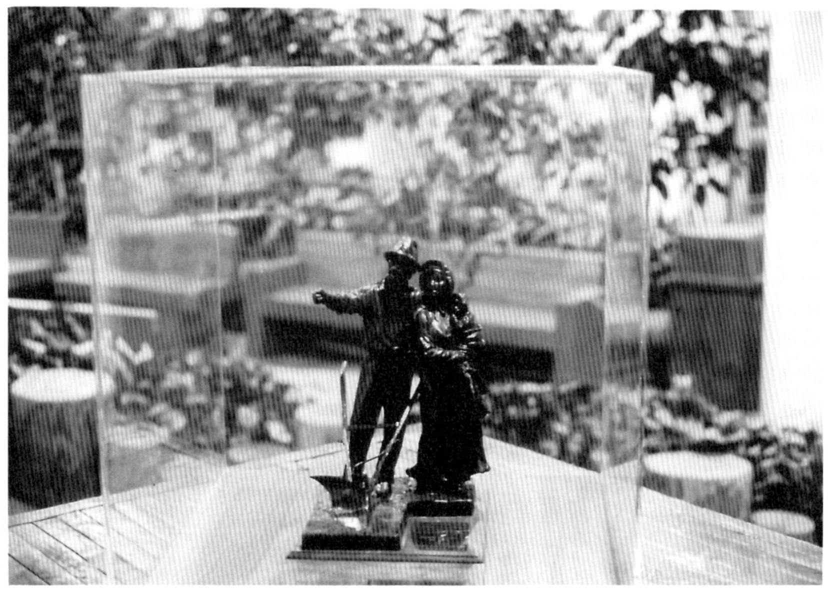

This 40-centimetre-high bronze is a miniature model of the heroic-size sculpture found in Stampede Park. It is a gift from the Calgary Jaycees and the Bank of Montreal.

Location: 317 - 7th Avenue S.W., Devonian Gardens
Date: 1987

66. Weather Vanes

Charlotte Whiten and Paul Kipps

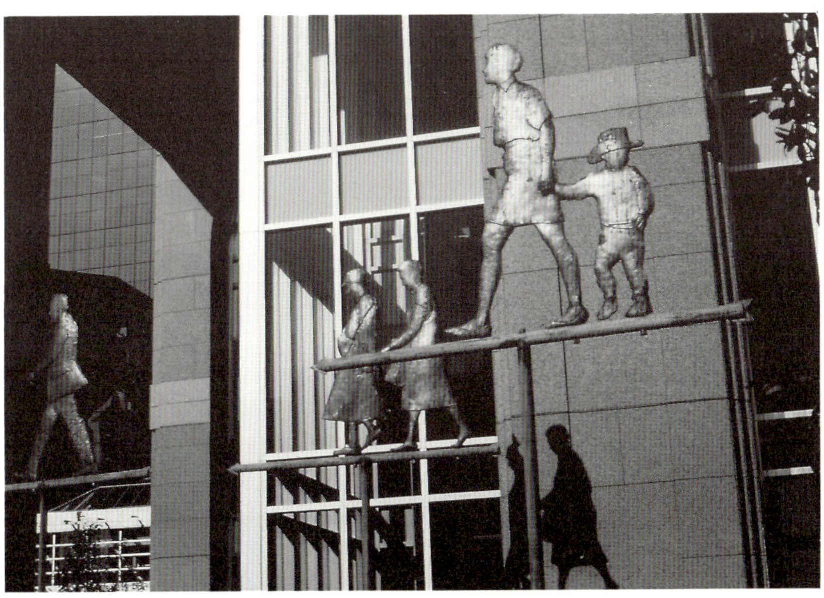

An unusual concept of "people sculpture" is presented at Bankers Hall. Eight life-size, two-dimensional figures are positioned atop tall poles, with four of the figures inside the southeast entrance and the others on the plaza outside. The intent of the project is to unite the people of Calgary with their indoor and outdoor environments, and with the unique weather patterns of their city.

These giant weather vanes are delicately balanced to align with the wind in the exterior pieces, and to respond to manual turning of the support poles of the sculptures inside the building.

Created by the artists from photographs and drawings of Calgarians, they depict a sampling of the community. Represented are, for example, a businessman, a woman holding the hand of a cowboy-hatted child, a mature couple and a lunch-break athlete. It is hoped that, by choosing people for the vanes, it will humanize the busy urban site.

Weather Vanes, of hammered copper, should soon acquire a green patina to blend with its unpolished brass poles.

Location: 9th Avenue and 2nd Street S.W. entrance to Bankers Hall
Date: 1991

67. Tribute to Land

Irene F. Whittome

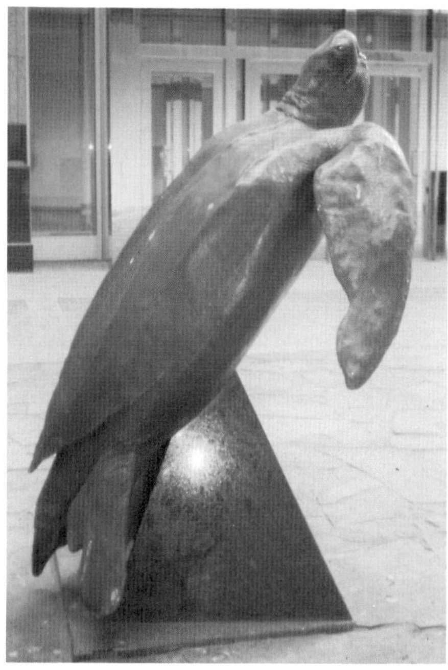

The massive bronze turtle rising from the floor of the exterior courtyard at Bankers Hall is part of an inter-relating artwork which also includes a stylized, horizontal bronze turtle inlaid in a granite panel in the foreground.

Inspiration for the piece is found in aboriginal mythology, where the turtle is the principal life-giving form. It is believed that the animal went to the centre of the earth to bring back the Tree of Life, which represents the Land.

In Iroquois culture, North America was referred to as the "Great White Turtle Island" because it was the piece of land that was supported by the turtle's back when it surfaced.

The artist explains that the work, which depicts the animal emerging from the centre of the earth, is a symbol of hope and represents a connection between earth and animal. It is her hope that viewers will find it a sculpture they can relate to, and that they will arrive at their own conclusions about the work.

The present location is temporary and upon completion of the Bankers Hall Development, *Tribute to Life* will be permanently installed in a sculpture garden on the corner of 3rd Street and 9th Avenue S.W.

Location: Bankers Hall, courtyard outside West Tower Lobby
Date: 1991

68. Friendship

Charles Hilton

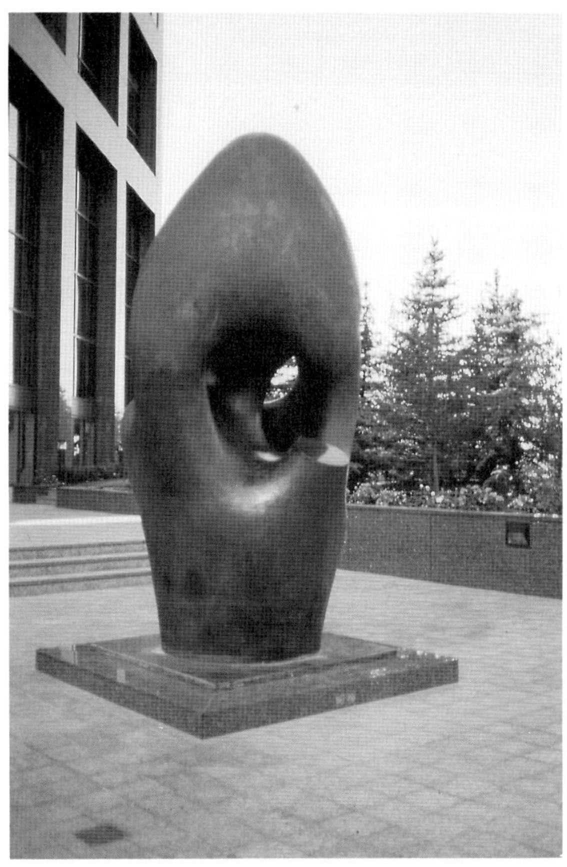

This massive, 3-metre-tall bronze was commissioned by Oxford Development Group in 1978, and was temporarily installed in front of the Provincial Museum in Edmonton until it could be moved to its permanent home in Calgary.

Hilton was coordinator of the 1978 Commonwealth Games sculpture symposium in Edmonton, an event dedicated to "abstractly exemplifying interpersonal relationships." The symposium inspired him to create this piece.

The dedication that accompanies the sculpture explains, "Friendship is the most cherished gift that one can give oneself; it is priceless." The artist says of *Friendship*, "It is made of unyielding, everlasting bronze, yet the fluid curves create a dominant impression of softness . . . a sculpture that is at once both gentle and powerful . . ."

Location: 3rd Avenue and 3rd Street S.W.
Date: 1980

69. Galaxy

Roy Leadbeater

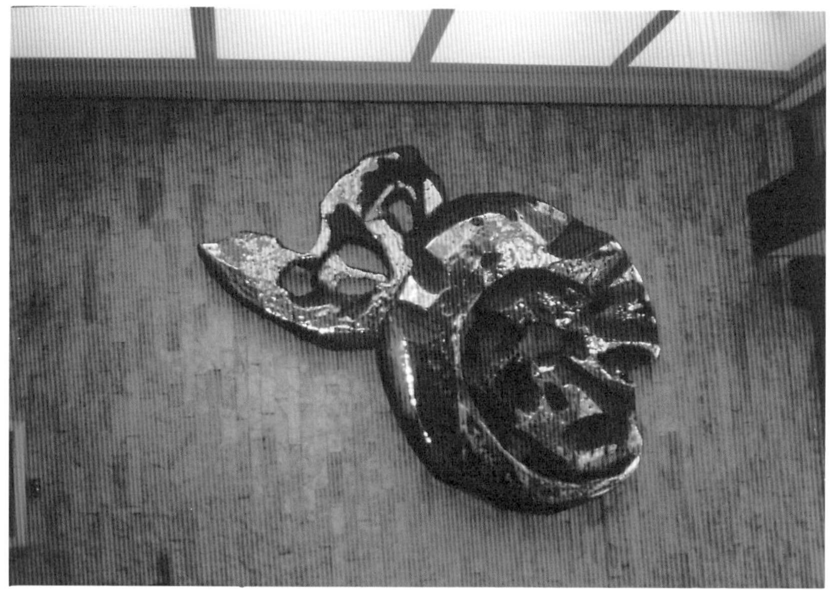

Shortly after receiving this commission from the Bank of Canada, Leadbeater was in the Toronto airport and picked up a copy of *Money* magazine to read on the plane. As this sculpture was to be related to banking, his purchase proved to be invaluable. The artist became intrigued with an article about the history of money — from wax seals to coins.

The cast-bronze sculpture represents the evolution of money and is also symbolic of the surface of a much-circulated coin, magnified to show every scratch and crevice.

The green patina in the piece is reminiscent of the coins stolen by pirates and lost in the oceans. *Pieces of Eight* was his first choice as a title for this sculpture, but it is not surprising the name was vetoed by the bank because it seemed inappropriate to associate itself with piracy.

Cast in the lost-wax technique at Basingstoke, England, and imported back to Calgary by air, the sculpture weighs over 1 tonne.

Location: 404 - 6th Avenue S.W., Bank of Canada
Date: 1971

70. Icarus

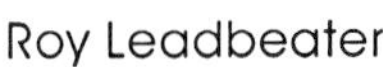

Roy Leadbeater

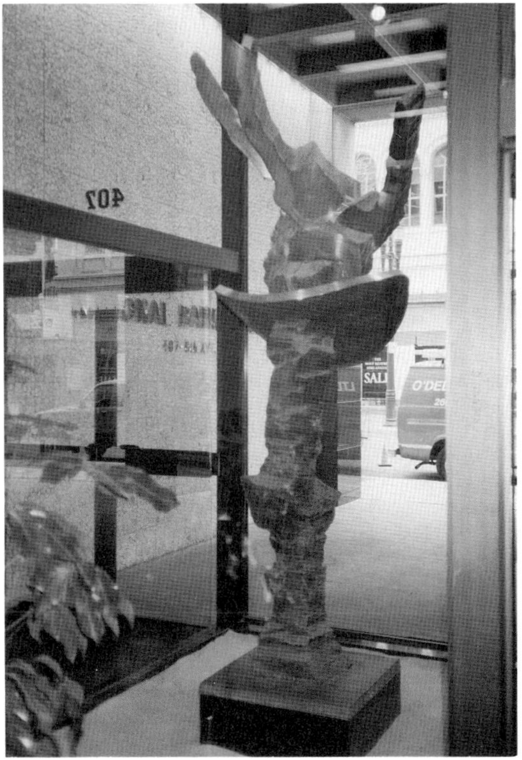

Icarus, according to Greek mythology, was imprisoned with his father, Daedalus. In order to escape, they fashioned wax wings for themselves and flew out of the labyrinth that held them prisoners. Icarus melted his wings by flying too near the sun and dropped into the sea.

The sculpture was completed without incident, then difficulties with the installation began. Problems arose because the piece had not been commissioned until nearly three years after the building was in use. *Icarus* was to stand in a glass cubicle at the front of the building, and all the glass had to be removed so the 3-metre-high piece and its 227-kilogram granite base could be set in place.

The sculpture had been designed as a fountain but a leak in the lead liner was discovered when the water was turned on. The liner was repaired; the sculpture was installed; the fountain was operative. Unfortunately, there was too much splash for the confined space so the full potential of the sculpture has never been realized.

Location: 407 - 8th Avenue S.W., National Bank Building
Date: 1970

71. Moonstairs

Jacqueline Badord

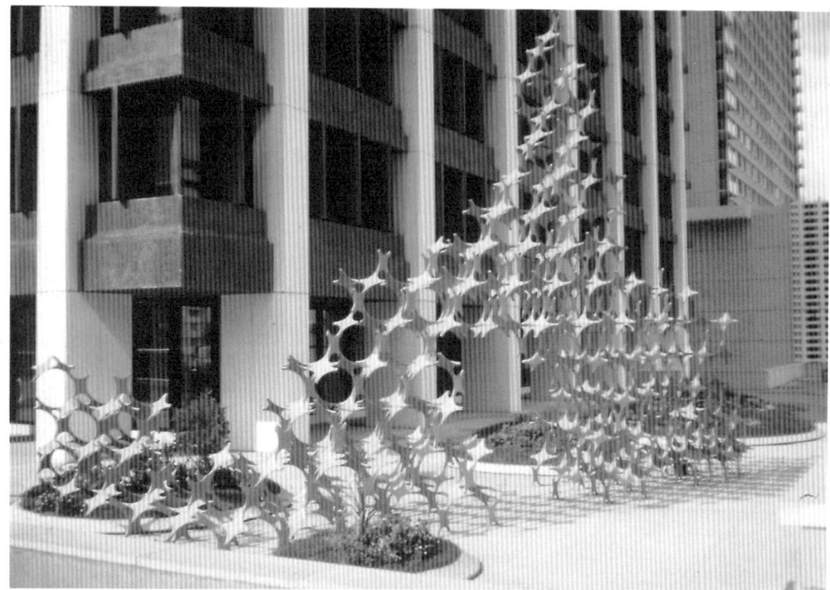

Moonstairs is made up of 800 aluminum modules cast in Paris from one basic design. These were then shipped to Calgary and assembled.

The module was conceived by Badord, a Paris artist, and sculptures created from it may be found in many locations throughout the world. Moonstairs, which climbs to a height of over 7 metres is the largest of these sculptures.

Badord, along with her husband, sculptor Oliver Descamp, and their architect-son Dominique, travelled to Calgary to construct the aluminum "immobile" on the Plus 15 pedestrian area north of Aquitaine Tower.

The artist described *Moonstairs* as "a design to occupy space, with the interpretation of it left largely to the imagination of the observer."

Location: 540 - 5th Avenue S.W., Aquitaine Tower
Date: 1969

72. Copper Wall

Sabatier of Paris

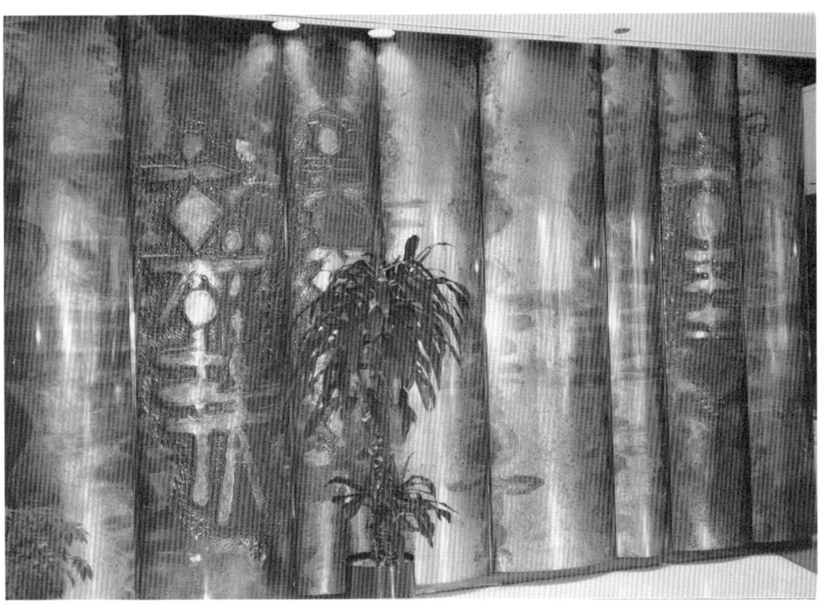

Copper panels, the work of Sabatier of Paris, cover the lobby walls in Aquitaine Tower.

The Parisian artist creates his murals with hammer, welding torch and acid wash. The copper art was prepared in France, then shipped to Calgary for installation.

Location: 540 - 6th Avenue S.W., Aquitaine Tower
Date: 1969

73. Aquitaine Landscape

Maurice Calka

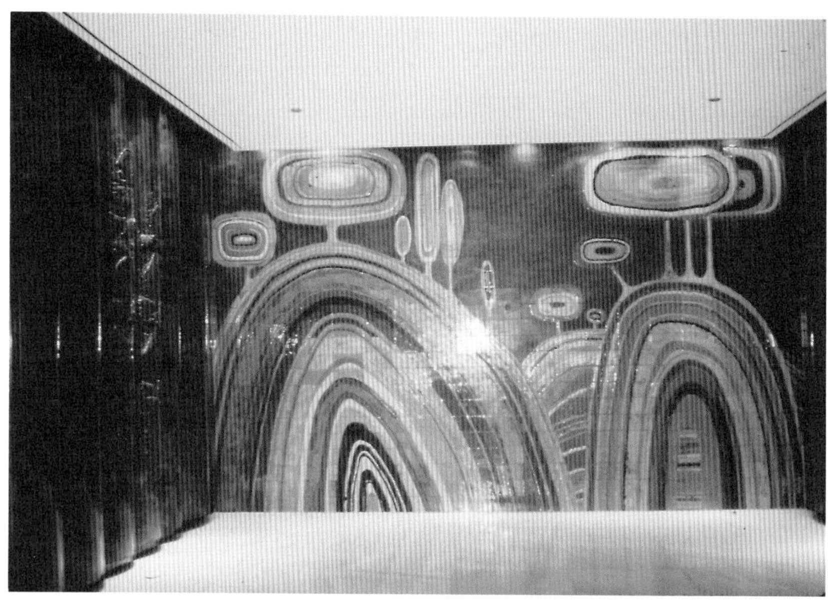

The large, brilliantly colored mosaic in the lobby of Aquitaine Tower is the work of a French artist, professor of arts at Beaux Arts, Paris, at the time.

The mosaic is his impression of a typical landscape in the French province of Aquitaine. The ceramic pieces were created in France, using a well-guarded, secret process to produce the unusual range and depth of colors. The mosaic was then assembled in Calgary by Calka.

Location: 540 - 5th Avenue S.W., Aquitaine Tower
Date: 1969

74. Mating Dance

Kevan Leycraft

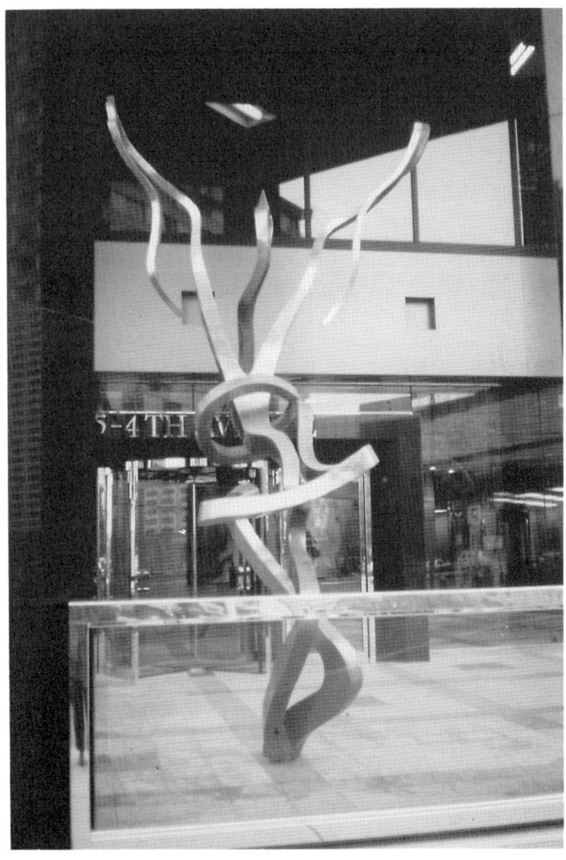

This abstract rendition of a whooping crane was created from over 300 kilograms of steel. The piece was commissioned by Edgecombe Properties for the northwest corner of the building.

Because the site catches the attention of Calgary's powerful west winds, the artist chose to make this a kinetic sculpture. He says, "When we get a strong chinook, this bird can dance." Passersby are intrigued by the fact that, no matter how strong the wind and how frantically the bird moves, no parts of the sculpture collide.

The stylized whooper with its wings raised high above its upstretched head stands at the elevated entrance of the building and rises over 4 metres above the sidewalk.

Location: 555 - 4th Avenue S.W., Selkirk House
Date: 1991

75. Pan and the Three Graces

Krystyna Sadowska

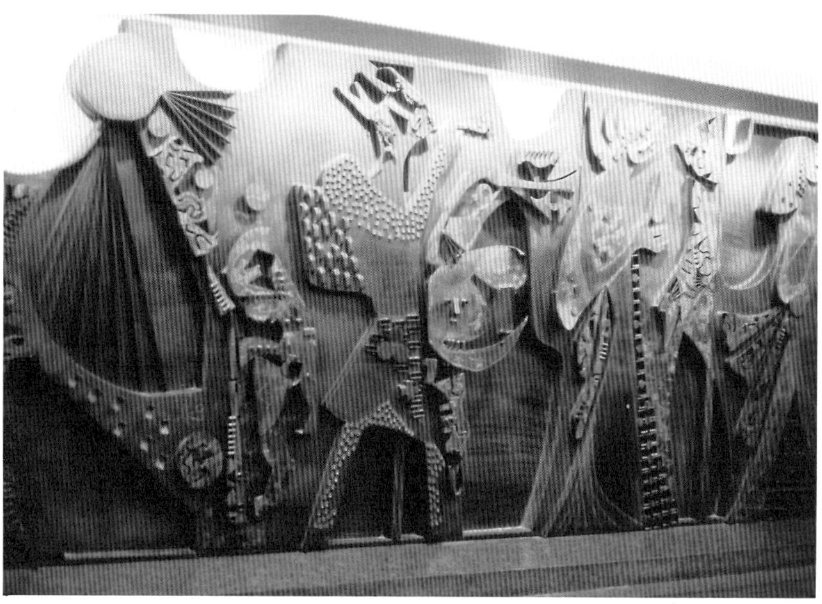

Inspiration for this imposing, welded-steel mural is found in Greek mythology. Pan, with the horns, hoofs and ears of a goat, was a rollicking deity. He ruled over woods, fields and fertility and was a marvellous musician. Pan and his pipes often accompanied the woodland nymphs in their dances. In this piece, he carries a flame to signify light and warmth.

The three Graces, daughters of Zeus, were the goddesses of joy, charm and beauty. They brought goodwill to gods and men as they presided over all happy social events.

In constructing the mural, the artist first sketched the scene, then enlarged it to actual size. The steel was then cut precisely to pattern and assembled using both the artist's own and standard welding methods. Examples of her techniques may be seen in the unusual texture and detail of the work.

Each of the large panels in the mural weighs over 360 kilograms, and the piece measures about 3 by 8 metres.

Location: 550 - 6th Avenue S.W., Calgary House
Date: 1965

76. Buffalo Trails

JoAnne Schachtel

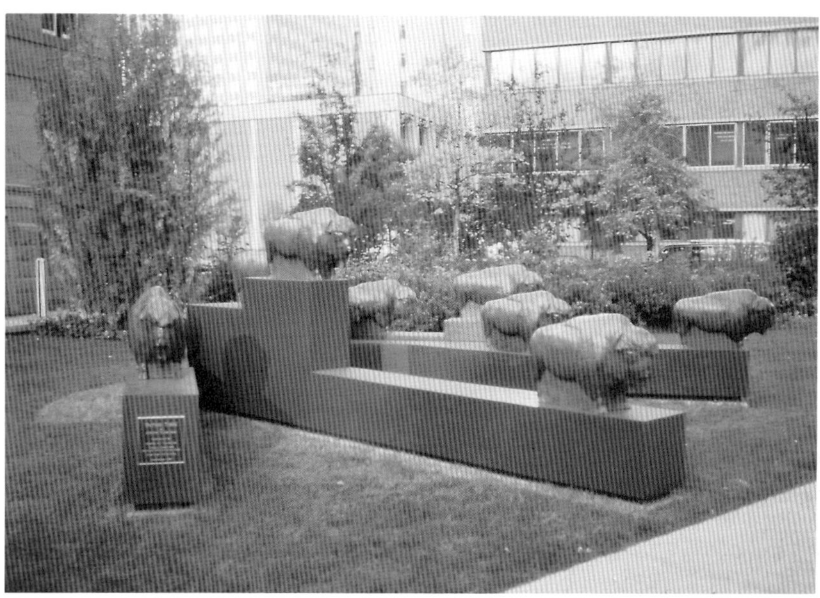

This display of thirteen plains buffalo, one-third life size, was a winner in the 1991 Calgary Downtown Business Revitalization Zone competition. Selected as one of two successful entries, the work is installed on the lawns at the Court House in downtown Calgary.

The buffalo are made of fiberglass and resin and were hand finished with a resin patina to give them the appearance of oxidized bronze. Although all were cast from the same mold, one of the group remains in the base color, a gold powder suspended in a resin base. It represents an albino animal, symbolic because early Indians believed if they killed an albino they would assume supernatural powers from it.

The grouping of buffalo on pedestals stands only about 2 metres in height, and the artist hopes the work will be "touched, sat on and enjoyed."

Location: 6th Avenue and 5th Street S.W., Court House lawns
Date: 1991

77. The Wonderful Energy Machine (1982)

Richard Prince

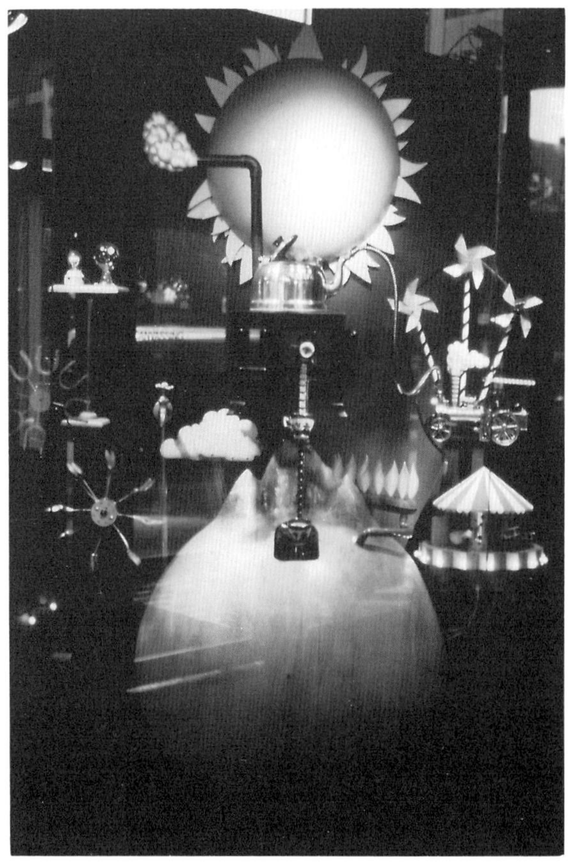

"The piece is not designed to explain anything in a scientific way, but rather to evoke the curiosity of young and old," says the artist. And that it most certainly does. Located at the entrance to the Energy Resources Conservation Board's "Energeum" museum, it is a composite of energy sources, both natural and man-made.

The earth is represented as an energy storehouse, dominated by a whimsically powerful sun. Other energy sources such as solar, steam, hydroelectric, gas, coal and petrochemicals are also included.

Created from a variety of materials, including wood, plastic and metal, it has many moving parts and is a source of continual speculation — "What is it?"

Location: 640 - 5th Avenue S.W., Energy Resources Conservation Board
Date: 1982

78. Boundary Waters

Hollis Williford

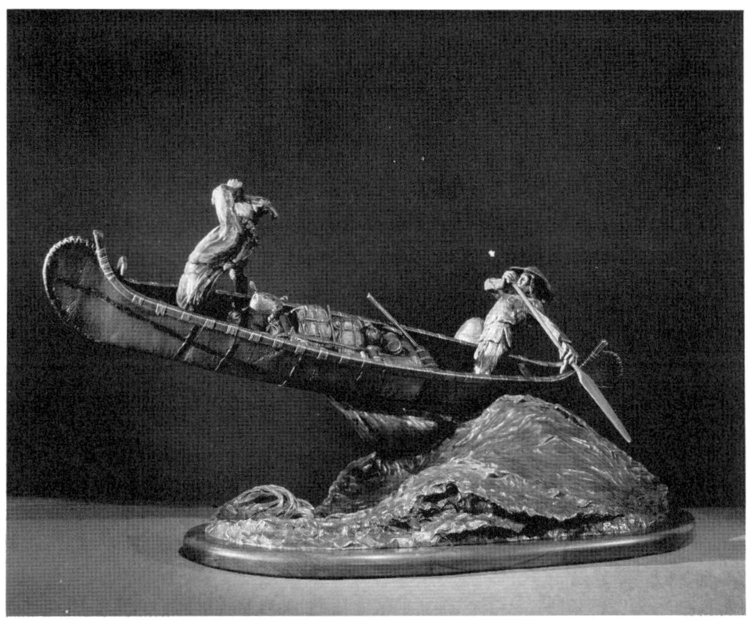

Williford says of the background to this dramatic, 1- by 1.5-metre bronze, "There is nothing connected with the development of North America's history that is more romantic and thrilling than the rise and fall of the fur trade. From the time the early French explorers came into the interior of the continent by the waterways of the Great Lakes country, until the last fur trader vanished from Mackinaw, it was a long succession of adventures, hardships and daring enterprise."

Traditionally the term "boundary waters" refers to canoe waters dividing Canada and the United States in the American Northeast. However, Williford uses it in the title of this sculpture to refer to "all the rivers, lakes and tributaries that encompassed the fur trade arena or the theatre of activity and commerce of what was at that time known as the Northwest."

In choosing their wild ride through the rapids, these two voyageurs are taking a chance that no fur company would ever have sanctioned because of the risk to valuable trade goods that could be portaged instead. The piece is the artist's salute to the spirit, courage and freedom of this reckless breed of men who challenged all odds.

As in several of Williford's large bronzes, the base is incorporated into the main work. In this instance, the swirling waters lift the canoe high into the water before drawing it back into the rapids.

The work was commissioned by Canadian Hunter Exploration Ltd.

Location: 605 - 5th Avenue S.W.
Date: scheduled for installation early 1992

79. Steeples

Roy Leadbeater

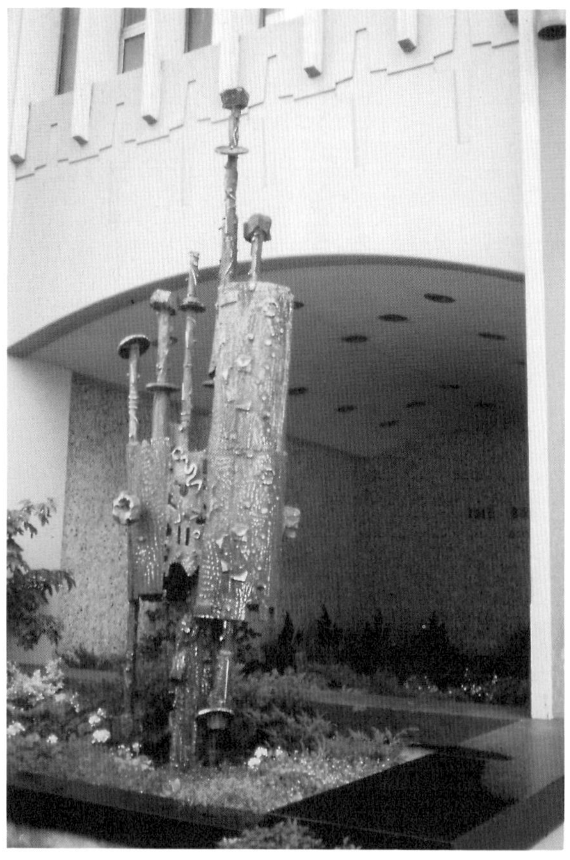

This piece was commissioned several years after the building was completed. It was designed to be a fire and water sculpture, with the intention being to use fire in winter and a combination of fire and water in the summer.

Although the design worked successfully, at present the concept cannot be fully appreciated because concern for conservation of resources precludes the use of natural gas for this purpose. The 4.6-metre-high *Steeples* has become simply a cast-bronze sculpture.

Location: 630 - 6th Avenue S.W.
Date: 1969

80. Sitting Eagle (1874 - 1970)

Don Begg

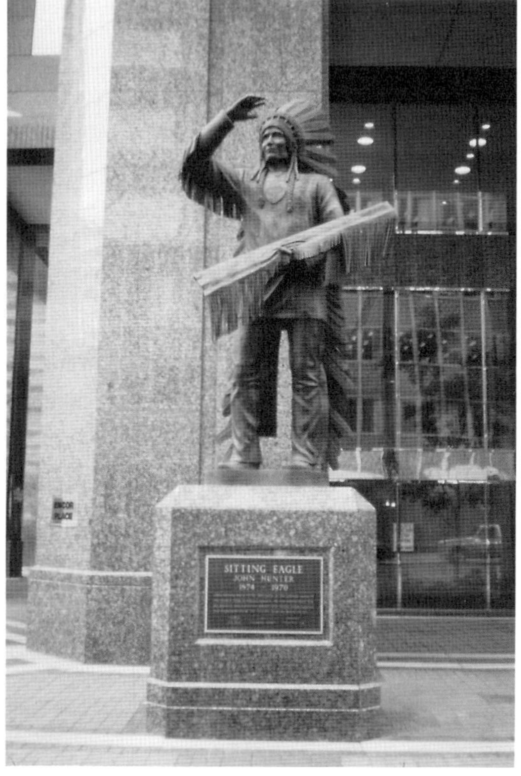

Sitting Eagle was born John Hunter in Morley, Alberta, and was a well respected member of the Chiniki band of the Stoney Indians.

In the words of his children and grandchildren, "He was a skilled tracker, hunter and fur trapper. During bad winters, he could be depended upon to generously help feed many of his neighbors. In later years, he established a cattle ranch which is still operated on the Stoney Reserve by one of his descendants."

A handsome man, he was much in demand for snapshots when he donned his beaded tribal dress at Banff Indian Days. He also attended the Calgary Stampede, winning many prizes for his traditional dress and tepee designs.

The 3.5-metre-high bronze is based on photos of Sitting Eagle when he was about fifty years old, and in his prime as an elder and leader of the Chiniki. The portrait sculpture was commissioned by The Cascade Group.

Location: 645 - 7th Avenue S.W., ENCOR Building
Date: 1988

81. & 82. Cityscape and Landscape

Brian Baxter

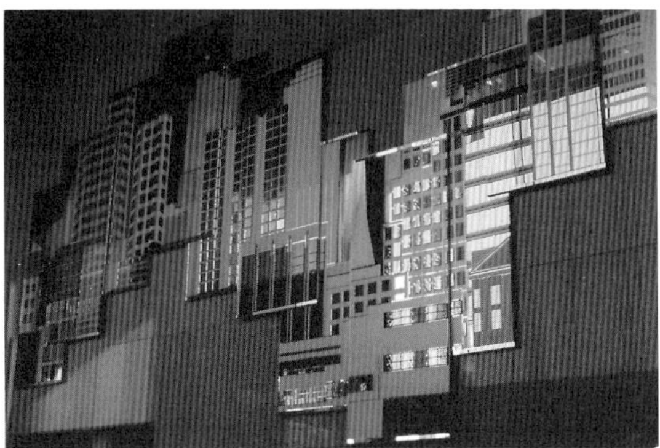

Murals of colored glass and mirrors add a dramatic touch to the rather bleak elevator lobbies in the north and south towers of Western Canadian Place.

Cityscape, located in the south tower, is a sophisticated depiction of the frontage of buildings in several Canadian cities. Created from sandblasted clear and colored glass, the work gives the illusion of mirrors sparkling on the lobby wall, with the reflection of the slatted ceiling adding texture to the windows in the sculptured buildings.

Landscape, in the north tower, is a colorful installation composed of twenty panels filled with symbolism. Provincial crests, hydroelectric lines, coal cars, fur pelts, trees, fish, livestock and farm crops are a subtle contrast to the colorful land weaving through the piece. From the multi-layered flatness of the prairie to the mountains and on to the blue ripples of the Pacific, it represents the resources and power of both humans and nature in Western Canada.

Location: 707 - 8th Avenue S.W., Western Canadian Place
Date: 1986

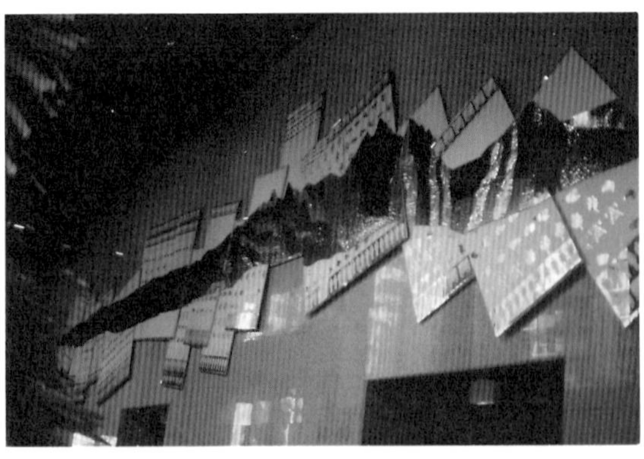

83. Soapstone Carving

Pierre Karlik

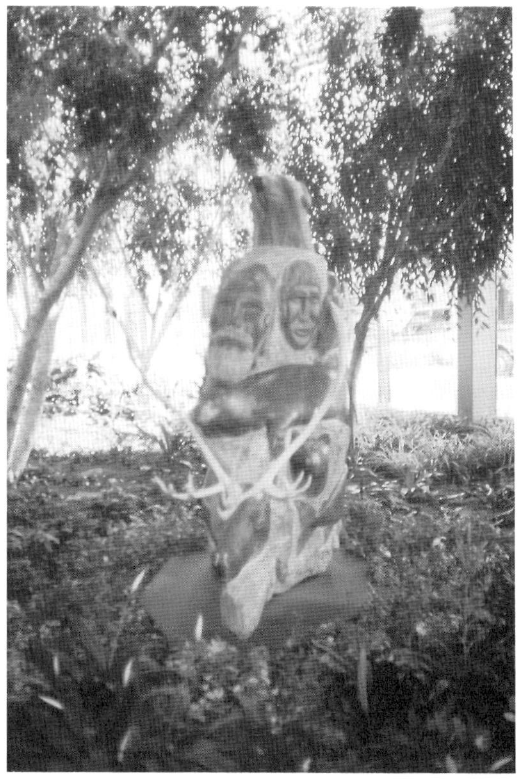

Originally commissioned by Aquitaine Company of Canada, the large carving was situated in the lobby of that company's building on 5th Avenue S.W. for a number of years.

The artist gives two reasons for the polar bear's dominance in this intriguing Inuit artwork. As Karlik explains, "The polar bear is the strongest creature in the Inuit culture, but it is also on top because it fits better according to the shape of the stone."

The carving is symbolic of the interdependence of life in the North. Emerging from the stone below the bear are an Inuit man, muskox, Arctic fox, hare, char, walrus, seal, ptarmigan, whale and caribou.

The raw soapstone, which was found 8 kilometres from Rankin Inlet, weighed nearly 4 tonnes. A dark grey, medium-soft rock, it was transported by sled and tractor to Rankin where Karlik did his carving. The completed work was then shipped to Calgary, and the artist was brought south to put finishing touches on the piece — authentic tusks on the walrus, whiskers on the seal and antlers on the caribou.

Location: 707 - 8th Avenue S.W., Western Canadian Place
Date: 1971

84. The Builders

George Pratt

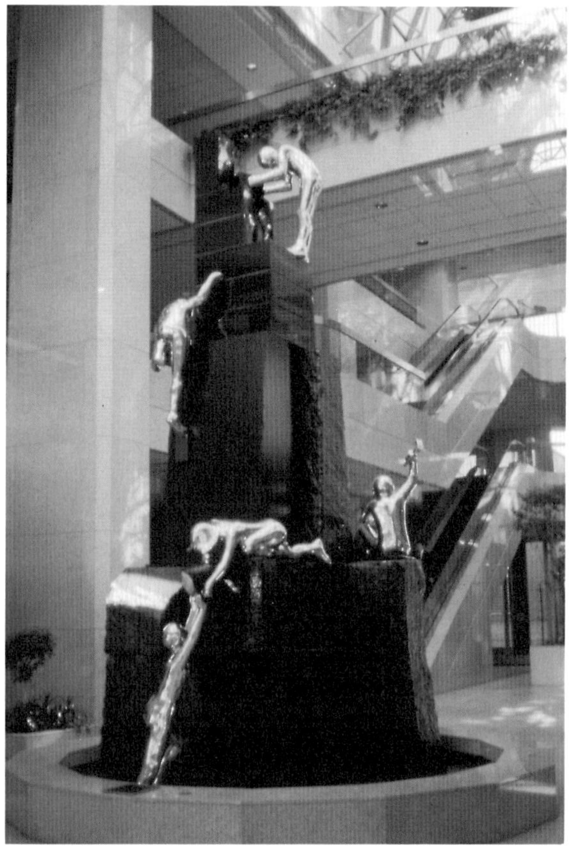

The granite for this piece was quarried on Nelson Island, British Columbia. The original stone was grey, with Pratt adding an ebonizing coat to dramatize the strength of The Builders and to symbolize oil, the underlying interest of its owners.

The sculpture is made of raw quarry blocks. Until the 5-metre level, the stone is rough-hewn, but then sawn surfaces are introduced. Toward the top, the blocks are highly polished and meticulously fitted. The artist's conception was to build and grow from raw earth to a finished edifice through cooperative human endeavor.

Six life-size bronze figures are imposed on the granite. These are meant to suggest a network of individuals combining their strength and industry to construct the very fabric of Canada. Together they heave the blocks from the ground, hew them to fit, lift them up again and finally fit them into place to create the finished product.

Location: 707 - 8th Avenue S.W., Western Canadian Place
Date: 1988

85. Nova Gate

Kosso Eloul

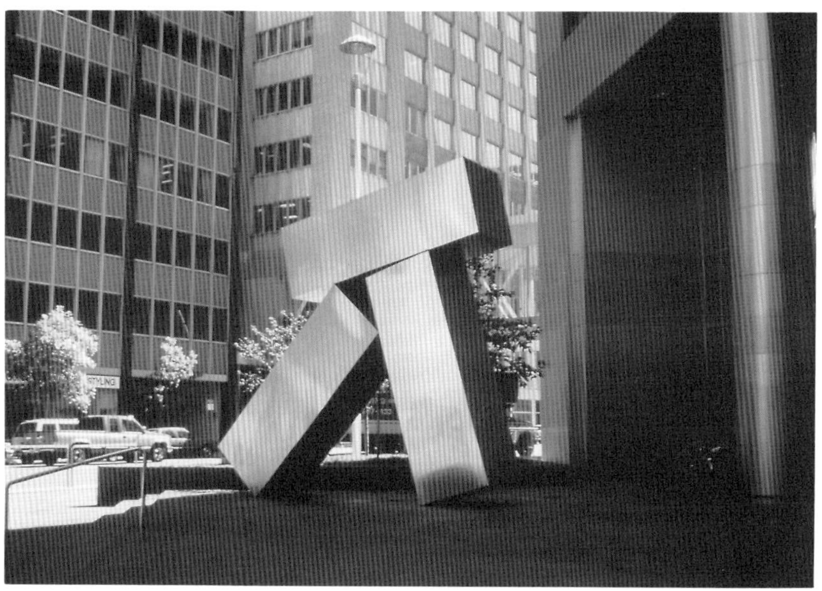

This massive, polished-steel sculpture dominates the small plaza in front of the Nova Building in downtown Calgary.

Intricate engineering holds the elements of the 4-tonne piece in place, with supports embedded in several feet of concrete beneath street level. Its size and tenuous balance present a powerful visual impact during the day, but in the evening it is bathed in soft street lighting, creating a more gentle effect.

The dynamic movement suggested by the sculpture is "symbolic of the energy and spirit of Calgary and The Nova Corporation," says the artist. "For the viewer, there is magic in 'What holds them together?' The answer is left open to the imagination."

Location: 801 - 7th Avenue S.W., Nova Building
Date: 1982

86. Mother and Children

David Panneok

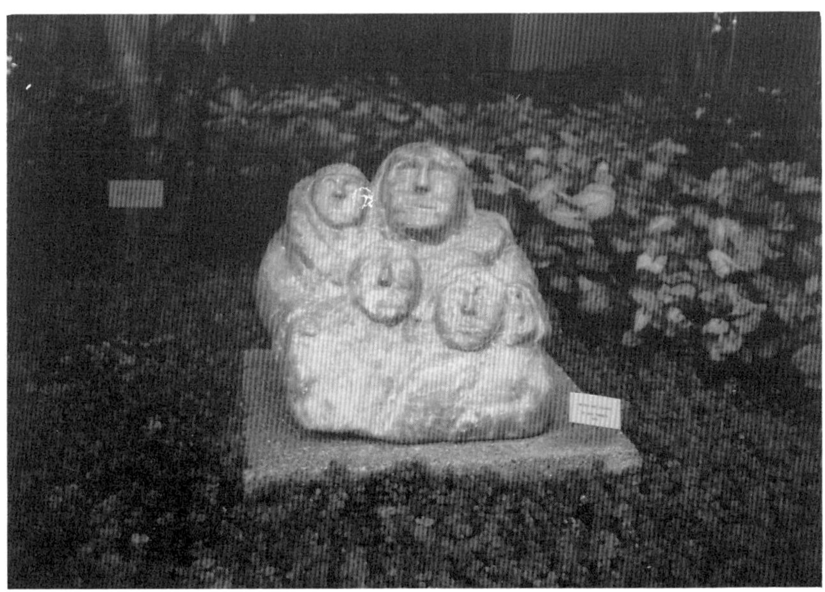

The Economic Development Department of the Government of the Northwest Territories asked Panneok to create this soapstone carving to raise money for the Arctic Winter Games in 1978. He agreed and, with just three days notice, flew to Calgary to begin the artwork. Carving the stone with hammer and chisels, he completed the assignment in two weeks in June 1977.

The gentle study of an Inuit woman and her family was commissioned by NOVA Corporation of Alberta.

Location: 801 - 8th Avenue S.W., NOVA Building
Date: 1977

87. Sundial

Bob Oldrich

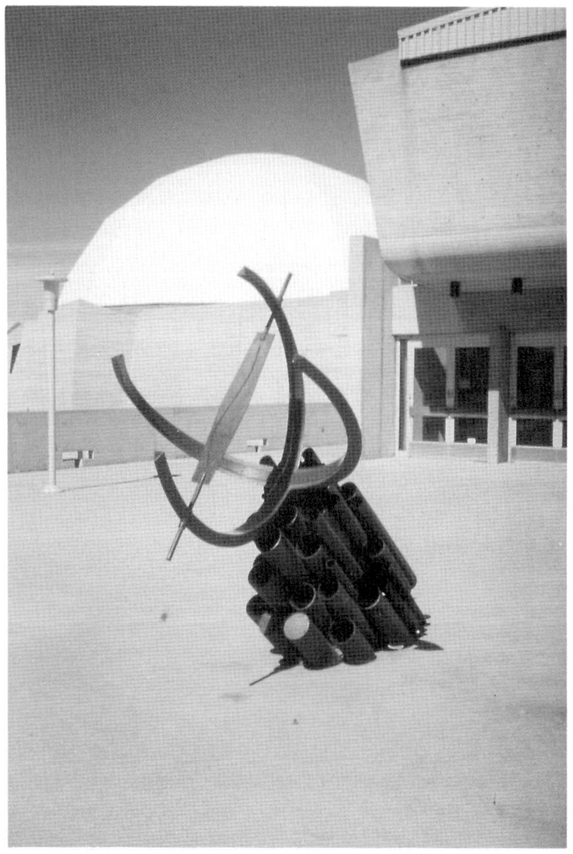

Made of steel and copper, to achieve an effect of aging, this art piece presented several problems for its creator.

Because a sundial must be functional, it required engineering input. "There was a large clock on a nearby commercial establishment that was less accurate than my sundial, but on a cloudy day, we'd have to ask them for the time," the artist recalled.

The choice of this sculpture, a Centennial gift to the City of Calgary by the Calgary labor movement under the auspices of the Calgary Labour Council, is an appropriate one for its location.

Location: 701 - 11th Street S.W., Alberta Science Centre
Date: 1967

88. General James Wolfe (1727-1759)

J. Massey Rhinn

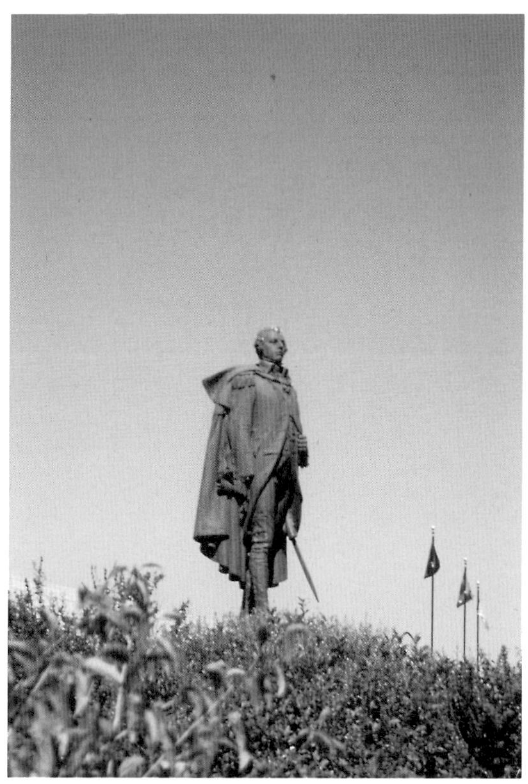

Outside the Alberta Science Centre stands a 3-metre statue of General James Wolfe. Donated by the late Eric Harvie, it was presented to the City in 1967. At the time, it was a cause of some controversy in city council when an aldermen suggested that the space-age planetarium was not a suitable site for the historic figure. However, another alderman pointed out that although Wolfe was no astronomer, "he had something to do with the Canadian centennial" and the statue remained at the Alberta Science Centre.

General Wolfe was in charge of the British expedition which defeated the French on the Plains of Abraham in 1759. At the moment of victory, General Wolfe was killed in battle and became an instant hero.

The sculpture was created in 1898, and stood for many years in front of the Astor Building on Lower Broadway, New York City.

Location: 701 - 11th Street S.W., Alberta Science Centre
Date: 1898, acquired in 1967

89. The Others

Jordi Bonet

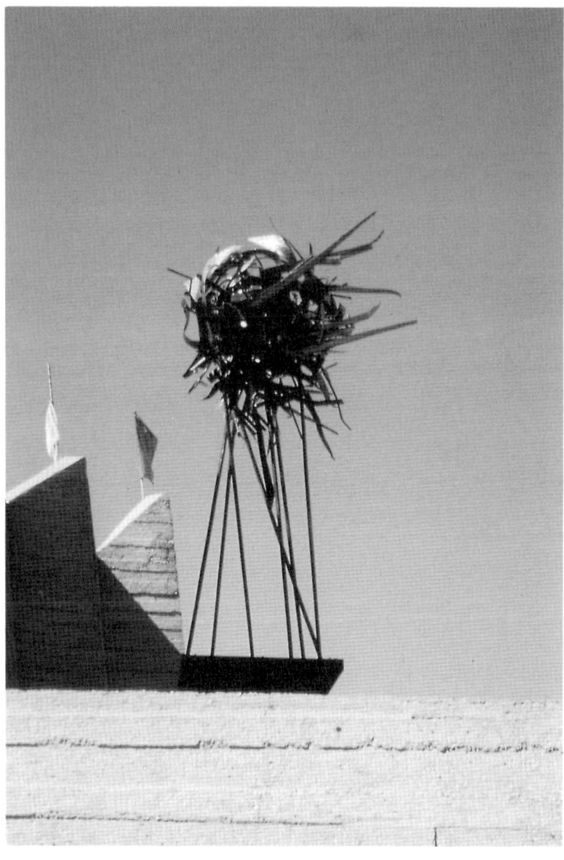

This unusual metal sculpture was a centennial gift to the City from the Calgary and District Dental Association. Installed in 1967, it is a mass of metal pieces welded into a spherical design to represent a planet. It stands on a 2-metre base of 2.5-centimetre metal posts.

Created specifically to stand outside the Alberta Science Centre, the finished work was something of a surprise to those who had seen other works of Bonet. "Very different from his usual style," said one of the dentists who served on the selection committee. "However, it suits the surroundings and it has aged well."

Location: 701 - 11th Street S.W., Alberta Science Centre
Date: 1967

90. Carved Wood Plaques

Nels Weismose

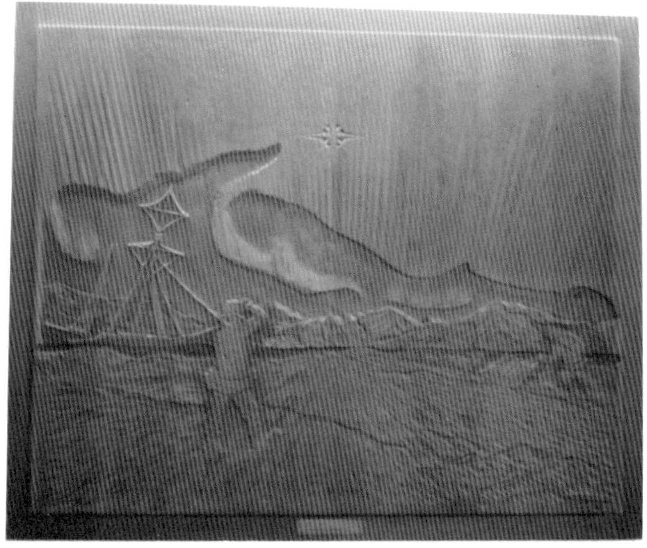

Northern Exposure - Aurora Borealis

Inside the Alberta Science Centre near the main lobby are three intricate wood carvings depicting famous early astronomers. They were a centennial gift from the now-deceased Calgary artist.

Tycho Brahe - a Danish scientist of the sixteenth century who left as his legacy a great series of planetary observations.

Ole Roemer - one of the least known of the world's great astronomers. Although many of his records were destroyed in a fire in 1728, his work greatly advanced observation techniques.

Galilei Galileo - an Italian astronomer, physicist and mathematician. He is renowned for his contribution to many disciplines, the major one being astronomy.

Another Weismose wood carving is found on the same wall. *Northern Exposure - Aurora Borealis* is approximately 1.5 by 1.5 metres and depicts an explorer shooting a star with his sextant. A sailing ship is anchored off shore to one side, and a dog team on shore completes the tableau.

Location: 701 - 11th Street S.W., Alberta Science Centre
Date: 1967

City Parks

91. Cracked Pot Fountains

Katie Ohe

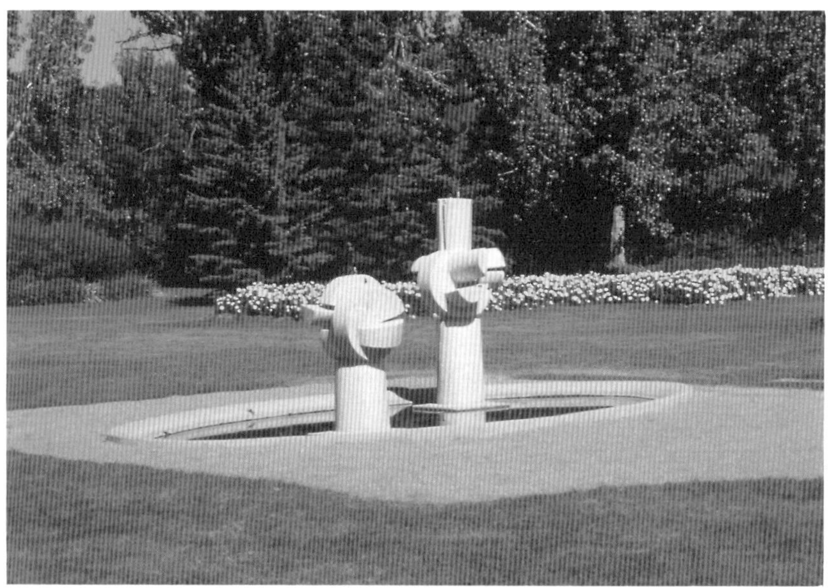

The pale pink, cast-stone fountains trickle lazily in the Prince's Island gardens. While working with pottery, Ohe became intrigued by the shapes formed when pots split or cracked, and deliberately included a crack in these spheres — hence the unusual name for a fountain.

They were originally created for a local shopping centre but, as the artist says, "They were out of context for a mall — not really in tune with their environment. I'm happier with their present location."

The fountains were presented to the City for use in one of its parks, and Prince's Island was chosen.

Location: Prince's Island Park
Date: 1964, placed on Prince's Island in 1965

92. Bird in Flight

Peter Smith

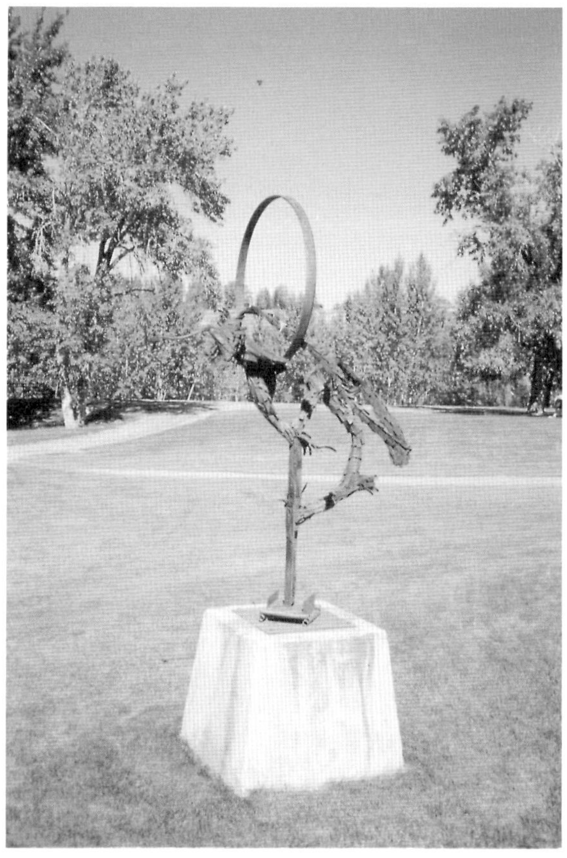

The artist describes this metal sculpture as "symbolic of the free spirit and soul." The welded metal sculpture was purchased by the City of Calgary for placement in Prince's Island Park.

Location: Prince's Island Park
Date: 1972

93., 94. & 95. Prairie Progression

Enzo DiPalma

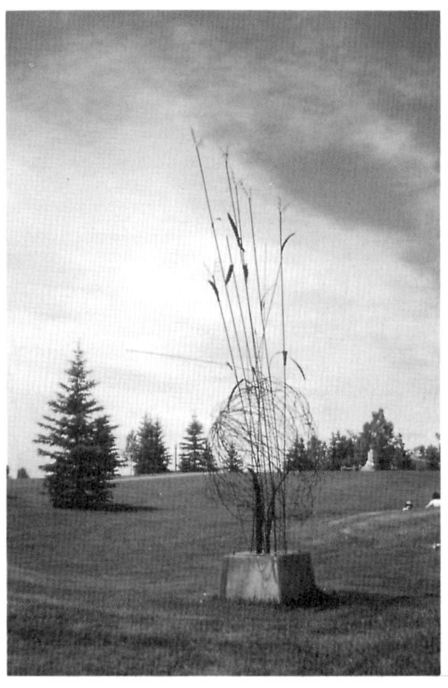

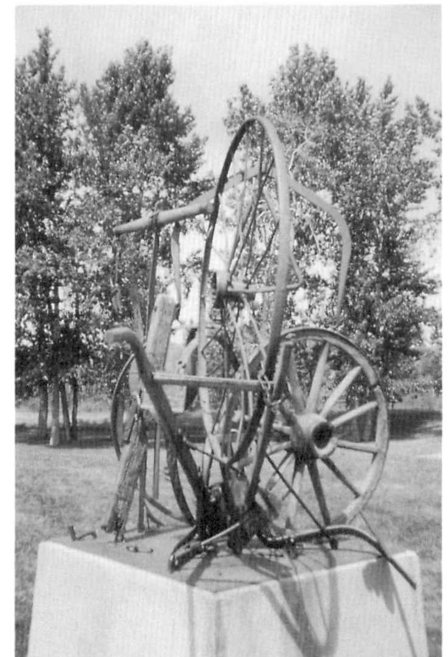

These three metal sculptures on Prince's Island have special meaning for prairie people. *Buffalo Grass and Tumbleweed* is deliberately out of proportion in order to convey the effect of buffalo grass swaying under a wind on the vast, rippling plain. The grass dominates the tumbleweed to symbolize the expanse of the land, however, the tumbleweed is solidly meshed and inseparable from the prairie.

Prairie Collage is a collection of found objects which the artist delighted in assembling. All items are authentic tools and artifacts used by settlers of the early 1900s. A model-T Ford carburetor is included as a reminder that industrialization resulted in the discarding of older, less sophisticated tools.

Ducks is DiPalma's statement on ecology. Although thousands of ducks migrated when he was a boy, very few were seen when he created the sculpture. He says of this work, "It represents our last two ducks, if conservation is ignored."

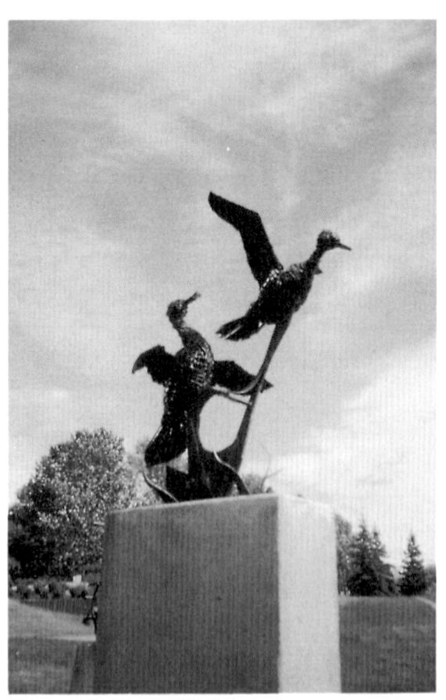

Location: Prince's Island Park
Date: 1969 & 1971

96. Copernicus (1473-1543)

Stanislaw Wyspianski

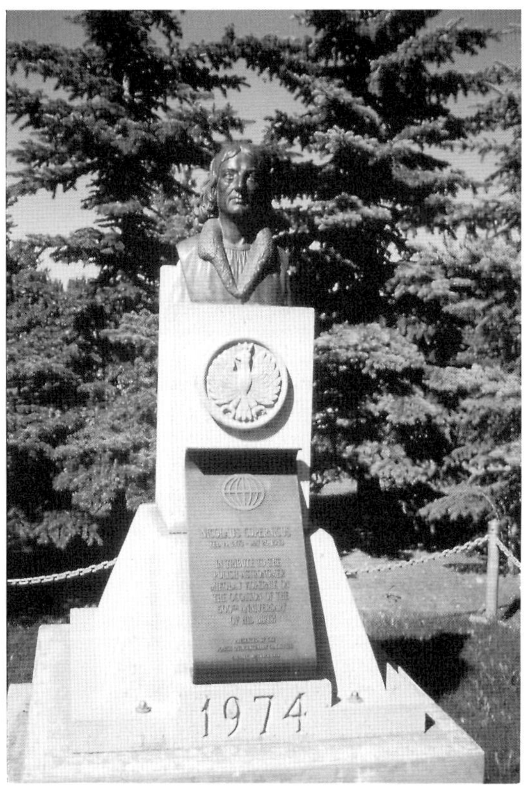

In 1975 the City's Polish community placed a bust of Nicolaus Copernicus on downtown Prince's Island. Copernicus advanced the theory that the earth and planets revolve in orbits about the sun, and the sculpture commemorates both the 500th anniversary of the birth of the famous Polish astronomer, and Calgary's centennial.

The bust was one of three cast from the mold of the original sculpture, which was over 100 years old. The mold was brought to Canada, then cast in bronze in a New York foundry. The original statue remains in the University of Krakow, Poland.

The City of Calgary donated the site in the park, along with funding to build the foundation. This was designed by a local architect, Henry Magillo. All other funds were raised by the Polish community, and volunteers from the group installed the sculpture.

Location: Prince's Island Park
Date: 1975

97. The Winner

J. Seward Johnson, Jr.

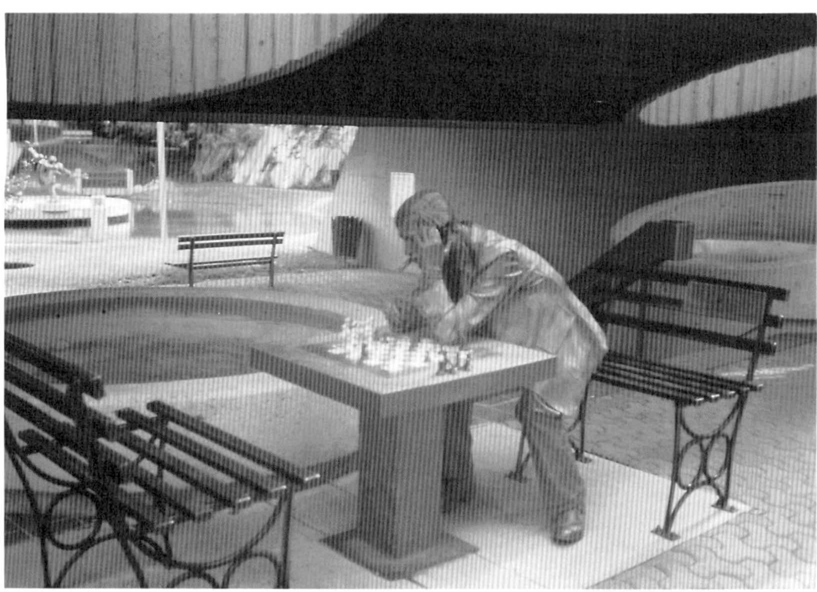

This popular bronze work is a good example of the artist's belief that public response to his sculptures is the completing element to the work.

The empty seat across from this inanimate chess player invites passersby to join the game and on a sunny summer's day, there may be a lineup as tourists stop to be photographed as part of the appealing tableau.

The "winner" is the person who has become the opponent, as the perplexed look on the sculpture's face reveals that he has just been checkmated. This interaction completes the sculpture's narrative just as the artist intended.

Location: 8th Avenue and 8th Street S.W., Century Gardens
Date: 1983

98. Alberta Family

Stanley Bleifeld

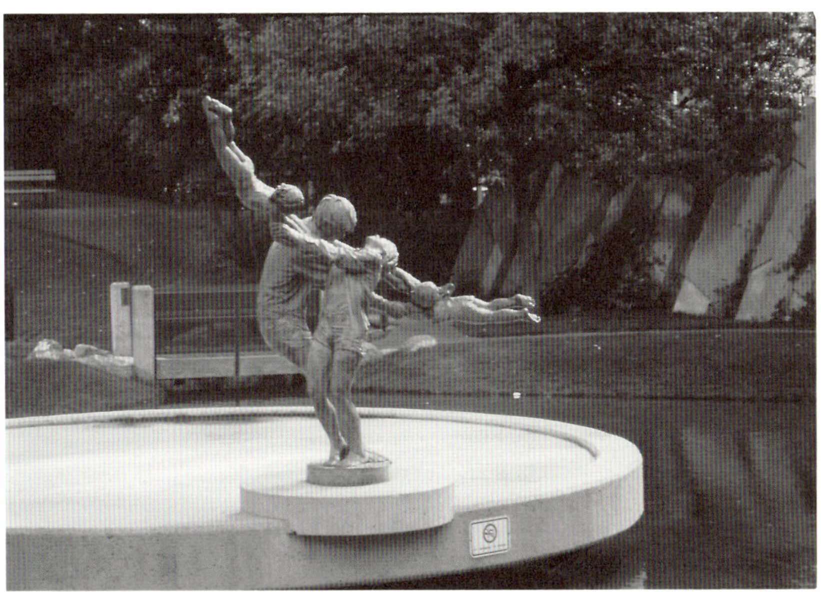

First seen by Calgarian Donald Harvie in California as a small work titled *Swinging Family,* this sculpture was recreated in its present size for the Devonian Foundation by the artist.

Cast in bronze, it is 2 metres high on a 1.7-metre circular base and stands in a pool of water in summer.

The artist says of the piece, "The subject is self-explanatory, and if it shows some exuberance and joy, it was what I felt about this phase of life."

Location: 8th Avenue and 8th Street S.W., Century Gardens
Date: 1981

99. Bears

Leo Mol

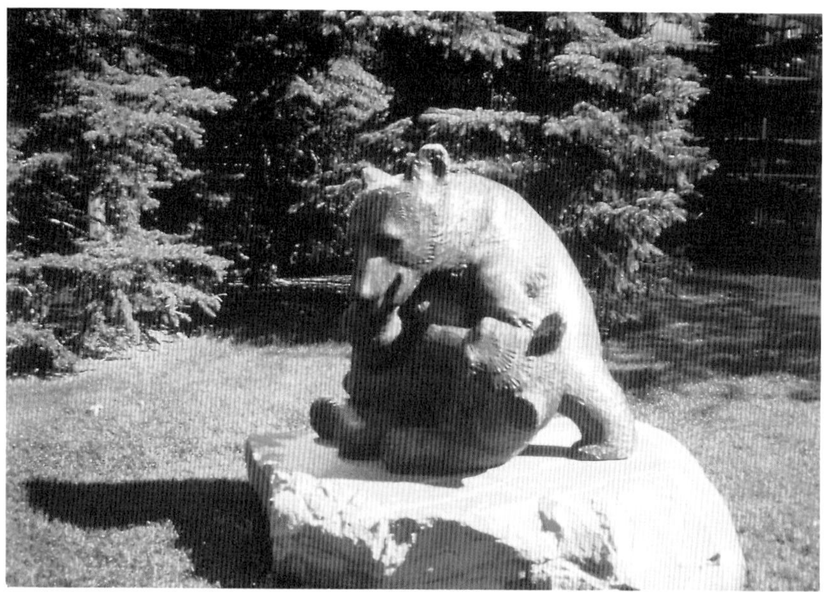

This playful pair of bronze bear cubs is mounted on a rock base and located in a sunny area of the Gardens. Mol is an animal lover, and his sculptures often include two or more for an interesting interaction of shape and form.

He has sculpted many different kinds of creatures, including deer, a European wild boar with its litter, and even a nanny goat, however, it seems bears particularly capture his enthusiasm. He explains that animals offer endless sculptural opportunities to the artist, and bears have a certain solidity and weight that he finds inspiring.

His first wrestling cubs were sculpted in the 1950s as a small, 10-centimetre-high ceramic. Since completing the Calgary *Bear Cubs,* Mol has done six smaller pieces featuring this animal, as well as a large polar bear mother and cub. The latter was purchased by the City of Churchill, in northern Manitoba, in honor of the huge white beasts that sometimes migrate through the city.

Two castings were made of the Century Gardens' sculpture, with the second remaining in Germany on the grounds of the foundry where Mol does most of his casting. A smaller version of the piece stands in front of the conservatory in Winnipeg's Assinniboine Park.

Location: 8th Avenue and 8th Street S.W., Century Gardens
Date: 1975

100. Dinny the Dinosaur

John Kanerva

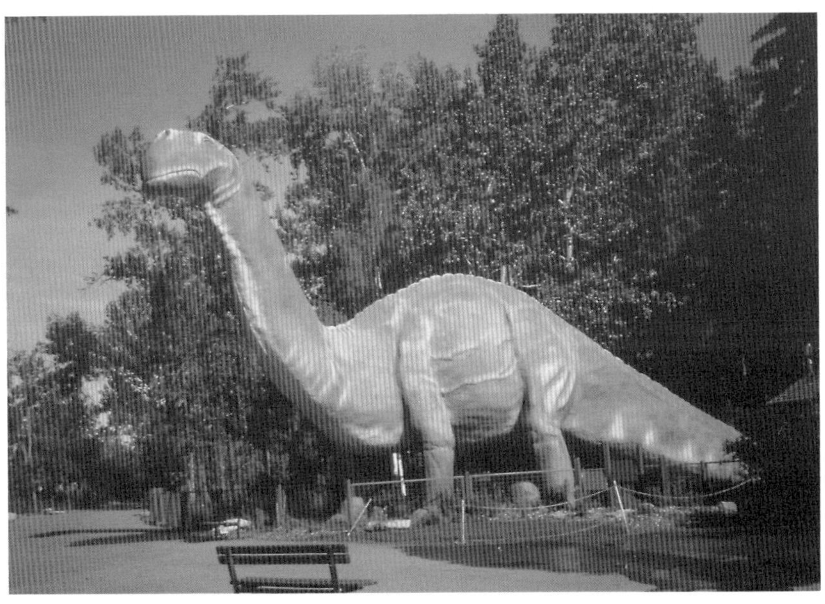

There is controversy over whether Dinny is a dinosaur, or even a brontosaurus, but, whatever his technical name, he is the only Calgary artwork recognized by the Province of Alberta as an official historic site.

The only survivor of Kanerva's prehistoric models once found in the now-dismantled Dinosaur Park, Dinny still stands guard over the zoo and is a magnet for thousands of photographers and children. Built in 1934, he is 12 metres tall, 36 metres long, and weighs a hefty 110 tonnes.

The unique figure was constructed from wire and cement after scale models had been carved in wood by Kanerva. It was a painstaking process and completion of the hollow shell of Dinny required six men working for five weeks. The artist then added "life" by shaping wet concrete in a manner comparable to pargeting a cement wall.

Kanerva's fifty-five smaller "dinosaurs" were in poor condition by 1986, and were demolished because of the difficulty in moving them to the Zoo's new Prehistoric Park, which opened that year. The many new and scientifically accurate creatures in this popular attraction are made of materials such as Styrofoam and fiberglass, however, the immovable cement Dinny continues to be a favorite and has become the familiar symbol for Calgary's zoo.

Location: Calgary Zoo
Date: 1934

101. ICU

Rich Roenisch

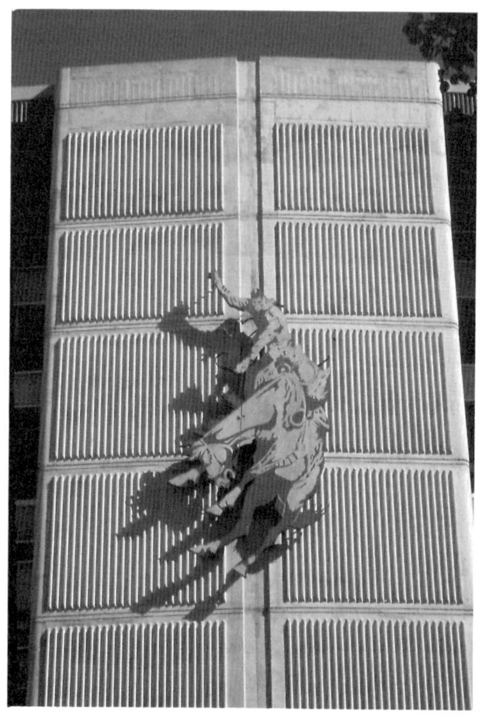

The 9- by 5-metre, engraved-steel plaque mounted on the Stampede grandstand is a replica of the familiar Calgary Stampede symbol. The original etching, used to promote the Stampede since about 1919, was made by the late Edward Borein, a noted California artist and friend of Stampede founder Guy Weadick.

Roenisch created the huge plaque from a scale drawing of 2.5 centimetres to 30 centimetres. He first constructed a full-size plywood pattern, then used this to cut out the steel model.

The unusual title comes from an old army practise of selling remount horses at public sales. The sales often went on for several days, with as many as 500 horses offered. If a bad horse (wild, bucking or mean) went through the ring one day and wasn't sold, he might show up the next day in a quieter mood and be bought by an unsuspecting buyer. To prevent this, the army began the practise of branding such horses on the neck with *IC* — inspected and condemned. The *ICU*, or *I See You* depicts a bucking horse and rider looking at one another.

Location: 17th Avenue and Macleod Trail S.E., exterior wall of grandstand in Stampede Park

Date: 1974

102. Bronc Twister

Rich Roenisch

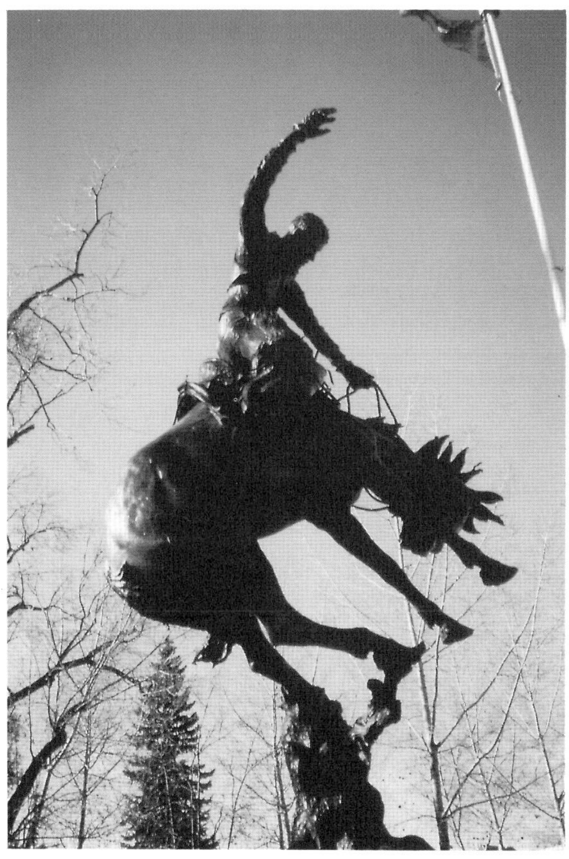

Based on the same original etching that inspired the *ICU* bas-relief on the grandstand, this life-size bronze statue was commissioned by W.W. Seibens and the Calgary Stampede.

It depicts a cowboy on a wildly bucking horse. The feeling of drama is graphically portrayed by the taut muscles of the horse and the "flying high" posture of the cowboy.

Location: 17th Avenue and Macleod Trail S.E., in front of Roundup Centre in Stampede Park

Date: 1980

103. Our Land — Our Future
Alberta Farm Family

Vilem Zach

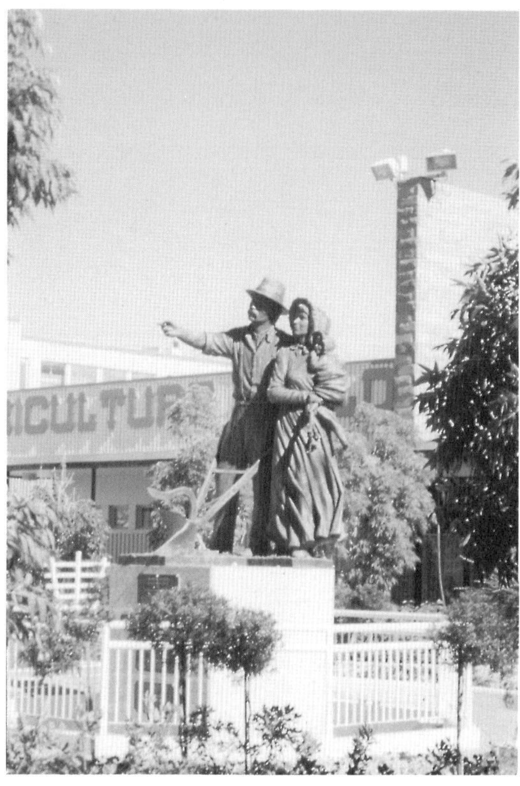

This bronze is the winner of a 1986 competition to celebrate both the 100th anniversary of the agricultural fair that grew into the Calgary Exhibition and Stampede, and the centennial of the arrival in Calgary of the Bank of Montreal. The 120 000-dollar sculpture was jointly funded by the Bank of Montreal and the Calgary Jaycees, with the Jaycee portion of the money raised through their annual Pot of Gold lottery, a Stampede project.

To prepare for the work, Zach studied the clothing of the 1880s at Glenbow Museum, and an actual plow on display at Fish Creek Park. From this research he sketched and later modelled a clay maquette of a farmer, his wife and baby gazing from behind the plow.

The work was then enlarged and cast in bronze using the lost wax method. Twenty-five miniatures were also cast.

Location: 17th Avenue and Macleod Trail S.E., in front of Administration Building in Stampede Park

Date: 1987

104. Boer War Memorial

Louis Phillipe Hebert

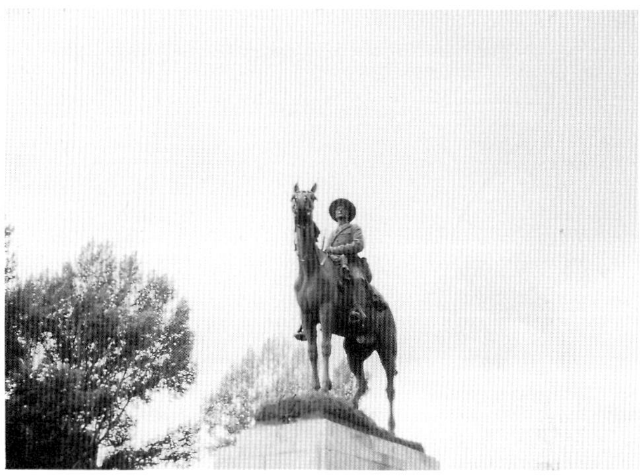

The Lord Strathcona's Horse Regiment, a unique Canadian contribution to the Boer War, was a force of 500 mounted "roughriders" which Lord Strathcona outfitted at his own expense. Headquarters were in Calgary, and the regiment became a source of great local pride.

After the war, in 1909, an unidentified man was found frozen to death in a field near the City. His only identification was a paper showing he had served in South Africa and had been discharged from the Strathcona's. Fellow veterans rallied to collect funds to provide him with a suitable burial.

Later, when his identity had been established, his family in Britain refunded the money, and it became the nucleus of a fund to erect a Boer War monument.

A typical Western pony, belonging to local entrepreneur Pat Burns, was shipped to Quebec for the artist's use. Thomas Henry Johnson, a recent arrival from Ireland, was chosen to pose for the soldier. Although he was a member of the Dragoons and had never served in South Africa, he was thought to be typical of the Canadian soldiers who had seen service in the war. Perhaps the choice was more logical than it appeared; most of the southern Albertans who had been with the Strathcona's were young British men and recent immigrants to Canada.

When Hebert visited Calgary, Eneas McCormick, a local businessman, also posed for the artist so he could see authentic Western horsemanship. Later, the families of both McCormick and Johnson were struck by the remarkable resemblance of the sculpture to each man.

At the time of its dedication, the statue was considered to be one of the four finest equestrian statues in the world. It is heroic-size, with the soldier being about 3 metres tall. Colonel Macleod Chapter IODE purchased the granite base.

Location: 12th Avenue and 4th Street S.W., Central Memorial Park
Date: 1914

105. World War I Memorial

Coeur-de-lion MacCarthy

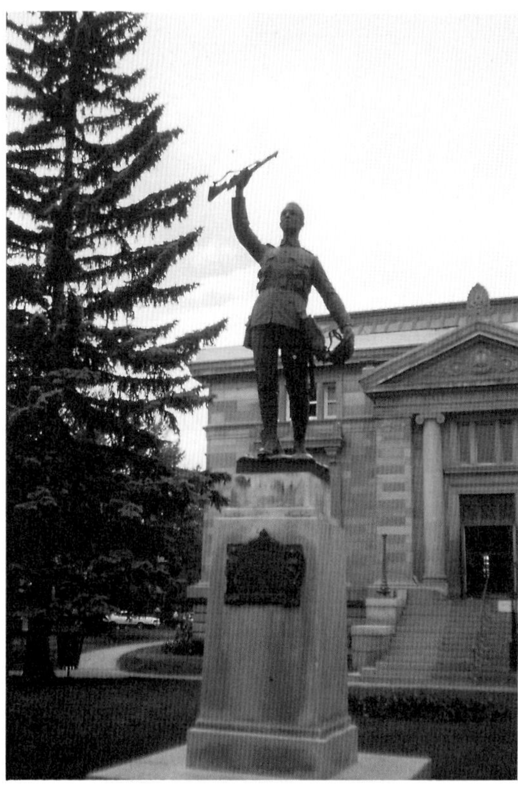

Unveiled on June 23, 1924, the memorial was a gift to the people of Calgary from the Colonel Macleod Chapter of the IODE, a women's patriotic and service organization.

The statue, which is by a Montreal sculptor, is 3 metres high from gun tip to base and stands on a 3-metre-high pedestal of Bedford stone.

According to a writer in a local paper in 1923, the design which was chosen depicted "a youth, virile, energetic, spontaneous, attired in his kit, who upon hearing the news of the signing of the armistice, has removed his helmet and raised his musket in the spirit of victory and glory." MacCarthy did a similar piece for Verdun, Quebec.

"Never Shall Their Glory Fade" is the inscription on the base of this memorial to the men who served in World War I.

Location: 12th Avenue & 3rd Street S.W., Central Memorial Park
Date: 1924

106. Book Totem

Rick Silas

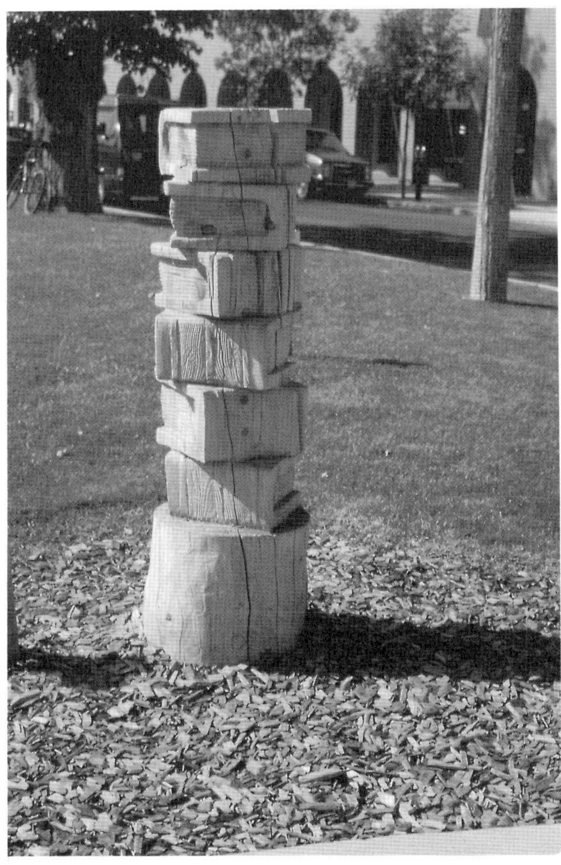

These two carvings of birch and fir were done on site at Tompkins Park. They are a reminder of the poplar trees which had recently been removed from the location.

The works were donated to the park by the artist after consultation with the City of Calgary. Silas now expresses a concern with the weathering process and hopes to see them in an atrium setting one day. The future of these sculptures is unkown at this time.

The sculptures show stacks of books of various shapes and sizes.

Location: 17th Avenue and 8th Street S.W., Tompkins Park
Date: 1988

107. Nimmons Cairn

Katie Ohe

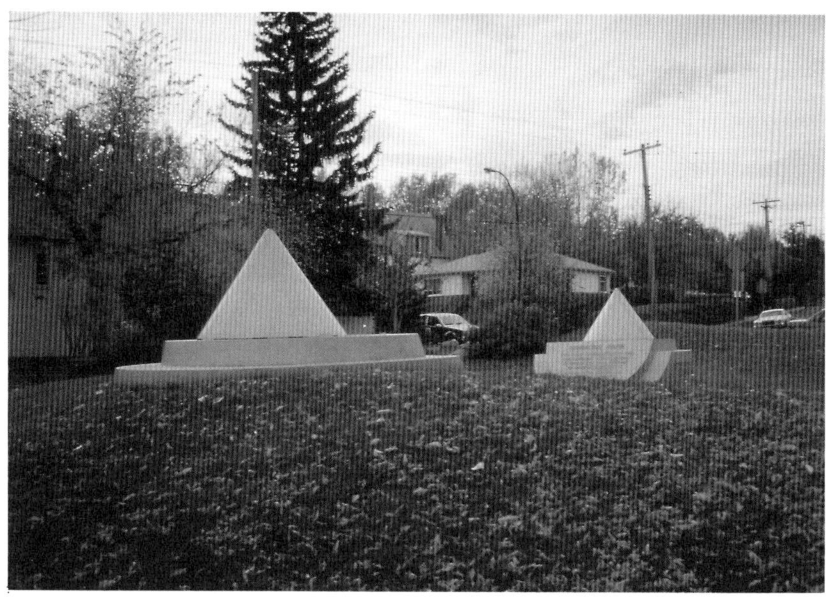

Located in Nimmons Park, a tiny, tucked-away oasis in the Bankview district, this cast-stone, two-part sculpture invites viewer participation. On a warm summer's day you may find a group of chattering youngsters setting out a tea party on the steps of one cone, while an intrepid team of kid-sized explorers scales the other.

The cairn commemorates William Nimmons, whose pioneer ranch encompassed the park area. Ohe had several reasons for choosing the shape of this Alberta Seventy-fifth anniversary commission. "The cone is symbolic of cairns, which were traditionally a heap of stones in a cone shape . . . and it is also symbolic of the union of heaven and earth, and of joy and disappointment."

In order to appeal to a sense of play, she kept the sculpture "human size" — the tips of the cones at eye level.

Location: 19th Avenue and 17th Street S.W., Nimmons Park
Date: 1983

108. Comet

Kathryn Fodchuk

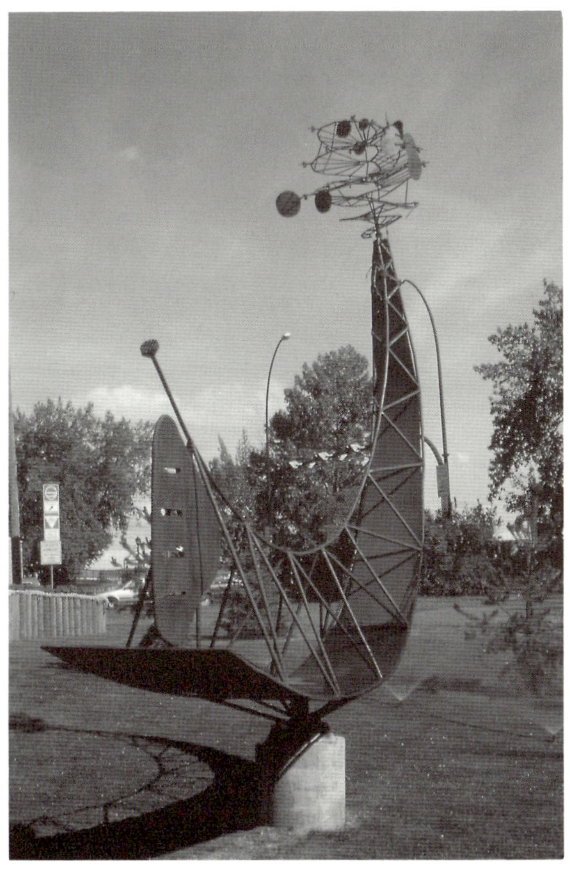

The title of this 2.3-metre-high, welded-steel sculpture evolved because of its resemblance to a shiplike space vehicle.

Comet once moved on ball bearings around its concrete base, but it became an irresistible, hands-on toy for local youngsters after its installation in this compact, no-name park. Eventually, the shaft cracked and became dangerous, so the piece was welded solid and immovable.

It was executed for the architectural commissions class at the Alberta College of Art and donated to the City of Calgary by Shell Canada Resources Limited.

Location: 10th Street and Memorial Drive N.W.
Date: 1983

109. Transition '67

Enzo DiPalma

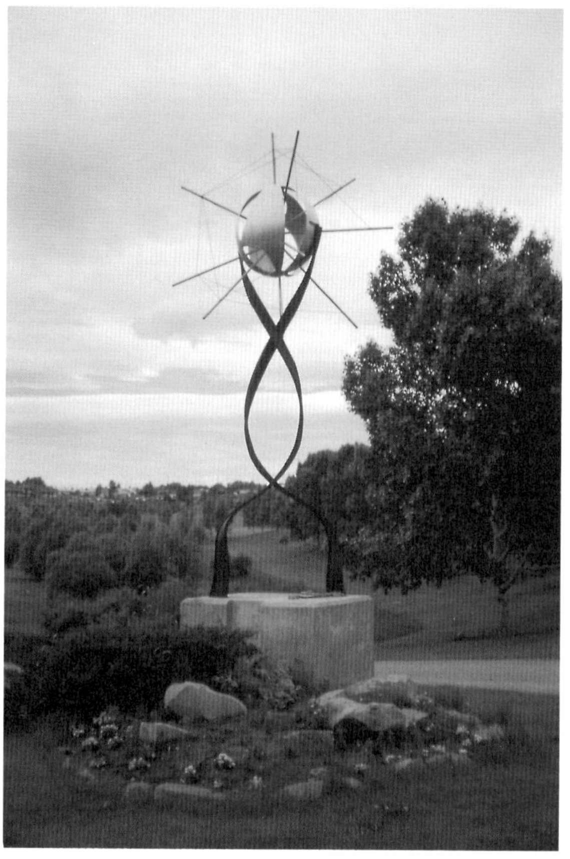

Can you remember how you commemorated Canada's 100th birthday? Members of the Britamco Club, employees of BA Oil in Calgary, will never forget their birthday present to Canada. *Transition '67* stands in Confederation Park as a permanent reminder of their generosity.

DiPalma describes this work as "an exploratory step into futuristic modern art, developing the theme of Canada's Centennial . . ." Designed to symbolize Canada's first 100 years of struggle and achievement, it takes as its theme the exploding fireworks so popular in 1967.

Constructed of steel and aluminum, it has proven to be flexible enough to withstand the climbing expeditions of a quarter-century of youngsters enjoying the park.

Location: 2807 - 10th Street N.W., Confederation Park
Date: 1967

Post-secondary Institutions

110. Enigma

Derek Besant

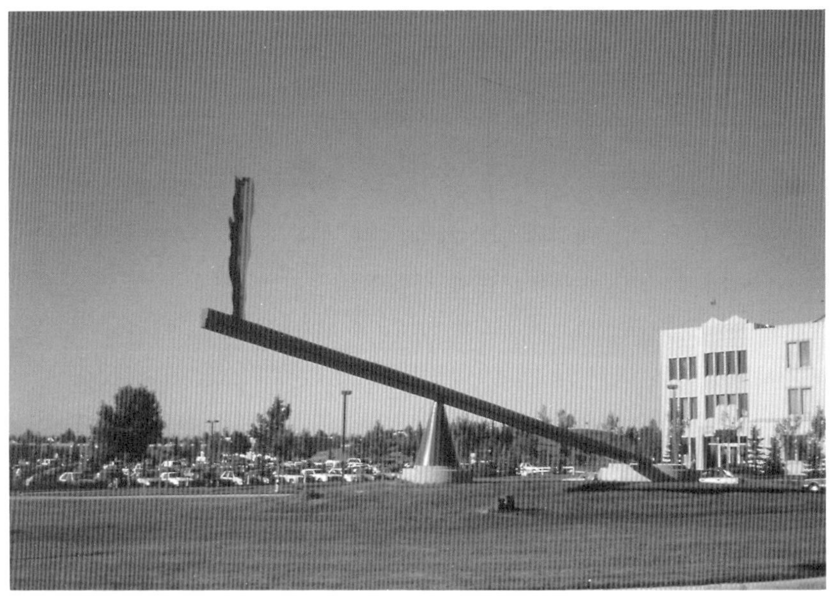

Enigma was chosen to be the signature sculpture for the east entrance of Mount Royal College. Situated on a grassy, elevated traffic island, the piece has four components: *Pool*, of cast concrete; *Beam*, a welded-steel armature; Cone, a steel support for *Beam*; and *Tornado*, thick plate steel attached to the end of *Beam*.

Two of Besant's research trips affected this work, one to Katsura, Japan, to spend time in its many sand gardens, and the other to northern Scotland to search out neolithic and standing-stone sites.

The artist explains, "There are relationships set up between the base components in *Enigma* that are universal and spiritual. The work had to occupy the site, yet let it breathe. There had to be a sense of coming upon something bigger than the sum of its parts, similar to the sites mentioned earlier. . . .

"The piece had to be clean and pure in its design . . . speak volumes yet remain mute; it should exude archaeology and simultaneously be lodged in the future and, more importantly, the present. . . ."

The project was funded by Amoco Canada Petroleum Company Ltd., with a matching grant from Alberta Advanced Education Endowment and Incentive Program.

Location: 4825 Richard Road S.W., Mount Royal College
Date: 1989

111. Homage

Derek Besant

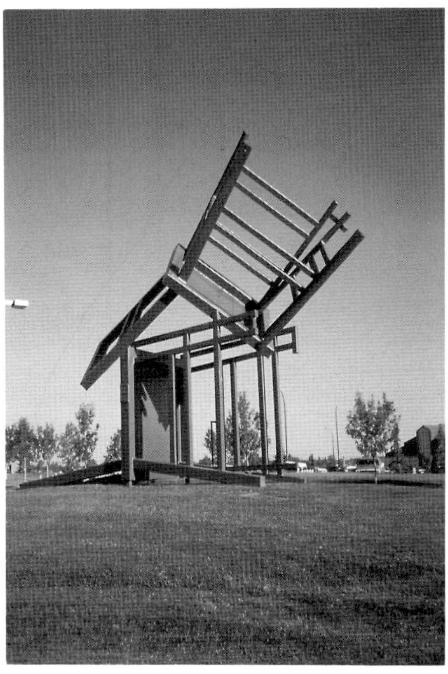

"If we can re-evaluate that which we know, perhaps we can see our own surroundings in a new way," is how Besant explains the concept of this signature piece, a duo of giant chairs balanced precariously.

He explains that the chair is a form he has worked with for several years; by simplifying it into a hybrid somewhere between drawing and sculpture, he has discovered the many possibilities it can reveal. "The balancing of two large-scale forms that are based on chairs created a dialogue that is architectonic," Besant explains.

Its academic surroundings demanded that the sculpture be intellectual and inspiring and the chair was chosen as a device to indicate figurative posture and a sense of proportion and balance. The scale makes a strong statement in staking out its territory at the western entrance to the college, however, the human quality of the chair gives it accessibility.

It is the artist's hope that, "*Homage* should always appear in a state of implied activity; caught at that moment when things could go either way. . . ."

It is made of steel, welded and painted. Each chair is over 5 metres high and weighs over 1 500 kilograms. It was funded by a grant from the Alberta Art Foundation, matched by the Alberta Advanced Education Endowment and Incentive Program.

Location: 4825 Richard Road S.W., Mount Royal College
Date: 1989

112. Untitled Bas-Relief

Walt Drohan

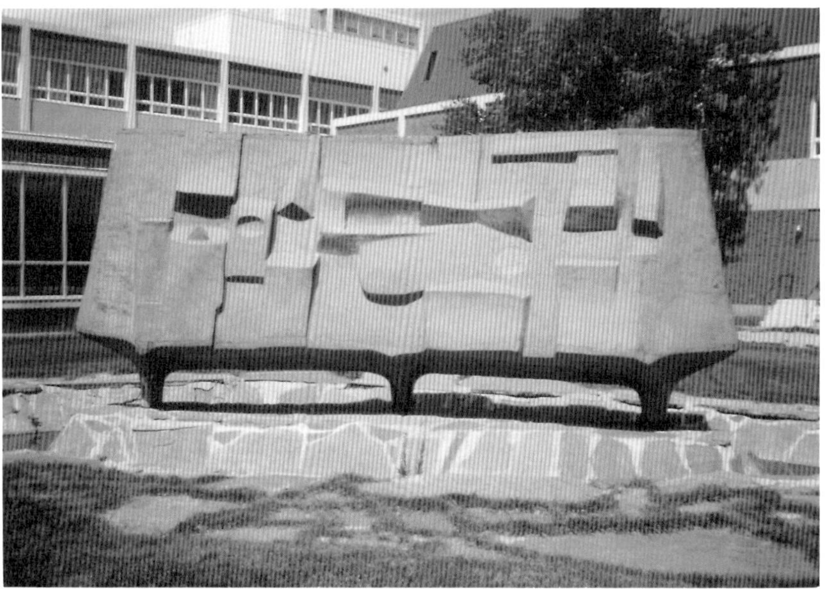

Located on the campus of the Southern Alberta Institute of Technology (SAIT) is a freestanding, concrete bas-relief. Supported by three metal posts, it is part of a planned fountain and represents the irregularities of a waterfall.

Location: 1301 - 16th Avenue N.W., SAIT
Date: 1965

113. Pleistocene Wedge

Marjorie Walrond

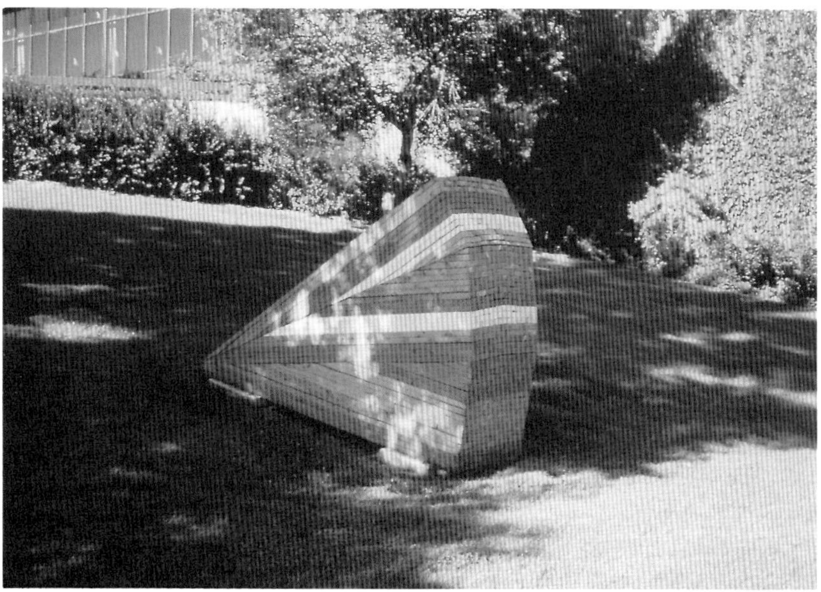

Commissioned by Petro-Canada and later given to the Southern Alberta Institute of Technology (SAIT), this piece was completed for an architectural commissions course the artist took in her final year at the Alberta College of Art.

The Wedge is made of solid, rough-cut spruce nailed and glued together. Approximately 3 by 2 by 1 metre in size, the form was sanded, stained and bolted into place on a cement pad, a process that took four months to complete.

Walrond suggests that the layers of the piece are symbolic of "the warming and cooling of the Pleistocene era, an epoch which fascinates us because of the evolution of humans."

She adds, "Making the Wedge was a huge undertaking, from unloading a flat of frozen waterlogged planks, to mastering my terror of radial arm saws. The pile of wood filled up half the sculpture studio and made a terrific picnic table for friends." Although vandals spray-painted it in 1988, sandblasting and restoration have rescued the sculpture.

Location: 1301 - 16th Avenue N.W. SAIT grounds, near the LRT station
Date: 1984

114. & 115. Two Untitled Pieces

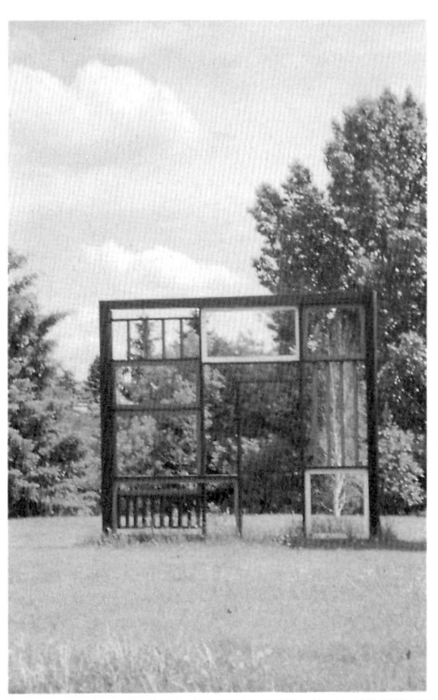

Two "mystery pieces" decorate the grounds of the Southern Institute of Technology (SAIT). They are works acquired from senior students in the architectural commissions course at the Alberta College of Art, probably in the 1980s. It is believed that the piece overlooking 10th Street N.W. near the LRT tracks is by Hansina Jensdotter while the other, in the northeast corner of the grounds, is by a male student. Titles of the pieces are not known.

Location: 1301 - 16th Avenue N.W., SAIT grounds
Date: probably early 1980s

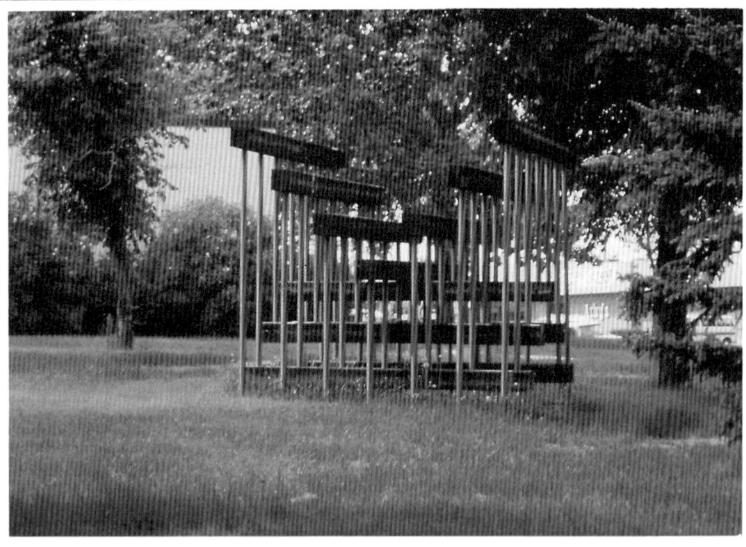

116. Emergence

Susan Velder

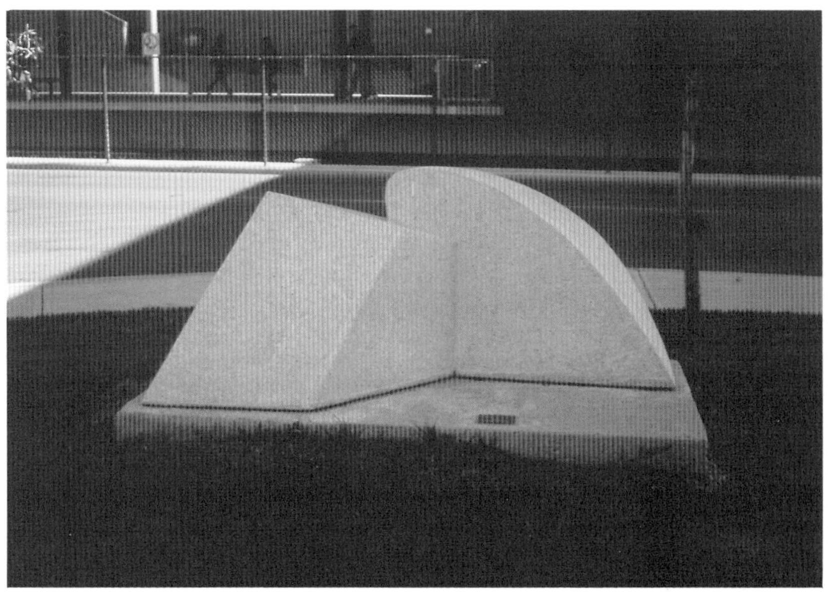

Found on the east side of the Alberta College of Art (ACA) near the Jubilee Auditorium, *Emergence* is an interpretation of seashells protruding from water or sand. It is created from a mixture of concrete, feldspar and dolomite applied by hand and trowel over a welded-steel armature.

The sculpture was completed in the artist's graduate year at the College.

Location: 1404 - 14th Avenue N.W., ACA
Date: 1977

117. Untitled

Harold Weiss

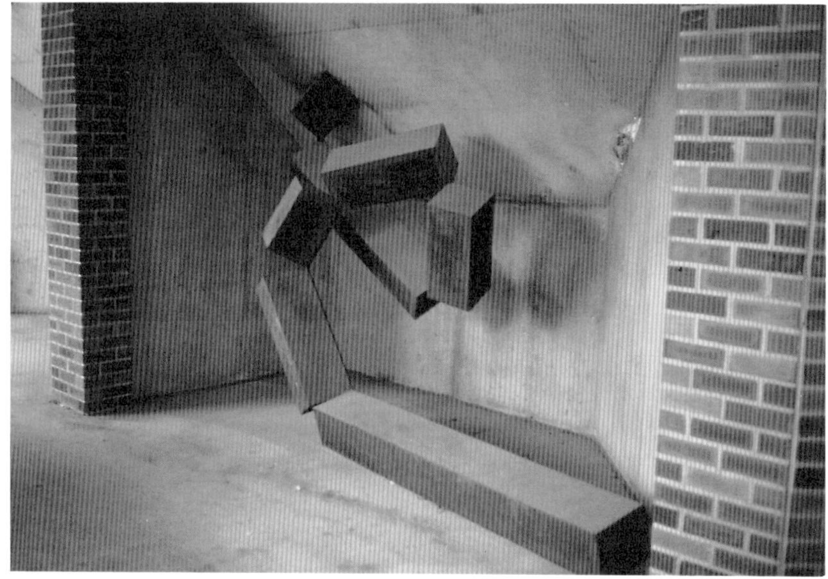

The original intent was to have one artist create a sculpture for both niches in the walkway to the Jubilee Auditorium from the parking structure. However, it was later decided that one should be left open for a second sculptor's work.

The welded-steel abstract in the first niche was the winner of a competition at the Alberta College of Art (ACA), and was chosen from maquettes produced by third-year sculpture students. The piece is unpainted and has been allowed to oxidize to its present warm rust color.

Location: Walkway from parkade to Jubilee Auditorium, ACA
Date: 1976

THE UNIVERSITY OF CALGARY CAMPUS

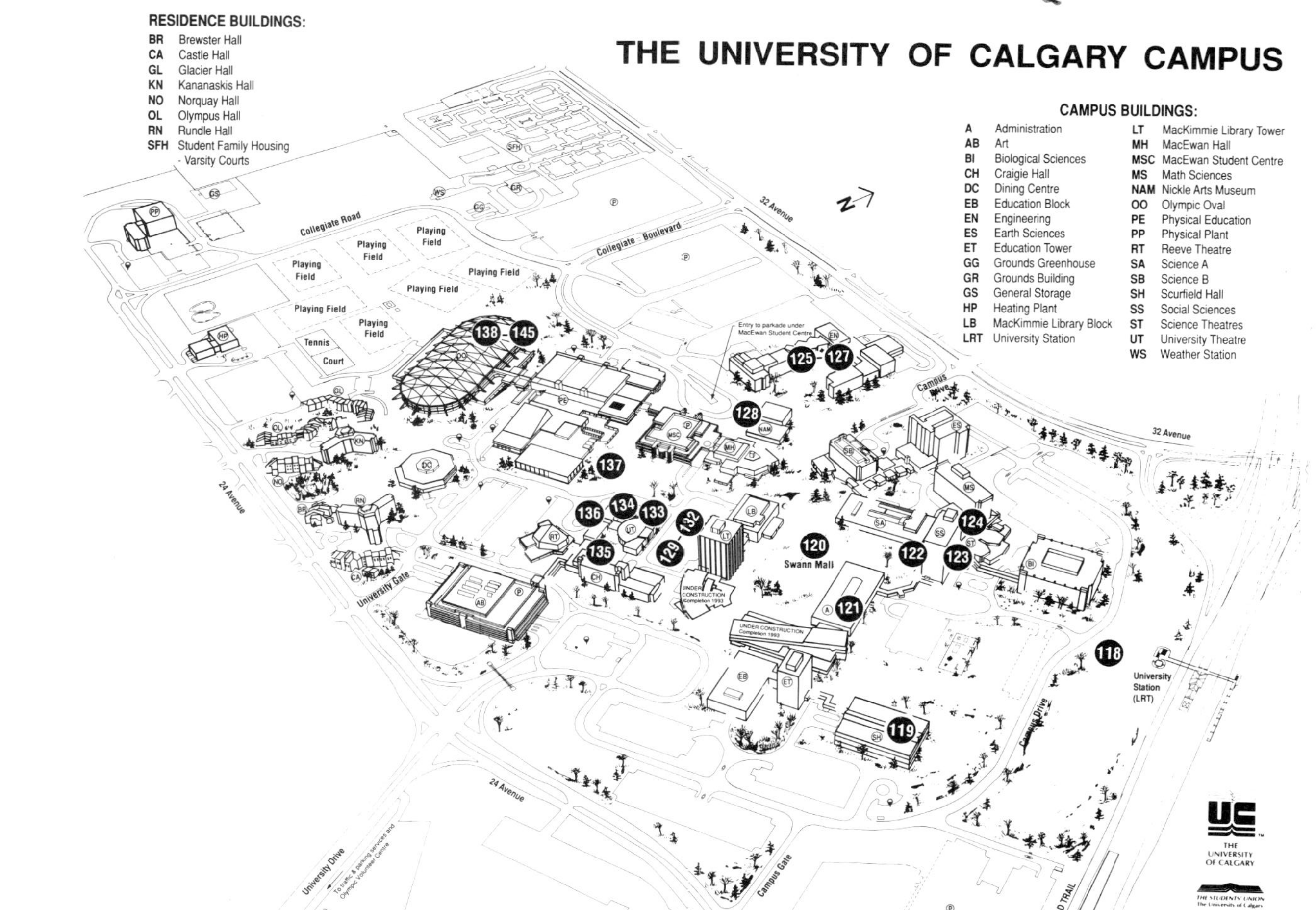

118. Cathedral Evening

Douglas Bentham

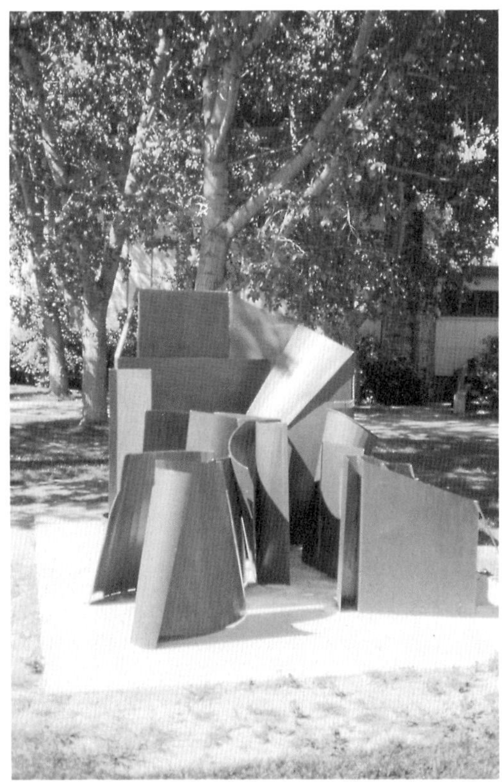

This sculpture of steel lacquered red, was completed over a six-year period. The artist says of the piece, "It is the culmination of a vision to create a public-scaled sculpture which, in its enclosing of space, would draw the viewer into a more intimate, one-to-one aesthetic experience. Much sculpture in the public realm becomes externalized as a result of a desire to relate to architecture, but Cathedral Evening has been geared in every aspect to be people-oriented."

It measures approximately 2 by 4 by 3 metres. First installed near the physical education complex, the piece is to be moved to a spot near the pathway to the LRT station shortly.

Location: University of Calgary, will be moved to the pathway to the University LRT station

Date: completed in 1987, installed in 1991 and 1992

119. Life's Journey

Shamas Malik

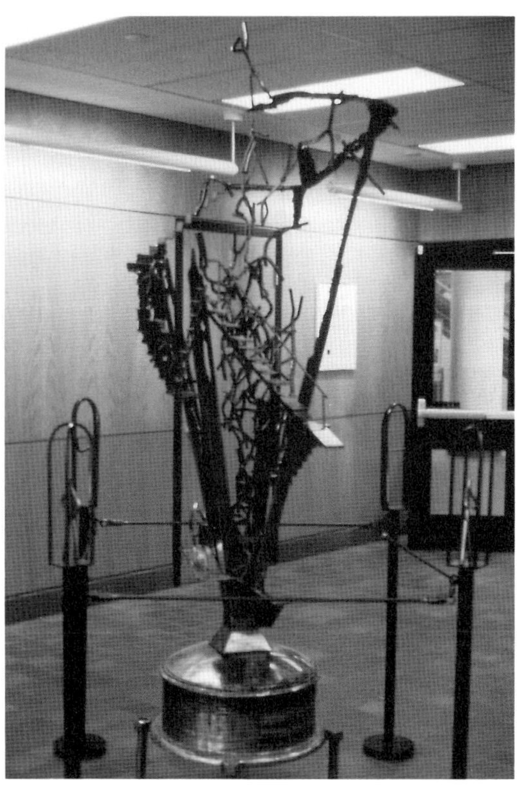

This sculpture started with the base, which sat in the artist's studio for several months while he tried to "figure out what should be on top of it." Finally the concept for the stairs, with his trademark, three-dimensional stick-man figures came to him in a "particularly confusing philosophy class." He says, "It seemed to me that the only points of agreement in philosophical thought are the facts that whether we are here or not, we are all born and we will all die." He continues, "However, what really concerns most people is what happens between those two known points and what interests me are the common elements which apply to any life or to any given day in that life."

Life's Journey is of welded steel and bearings, and measures 1 by 1 by 2.4 metres. It depicts a series of stylized steel figures clambering and clawing their way up a series of staircases and ramps, and the emergence of a triumphant one at the top of the sculpture. It is Malik's first work of this scale, and his first kinetic sculpture. It was purchased by the Faculty of Management, University of Calgary.

Location: University of Calgary, Scurfield Hall

Date: 1990

120. Untitled Steel Sculpture

George Norris

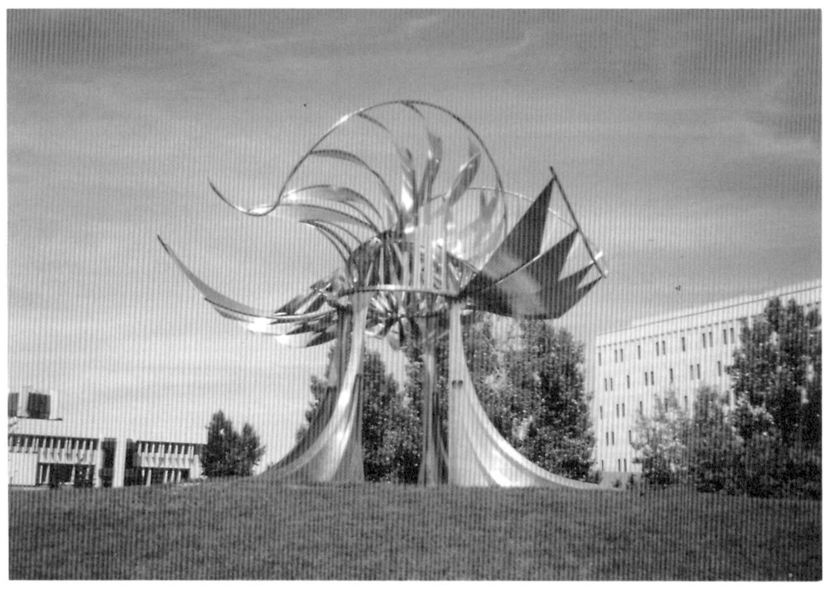

"It's an open book." "No, it's a prairie chicken!" "It is not! It's an Indian headdress."

The meaning of the large stainless steel sculpture which dominates Swann Mall has been the subject of speculation since the piece was installed but, according to the artist, there is no right or wrong answer. The piece is anything the viewer wants it to be, since Norris has declined to label it or explain it.

His only comment on the sculpture is that "it concerns itself with 'revelation,' a central concern of any educational institution."

Norris was delighted when the jury not only selected his sculpture from 200 entries in a competition, but also agreed with his broad concept for development of the mall, and gave him the opportunity to work with university planners on its realization.

The specially constructed grassy knoll on which the sculpture stands has become a campus focal point.

Location: University of Calgary, Swann Mall
Date: 1975

121. Sophocles, Plato and Krito

Nikolas Pavropoulos

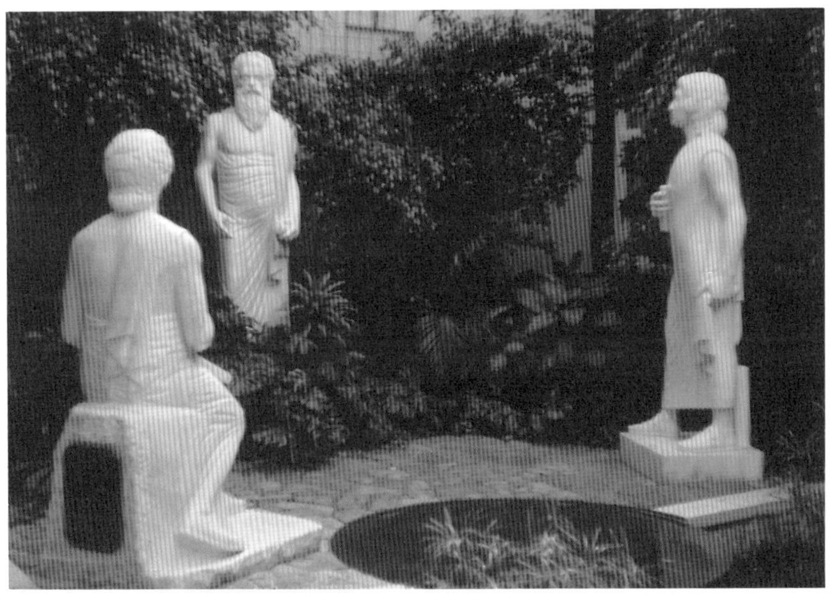

Three massive marble statues command centre stage in the gardens of the atrium of the University of Calgary Arts and Administration Building. They were a gift to the students of the university from Jimmie Condon (known to everyone as "Jimmie") longtime restaurant owner and patron of amateur sports in Calgary.

Jimmie came to Calgary from Greece in 1911 and spent a lifetime encouraging Calgary youth, both girls and boys, to achieve their best through competing in organized sport.

In the same spirit, he commissioned Nikolas Pavropoulos, an Athenian sculptor, to create the heroic likenesses of Socrates and his students Plato and Krito. Jimmie's hope was that the statues would encourage University of Calgary students to aspire to similar academic achievements.

Each Greek scholar is carved from a single piece of Pentelic marble, and weighs at least 2 tonnes. When they arrived in Calgary after a trip by ship, train and truck, they were somewhat rubbed and damaged and Pavropoulos came from Greece to make repairs.

Special equipment was designed to allow movers to transport the pieces and stand them in place at the university.

Location: University of Calgary, Arts and Administration Atrium
Date: 1980

122. Porcelain Mural

Ed Drahanchuk

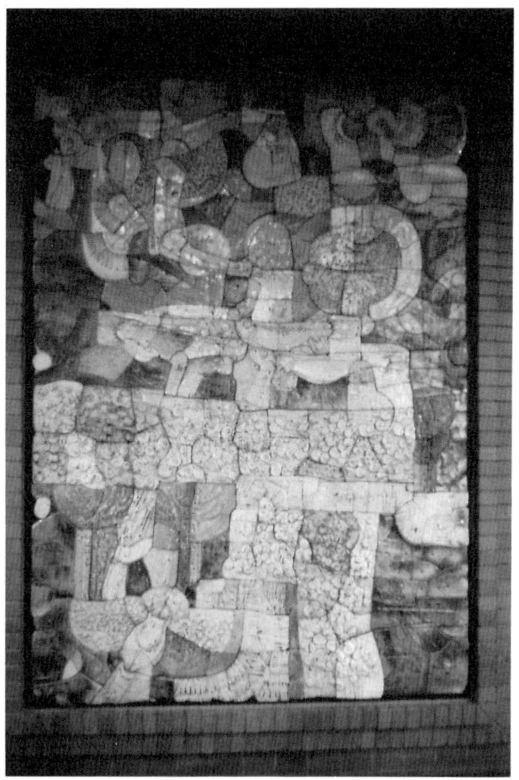

Although most Drahanchuk works of this period are in earth-tones, through the use of Celadon glazes this mural includes blues and sea greens to enhance its fossil theme.

The clay used in modelling the pieces of the mosaic was of a consistency similar to sour cream, and extremely fragile. Great care had to be taken to prevent cracking during the drying process and the porcelain went through a process of repeated firing and glazing to acquire strength, depth, lustre and color.

The piece was earlier selected from sixty submissions in a competition to purchase an appropriate artwork for the ground floor lobby of the Hudson's Bay Oil and Gas Building. In May of 1976, when the company moved to new quarters, the mural was presented to the University of Calgary.

Location: University of Calgary, Sciences complex
Date: 1973

123. Zipper

Katie Ohe

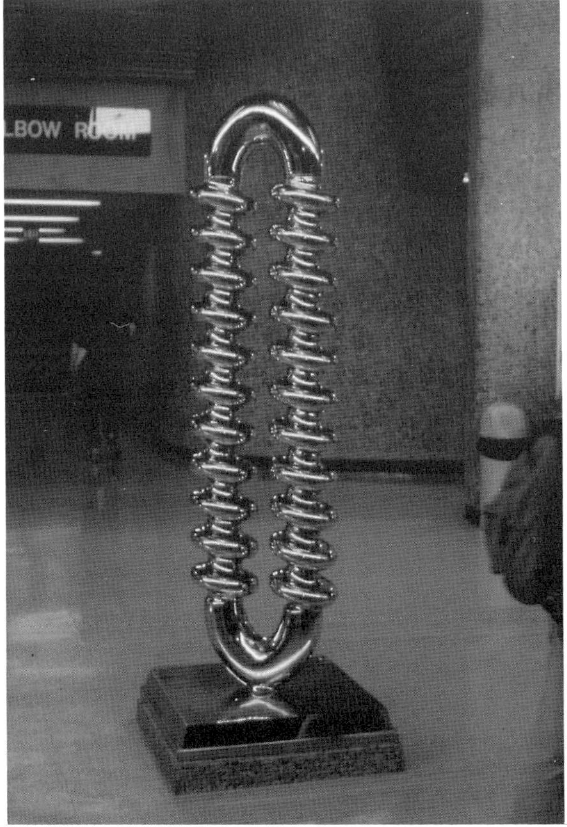

Zipper, which stands over 2 metres high, is a semi-kinetic chrome sculpture. It was created from prefabricated steel elbows which were cut and welded.

Like most Ohe works, it invites touch. As she points out, "When you touch, something must happen. Touch causes motion and, through motion, we realize spatial changes and new form relationships. The scale and proportion must be right! The piece, in this instance, must be touchable. If it weren't of a human scale (too large or too small) one would lose that sense of involvement, that desire to touch."

Zipper is a vertical oblong shape and a gentle touch sets it spinning slowly, causing the space enclosed by the form to change. The artist explains, "The vertical columns are composed of undulated, diagonal, vertical forms, which, as they revolve, cause an optical illusion, creating the sense of an overall oval twist."

Location: University of Calgary, Science Theatres area
Date: 1975

124. Sculptured Wall Panel

John Crate and Robert Spaetgens

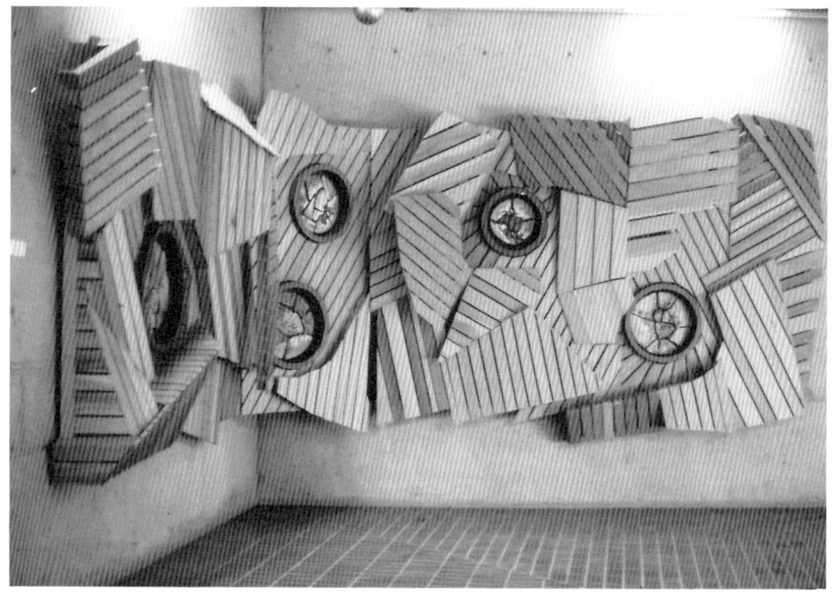

This multi-media sculptured wall panel was the winning entry in a 1976 student's art competition at the University of Calgary.

The panel, designed by two fourth-year Fine Arts students, is constructed of cedar and ceramic, and is in five pieces bolted together and lifted onto wall brackets.

The men conceived the idea for the piece together. Cedar was chosen to lend warmth to the concrete corridor, while round ceramic medallions were added to soften the rather angular background and relate to the round skylight above.

The piece, 2 by 6.5 metres, took only two months to complete. The deadline for installation was February 1st, 1976 and they finished with just fifteen minutes to spare.

Location: University of Calgary, Sciences complex, pedestrian corridor between Science Theatres and Math Sciences

Date: 1976

125. Conic Free Form

Katie Ohe

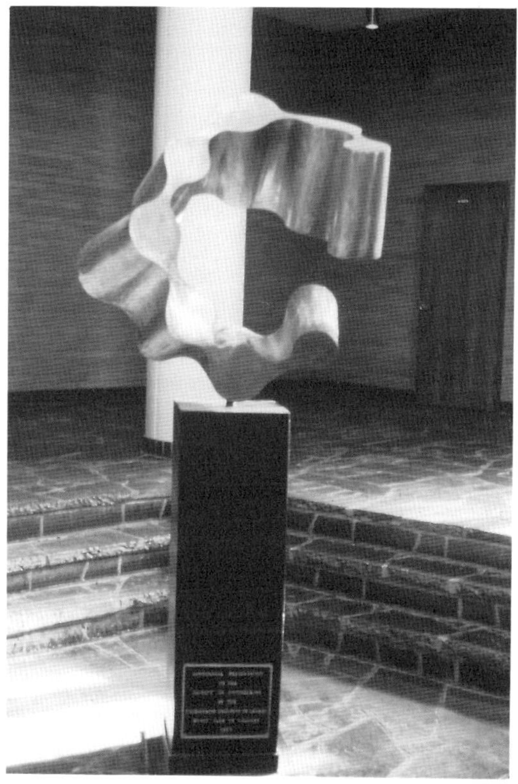

"The 'Manifestation of the Wheel' is my personal title for this piece," the artist says. The metal sculpture was commissioned by the Engineering Institute of Canada Wives Club of Calgary as a centennial presentation to the Faculty of Engineering. It proved to be a difficult assignment.

"It began as a cubic-like structure but that, at the time, had little meaning for me," Ohe explains. "It went through many form changes before a meaningful concept took shape. Gradually, a circular shape composed of a cylindrical form evolved. The final result is a polished steel sculpture which rotates on its base conveying the sense of a wheel."

She recalls, "When I took my clay model to the aluminum sprinkler company that helped with its construction, the technician just shook his head. He told me, 'It can't be done . . . but we'll do it!'"

The work is located in the main foyer of the Engineering Building.

Location: University of Calgary, Engineering Building
Date: 1968

126. Untitled

Engineering Students

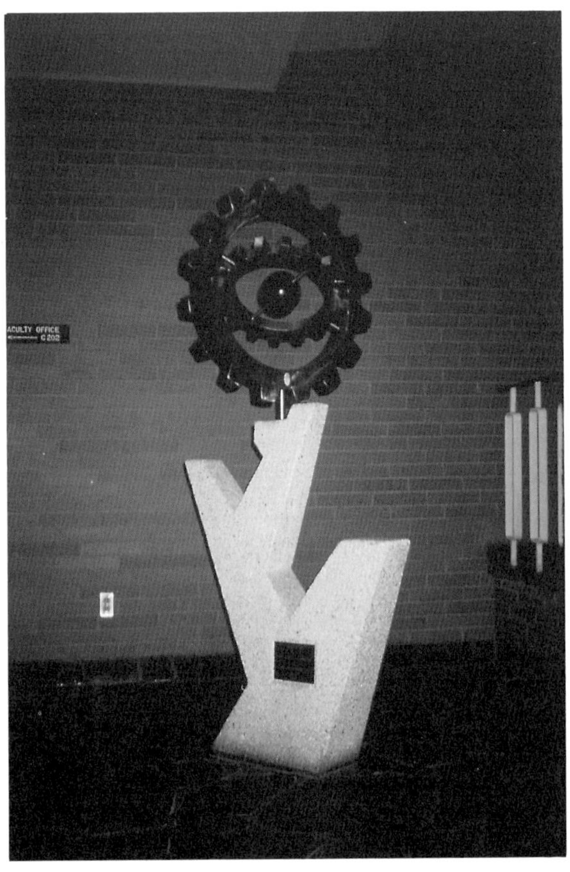

In 1970 the graduating engineers from the University of Calgary constructed this semi-kinetic metal sculpture, symbolic of the cog that is the logo of the Faculty of Engineering.

The piece, which involves all the disciplines from engineering, was designed by Bill Mah. Finances were provided by Engineering Students' Services, and the work was done by volunteer students and staff members.

It was presented by the graduating class of May 1970, and is in the main foyer of the Engineering Building.

Location: University of Calgary, Engineering Building
Date: 1970

127. Firetell

Stephen Cruise

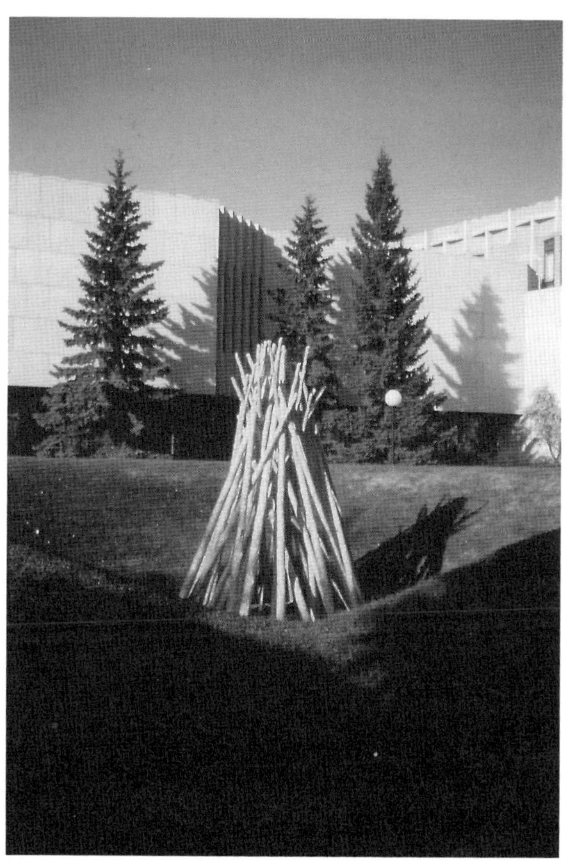

Fire has mystic qualities symbolic of the beginnings of man and, using sticks of fiberglass with a wood core, Cruise has created an instant ancient site. The piece is ringed by an artificial, grassy hillside that provides a very private site for the colorful red and yellow work. It is hoped that, as the work becomes familiar, students will gather comfortably around the campfire and use it as a contemplative place.

Firetell was the winner of a national, juried competition.

Location: University of Calgary, Engineering Building
Date: 1986

128. Pieces of Eight

Roy Leadbeater

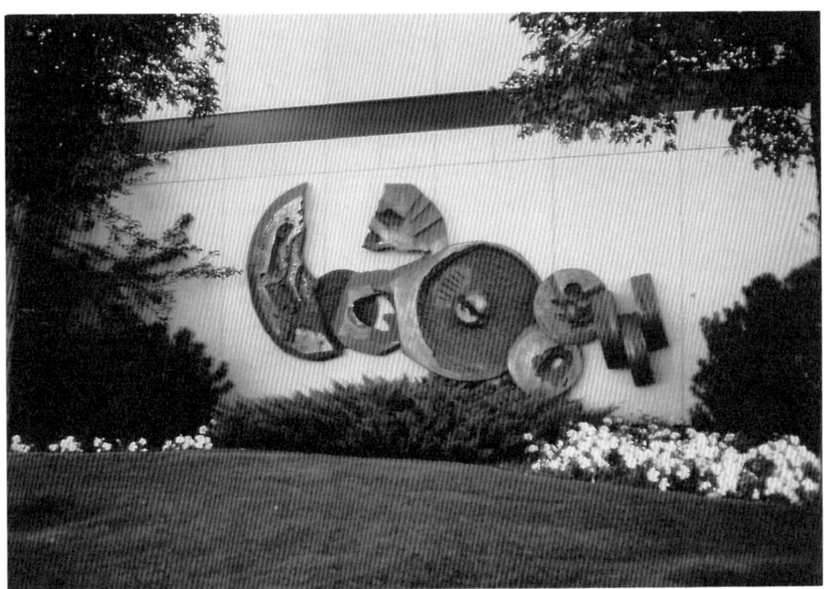

This massive bronze is found on the front facade of the Nickle Arts Museum. It depicts what happens to coinage when it passes through human hands, an appropriate theme for the site as the museum contains a fine collection of ancient coins donated by its benefactor, the late Carl Nickle.

Because of the completion deadline, the styrofoam pattern of the sculpture was airlifted to a foundry in Basingstoke, England, for casting. The resulting rough-bronze sculpture was then returned to Leadbeater for finishing.

The work was mounted in bitterly cold January weather and a temporary, heated enclosure was built so it could be completed on time. The several pieces of the sculpture were set in place using stainless steel dowels set in a cement grout.

The piece is 6 metres long, 3 metres high and weighs about 1 tonne.

Location: University of Calgary, The Nickle Arts Museum
Date: 1979

129. Locus VII

Catherine Burgess

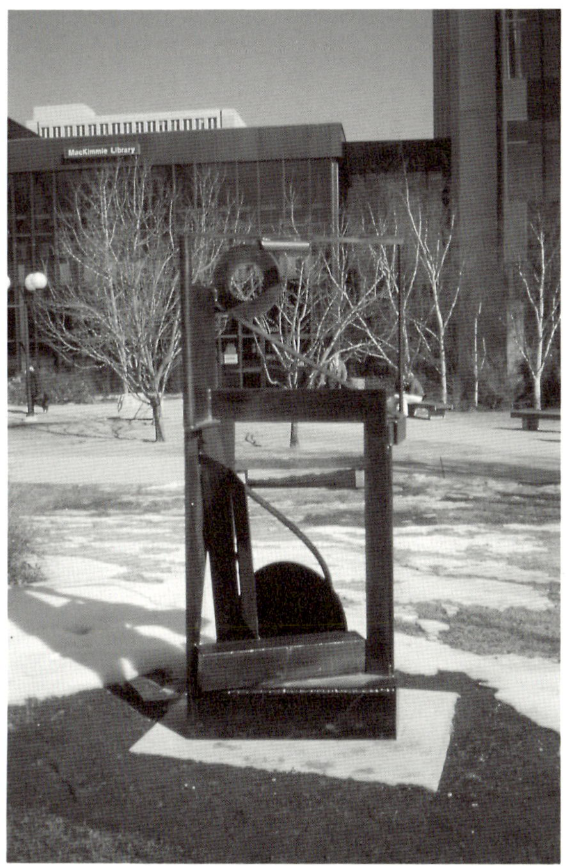

The artist's interest in the expressive nature of architectural space and form has led her to use geometry to create an enclosed space that acts as a sanctuary.

This welded-steel piece is the seventh, and one of the largest, in a series of sixteen pieces with "sense of place" as their general theme. It is a continuation of her previous series, which included a number of altarpieces dealing with the theme of "sanctuary."

Locus VII is one of the largest pieces from the Locus series — 178.5 by 64 by 78 centimetres — and a rare example of a vertical sculpture in her work.

Location: University of Calgary, Sculpture Garden
Date: 1989

130. 644.89

Ben McLeod

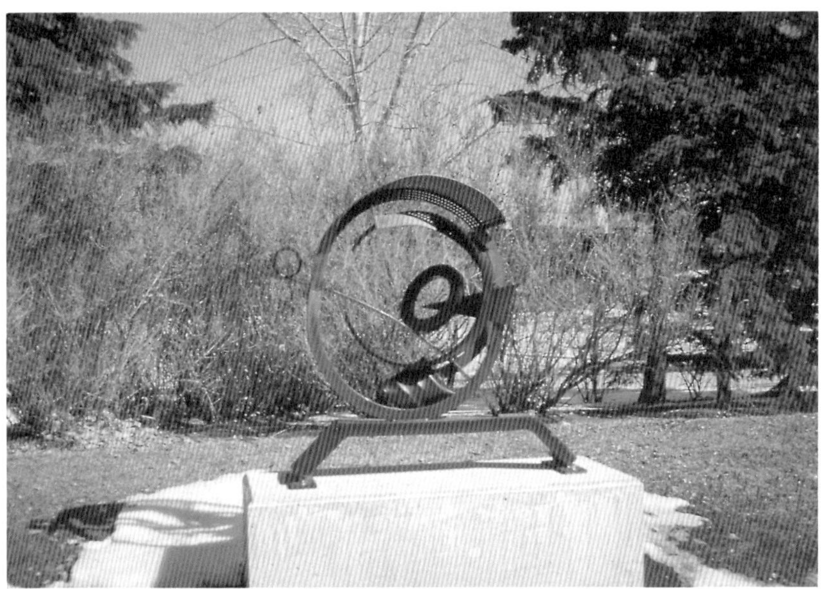

There is no mystery about the title of this abstract piece; the number 644.89 simply indicates the artist's cataloguing system. It refers to the number of the sculpture and the year it was completed.

When creating a sculpture, McLeod looks for the inner conflict and focus of energy of the materials and establishes this relationship in the work.

The piece is of steel painted red and black.

Location: University of Calgary, Sculpture Garden
Date: 1989, installed in 1990

131. Rani

Isla Burns

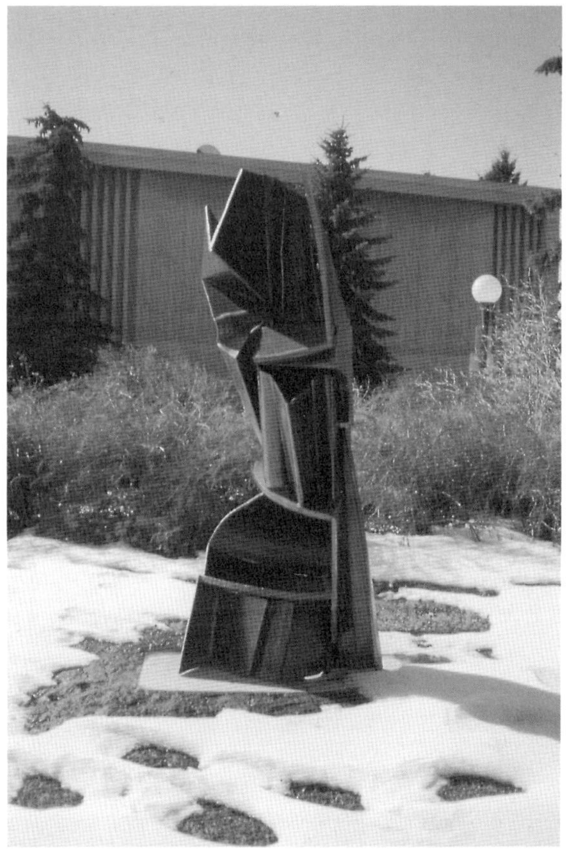

This welded-steel abstract, located on the west side of the Sculpture Garden, measures 213 by 79 by 64 centimetres.

The artist once said when asked to explain her works, "We have the ability to look at a plant or flower without asking what or why, without questioning the meaning and reason of that particular shape or form as opposed to another. We accept nature's arrangements unquestioningly. The beauty has purpose and mystery. Likewise, if we can approach abstract art as openly as we do nature's offerings, the beauty, purpose and meaning will reveal itself, and the mystery will be accepted and enjoyed."

Location: University of Calgary, Sculpture Garden
Date: 1986, installed in 1990

132. Blowing

Alan Reynolds

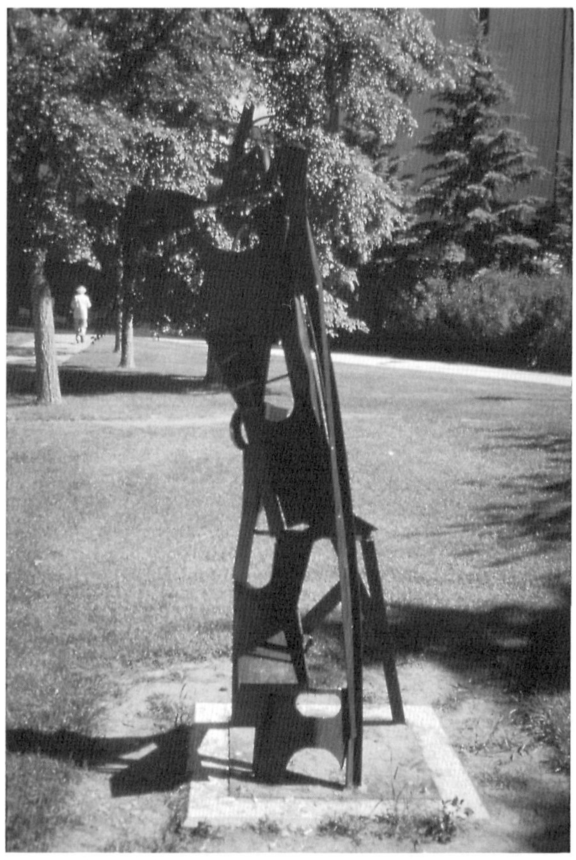

This abstract sculpture is made of welded steel painted black. The artist feels that art is an extension of his being, and finds it inappropriate that many people "expect sculpture to somehow excite them." He says, ". . . This ain't rock music. Sculpture has to have the power of silence."

Reynolds tries to distill life experiences and incorporate them into his work, but not in a literal way. Shapes that he sees, and relationships he experiences, are transformed when he includes them in his modernist pieces.

Most of his works are in the collections of private individuals.

Location: University of Calgary, Sculpture Garden
Date: 1990

133. Nirvana

Steven Heimbecker

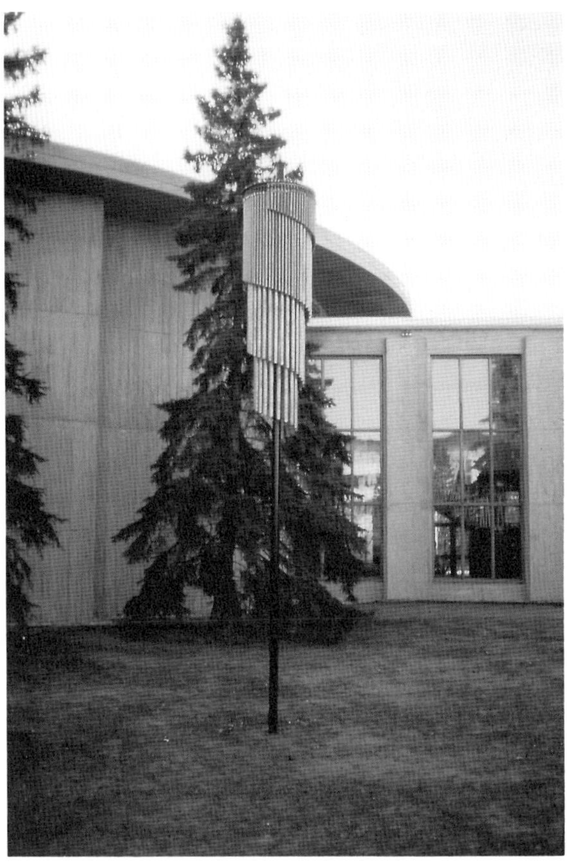

In eastern philosophy, Nirvana is the ideal human state — oblivious to anguish, care and pain. The word derives from two words meaning to blow out or to cool.

Heimbecker's *Nirvana* is a graceful wind sculpture. A spiral of 145 galvanized-steel chimes nearly a metric tonne in weight, the pipes range in length from 15 centimetres to 2.5 metres. The kinetic piece, which is nearly 7 metres high, has been engineered to sway in the breeze like a tree, with the smallest of winds able to coax out its mystical, Asian music.

Location: University of Calgary, north side of University Theatre
Date: 1989

134. & 135. Serpentine and Discobolus III

Doug Moen

Welded metal sculptures by Saskatchewan artist Doug Moen stand outside the University Theatre. The 1.5-metre-high pieces were purchased as part of the university's permanent art collection.

Moen said of his work, "I work freely, making no maquettes and only a few drawings. Working my ideas out on the production line keeps my work spontaneous, and lets it choose its own moment of existence."

Serpentine is on the northeast side of the theatre, while *Discobolus III* is on the southeast.

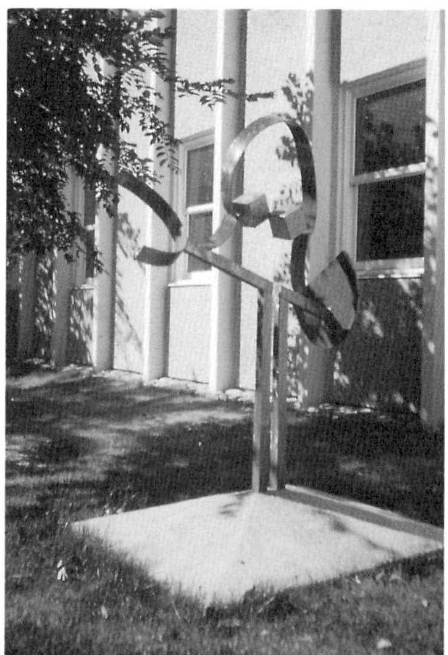

Location: University of Calgary, behind University Theatre

Date: 1970

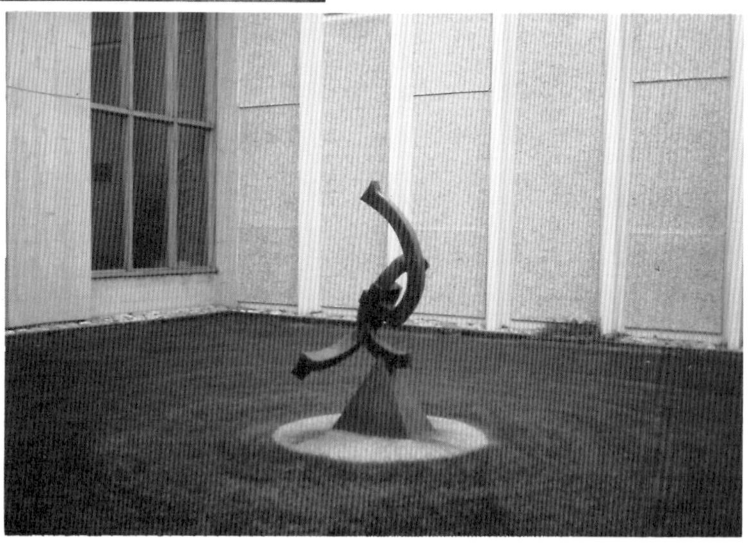

136. Rhythm One

Ed Drahanchuk

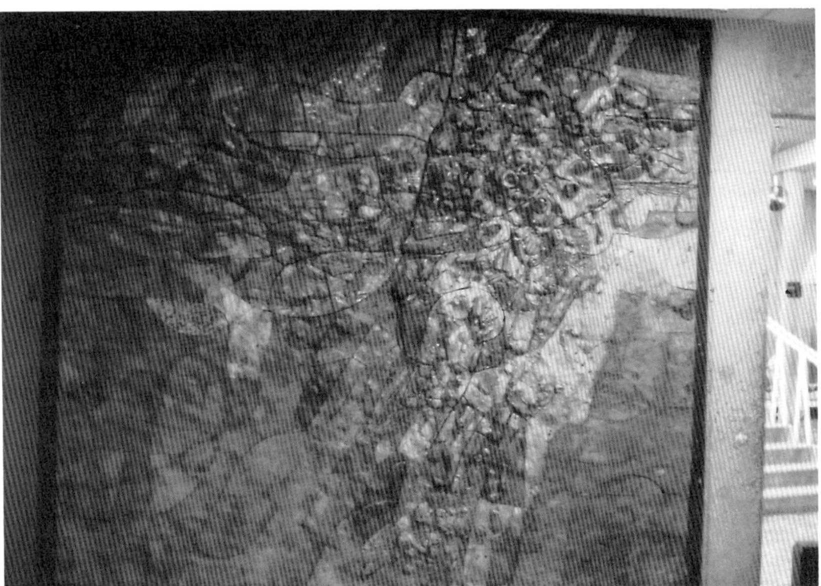

This large ceramic mural is found in the theatre lobby in Calgary Hall.

The artist said of the work, "When I do a large piece of work like this mural, I like to mull it over in my head for at least a couple of months — sometimes seven or eight months. I envision what it would look like, change things and consider the problems of construction. When I go for a walk in the woods, what I see becomes patterns of designs. What I feel in the woods makes the designs live."

Location: University of Calgary, Calgary Hall
Date: 1970

137. Olympic Arch

Colette Whiten and Paul Kipps

Designed by architects A.J. Diamond and Partners, this arch is "supported" by eight life-size bronze figures sculpted by the artists.

Whiten and Kipps chose athletes from Toronto's West End YMCA to act as models, then each athlete spent a total of at least ten hours posed in a straining position while the artist covered sections of their bodies in plaster of paris to make a mold. The molds were then shipped to a local foundry and cast in bronze.

The large, rust-colored arch was originally the official entrance to the Athletes' Village at the University of Calgary during the 1988 Olympic Winter Games. The work, which was funded by TransCanada PipeLines Ltd., was one of two arches chosen by jury from fourteen submissions representing architecture in Canada. Before the competition results were announced, the athletes who had posed for the sculpture sent the artists a telegram urging them to "Go for the bronze."

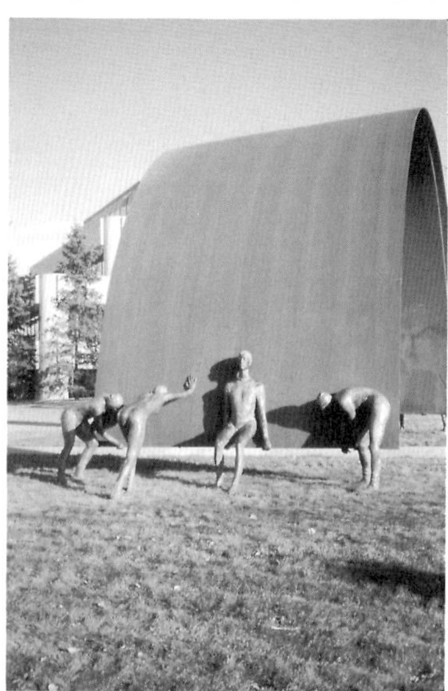

After the Olympics, the arch was moved downtown to a controversial location in front of the Municipal Building. Then, in 1991, as part of the university's 25th Anniversary celebration, it was returned to the university to a permanent site in front of the physical education complex.

Location: University of Calgary, physical education complex

Date: 1988, installed at University of Calgary in 1991

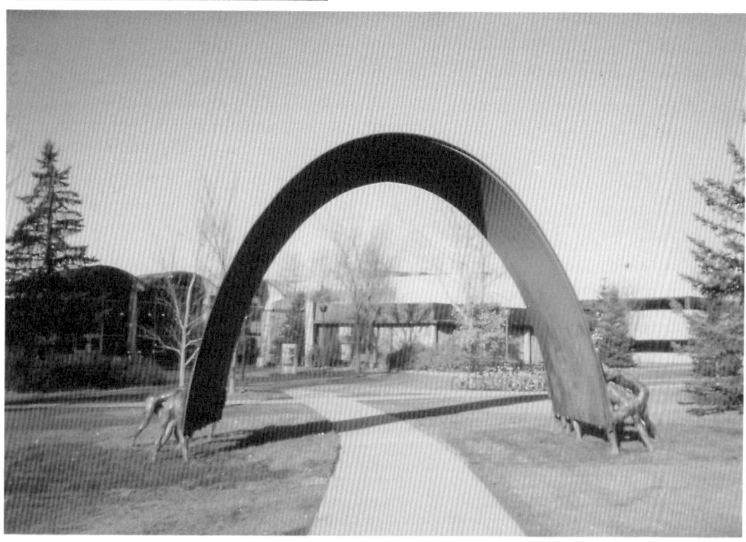

138. Spire

Bob Boyce

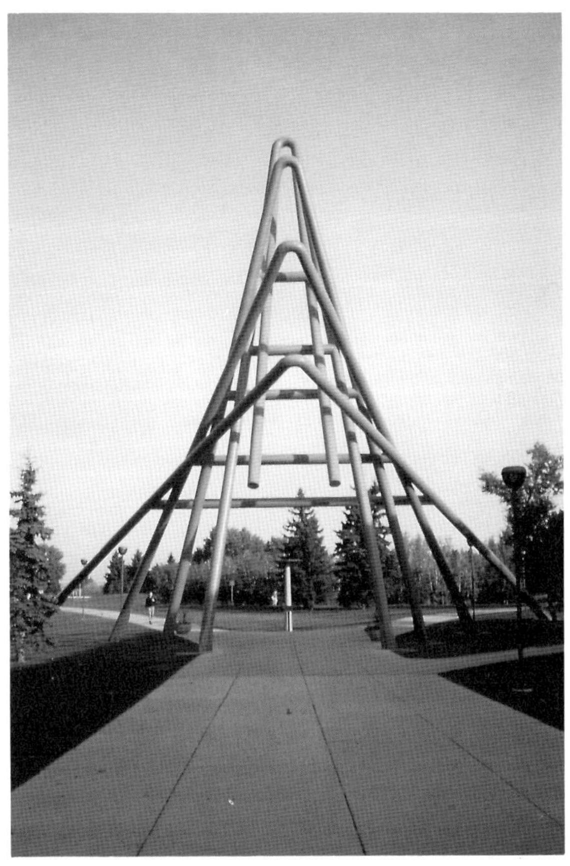

Winner of a competition to provide a suitable entrance piece for the 1988 Olympics' futuristic speed skating oval, the fiery-red *Spire* rises a symbolic 19.88 metres into the air.

It depicts the progression of human movement — crawling, walking, running, jumping and flying. Five jutting bipods represent the five rings of the Olympics, while the outline is a spaceship heading to outer space. The interior of the piece is man discovering his inner space.

Location: University of Calgary, Olympic Oval
Date: 1987

139. La Patineur de Vitesse '84
The Speed Skater

Germain Bergeron

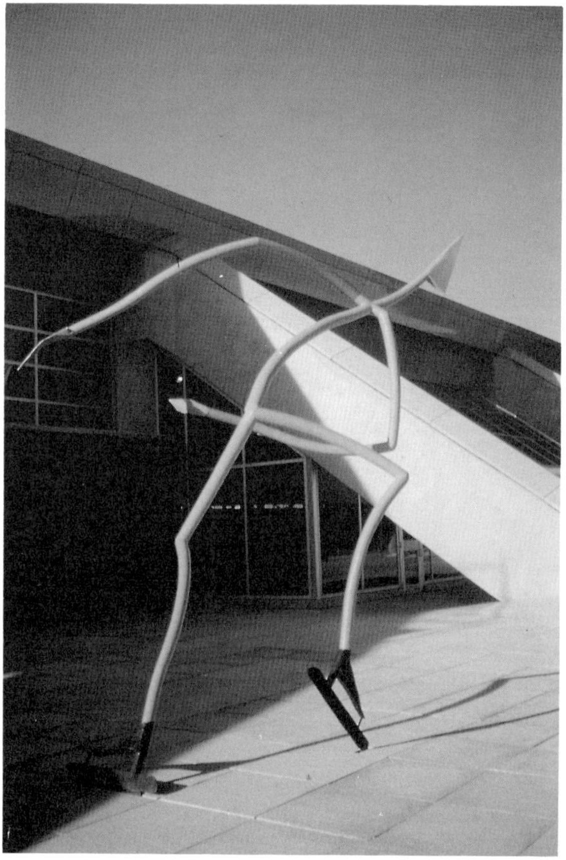

This muted-red metal sculpture stands poised to skate on the plaza on the south side of the Olympic Oval.

It is 6 metres high, and is the artist's tribute to Canadian speed skater Gaetan Boucher, who won two gold and a bronze medal in the 1984 Winter Olympics.

Location: University of Calgary, Olympic Oval
Date: 1987

140. Rocky Mountain Mining Mask

Don Proch

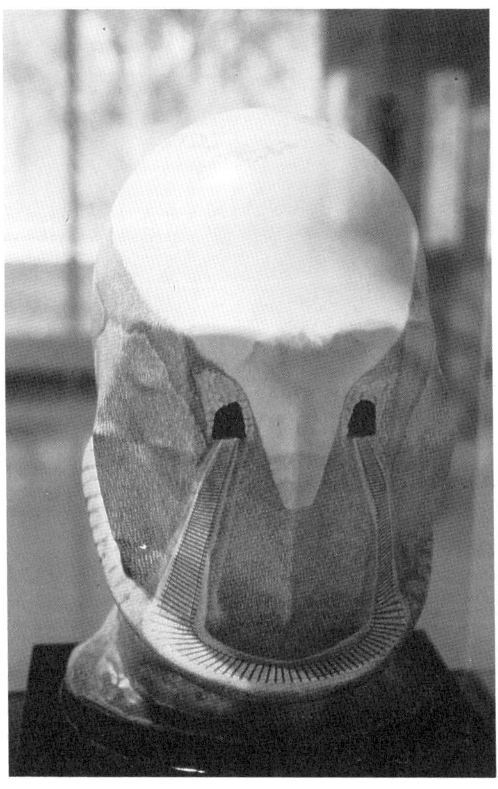

Masks have become Proch's hallmark and he has created them on a wide variety of prairie subjects. Unlike the goalie masks they resemble, Proch's three-dimensional sculptures reveal more than they conceal. The Rocky Mountain Mining Mask is a glossy, ridged landscape of the mountains, its design a powerful image of the world as seen by the wearer of the mask.

A railway track loops around the nose, leading from and into tunnels that are the eye spaces. Minute fir trees cover the mountainside, each tree distinct and clear, yet giving an impression of the granite texture of the Rockies. Snow covers the top of the skull, while a snow-fed river drops down the back, leading out of the mountains and on to the western foothills.

The mask is constructed of graphite, silver point, fiberglass, clear lacquer and silver wire. It is in the collection of the University of Calgary, purchased with funds from the Government of Canada and a donation from Dr. William Campbell of Winnipeg.

Location: University of Calgary, Olympic Oval
Date: 1990

141. The Speed Skater

John Weaver

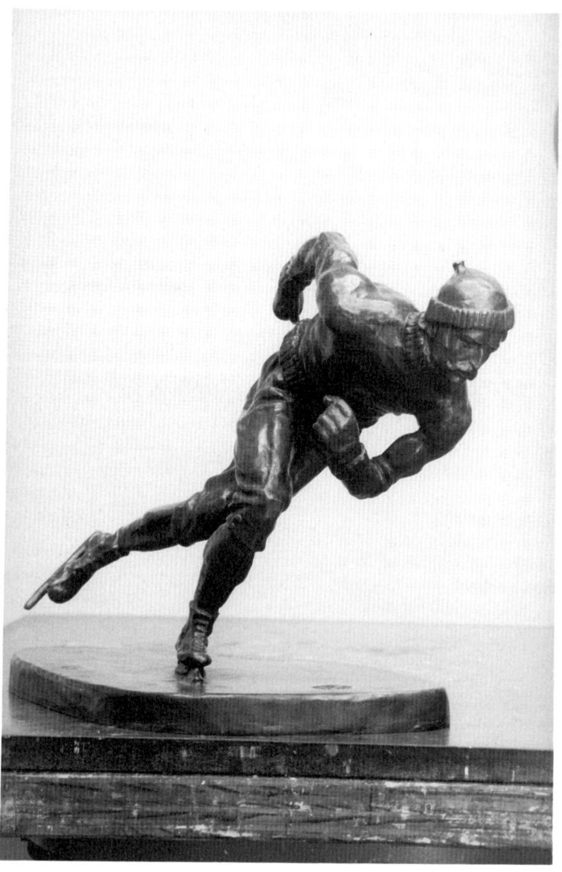

Although it is a part of the *Spirit of the Winter Olympics* series depicting Winter Olympic sports' competitors, *The Speed Skater* stands on its own merit at the Olympic Oval. A tribute to Winter Olympic competitors, it recognizes Calgary's intention to carry on the sporting traditions that produce excellence.

Weaver said of the piece, "This intrepid fellow is intent on going to the 1928 Olympic Games in St. Moritz, Switzerland. Three years before, in 1925, there was only one Canadian entry in the speed skating event of the 1st Winter Olympic Games in Chamonix, France: C. Gorman. Perhaps, with much work, this man can offer C. Gorman company."

The series was commissioned to support the 1988 Winter Olympics, and sales of the sets of sculptures raised 500 000 dollars in support of amateur athletics.

Location: University of Calgary, Olympic Oval
Date: 1988

142. The Athlete

Robert McKenzie

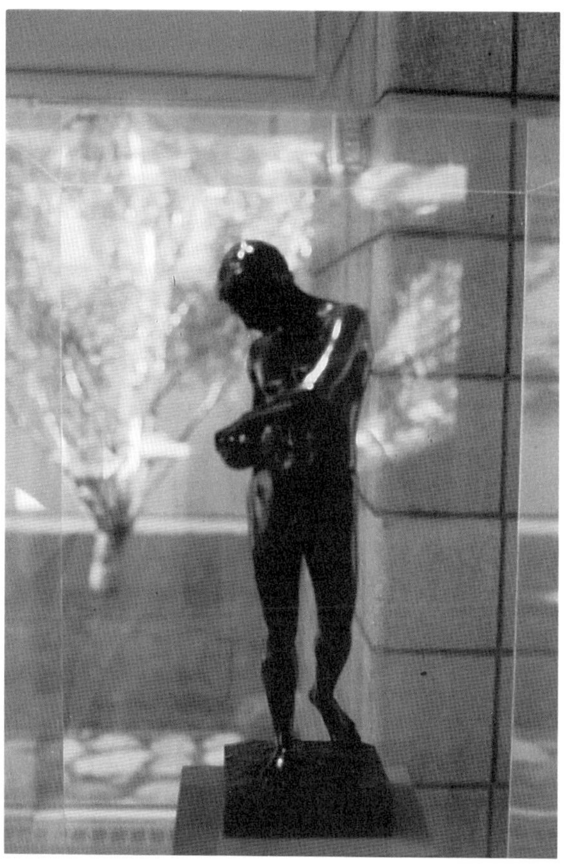

The Athlete is a copy of McKenzie's second major sculpture, which was created for the Society of Directors of Physical Education in Colleges. His commission was to sculpt a model of the ideal athlete and he was furnished with measurements of 400 excellent athletes from Harvard University. The composite was completed in 1903, and exhibited at the Paris Salon, the Royal Academy, and the Roman Art Exposition. Copies were acquired for the Museum of Natural History, New York City; the Ashmolean Museum, Oxford, England; the Art Gallery of Ontario, and many private collections.

Location: University of Calgary, Olympic Oval
Date: 1903, present site 1987

143. Brothers of the Wind

Robert McKenzie

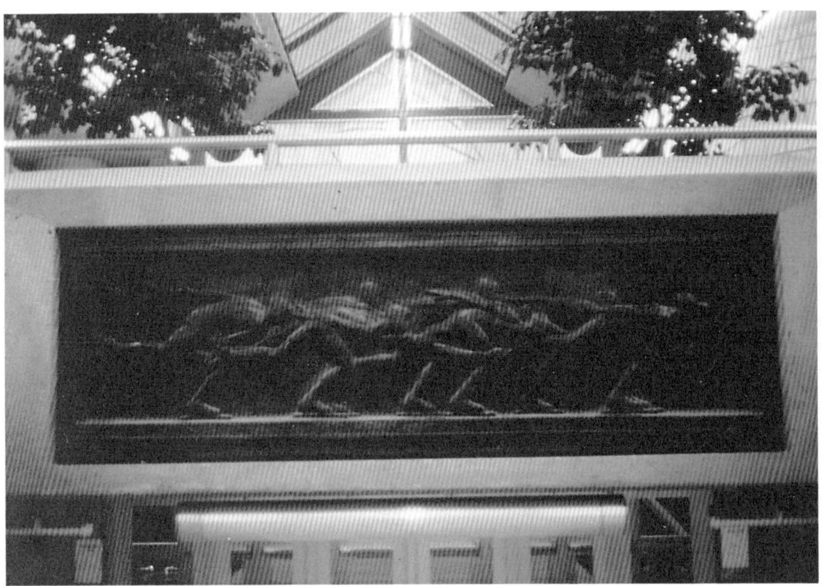

This large bronze frieze, depicting eight speed skaters in competition, was created for the Philadelphia Skating Club in 1925.

Location: University of Calgary, Olympic Oval
Date: 1925, present site 1987

144. Pagoglyphs (Marks on Ice)

Brian Baxter

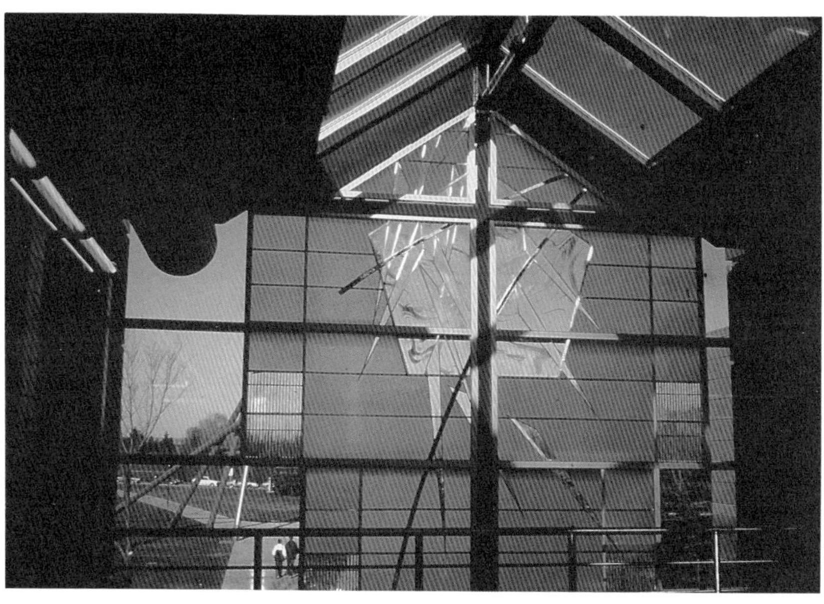

Two wintry, leaded, art glass pieces, set high in the north and south windows of the Oval, represent the marks an ice skater might make in a crystal-clear surface. The piece measures approximately 5 metres by 4 metres.

Location: University of Calgary, Olympic Oval
Date: 1987

145. Heroic Entrance

Barbara Astman

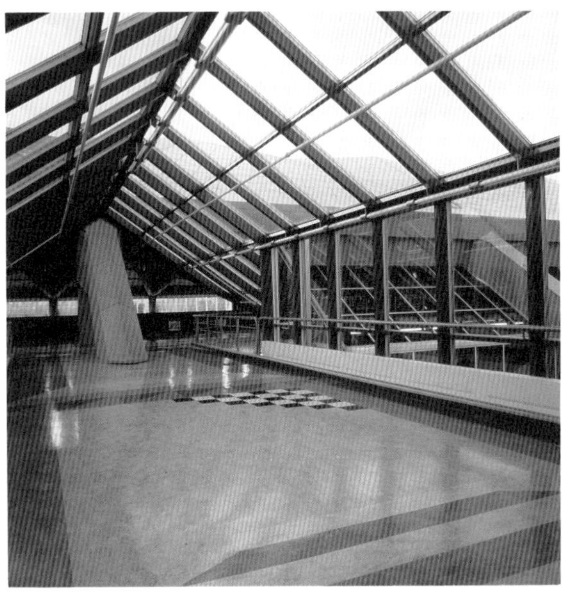

The striking "art floor" at the entrance to the speed skating oval is a mosaic created from a marblized linoleum called Marmoleum. This is an exceptionally durable flooring made from natural materials — jute, cork, linseed oil, wood flour, pine resin and pigments. Not only are the tiles slip resistant and sound absorbent, they also resist cigarette burns, retard fire and destroy bacteria. As well, Marmoleum can be permanently bonded to itself, so through the use of heat welding, a variety of colors could be juxtaposed to form the design.

"The intent of the floor I have designed is to enhance the excitement, splendor and spirit of the Games . . . it is meant to complement and reflect the impressive design of the Olympic Oval itself, and to enhance the public's enjoyment and appreciation of both the space they occupy and the historic events they are about to witness," Astman said.

The black-and-white checkerboard pattern is reminiscent of the past — the historical aspect of the Olympics. An illusion of stairs worked into the design encourages the flow of crowds into the Oval and creates an impression of climbing up to the arena.

Location: University of Calgary, Olympic Oval
Date: 1987

Northwest

146. Bas-Relief

Katie Ohe

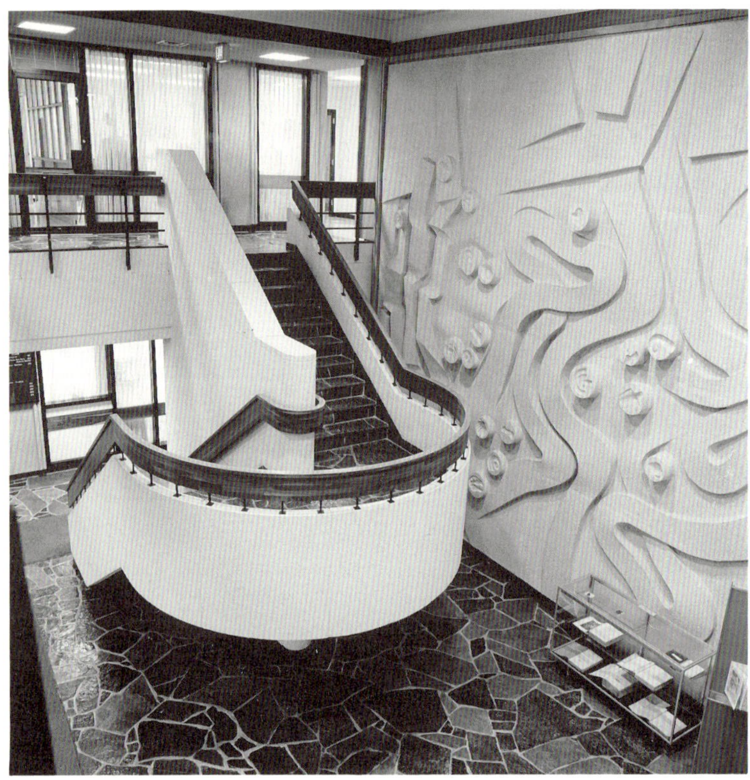

Commissioned by the federal government, this cast-stone mural, which measures 6 by 9 metres, covers an interior wall on the first floor lobby of the building. The mural is a stylized geological map of Canada with symbolic forms of fossils scattered in appropriate areas.

Ohe studied geological maps and fossils to learn about the structure of rocks, mountains and plains. She decided she didn't want literal mountains like those found in relief maps, so mountains are arranged in shifts, folds and faults. The plains are a broad undulating surface, while the feldspar region around Hudson's Bay is a ribbonlike shape in a circular swirl. The dolomite formations of the Maritime region and the Northwest Territories are also ribbonlike, but based on a parallel composition. The undulating swells of oceans rise over the coasts.

Crushed stone in concrete gives a pale pink color to the feldspar area and a tan shade to the dolomite formations.

The cylindrical forms projecting from the surface of the relief are representative of geological cores.

Location: 3303 - 33rd Street N.W., Geological Survey of Canada
Date: 1967

147. Encounter

William McElcheran
(aka William Mac)

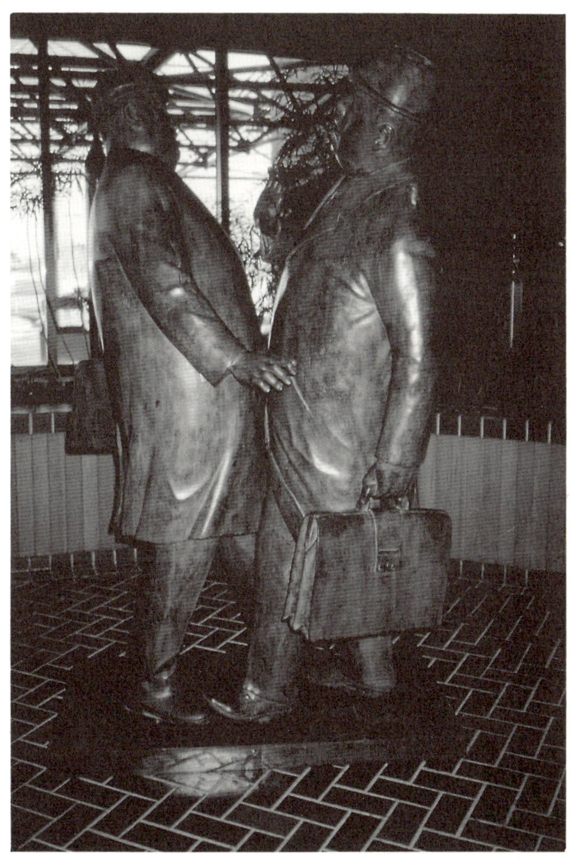

Like *Conversation,* McElcheran's sculpture on Stephen Avenue Mall, this piece depicts a meeting between two portly, briefcase-carrying businessmen. While the downtown piece shows them in conversation, in *Encounter* they have come upon one another unexpectedly, likely with their minds on important appointments. They collide in the lobby of the Foothills Hospital Special Services Building and stand toe-to-toe, belly-to-belly trying to regain their balance and dignity.

The amusing study was purchased through an art program set up to place Canadian art for the enjoyment of patients and visitors in the cancer centre.

Location: Foothills Hospital, Special Services Building
Date: 1984

148. Genesis

Anubhava Loving Peace
(formerly Judi Christensen)

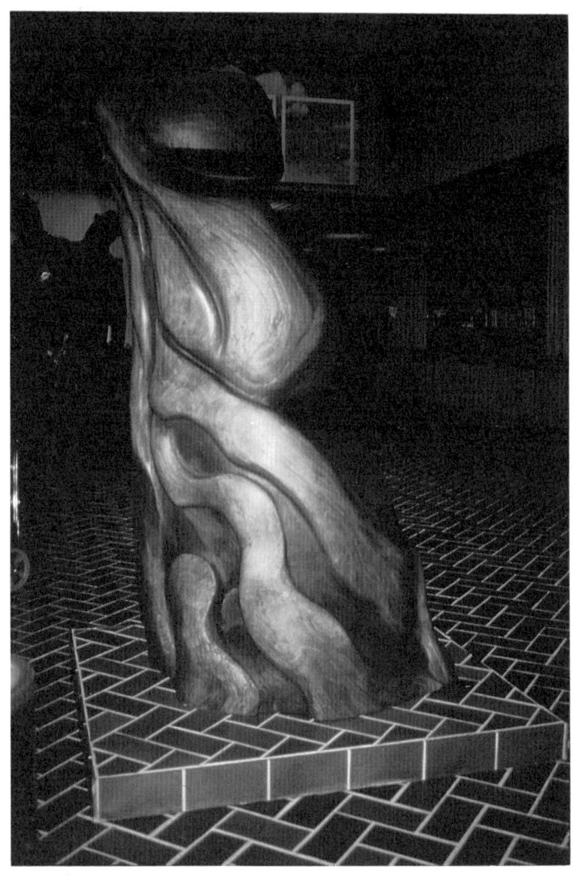

The 1.2-metre, abstract *Genesis* is created from Barbadian mahogany, a harder wood than the South African variety. The artist explains that "the form was inspired by landscape and human relationship to it, and by the soul's growth through an interaction between form and formlessness."

Location: Foothills Hospital, Special Services Building
Date: 1984

149. Tree of Life

Ross Weaver

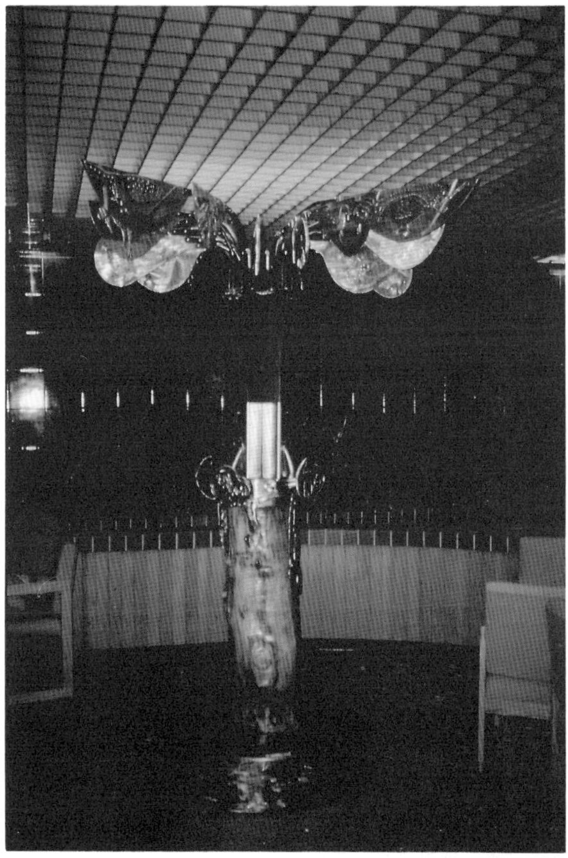

Located in the Special Services Building at Foothills Hospital, where many of the patients are being treated for cancer, *Tree of Life* provides a welcome lighthearted touch.

Its main theme is birds and our attitudes to life with birds. The piece is bursting with things to look at and enjoy. On both sides of the aluminum leaves, and on the trunk and base, you find birds flying in trees at night, admiring themselves in water and feeding their young. As well, you may spot cheerful butterflies or a cat sliding downhill.

Created from bronze, aluminum, steel and wood, the 2-metre sculpture is intended to be an optimistic artwork for patients and visitors.

Location: Foothills Hospital, Special Services Building
Date: 1984

150. Pocket Jungle

Tony Bloom

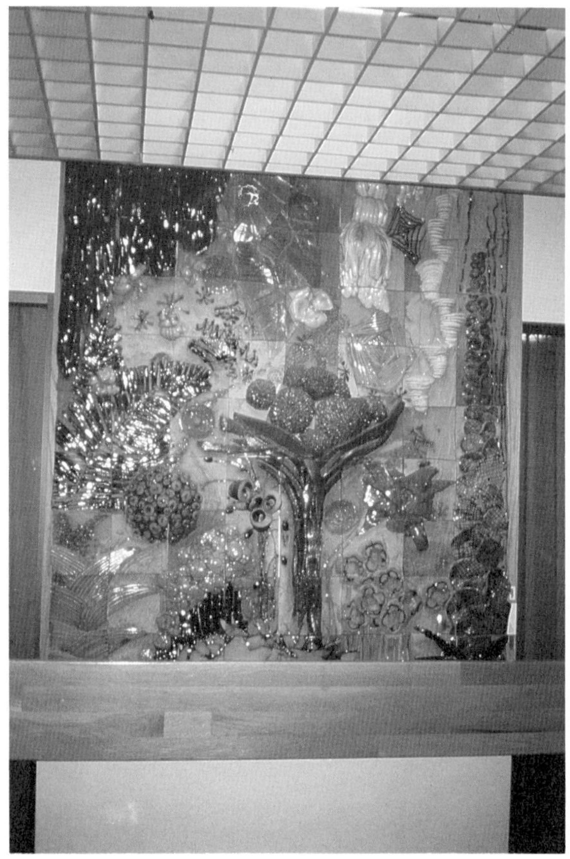

"A small jungle of flowers and ferns seemed appropriate for the setting, with its nearby planters of real vegetation," Bloom says. Because the area attracts many cancer patients and their visitors, this happy piece is meant to cheer and amuse its viewers.

The artist points out that his brightly colored, almost 2-metre square ceramic mural contains "messages, jokes and things to find," such as bees on the flowers and the "zzzz" of snores on a drowsy, heat filled day.

Location: Foothills Hospital, Special Services Building
Date: 1984

151. Hippocrates

Nikolas Pavropoulos

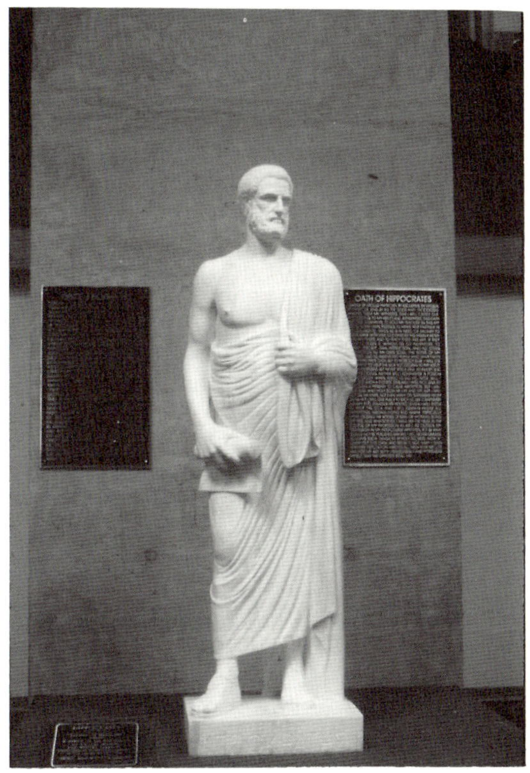

Hippocrates, the father of medicine, lived in Greece from about 460 to 377 B.C. Even today, in many medical schools doctors affirm a modern version of his ancient oath at graduation.

The noble physician towers over University of Calgary medical students as they cross the lofty mall in the university's Health Sciences Centre adjoining the Foothill's Hospital. The 3-tonne sculpture was carved in Greece from a single piece of Pendelic marble.

The statue was commissioned by Jimmie Condon, a Greek immigrant who came to Calgary in 1911 and spent his lifetime encouraging the youth of Calgary, both girls and boys, to strive for excellence in sports. He visited Greece in order to choose the artist to sculpt his dream — a statue of Hippocrates that would inspire future doctors to give their utmost to their profession.

Location: 3350 Hospital Drive N.W., Health Sciences Centre
Date: 1980

152. Robert the Bruce (1274-1329)

Charles D'Orville Pilkington Jackson

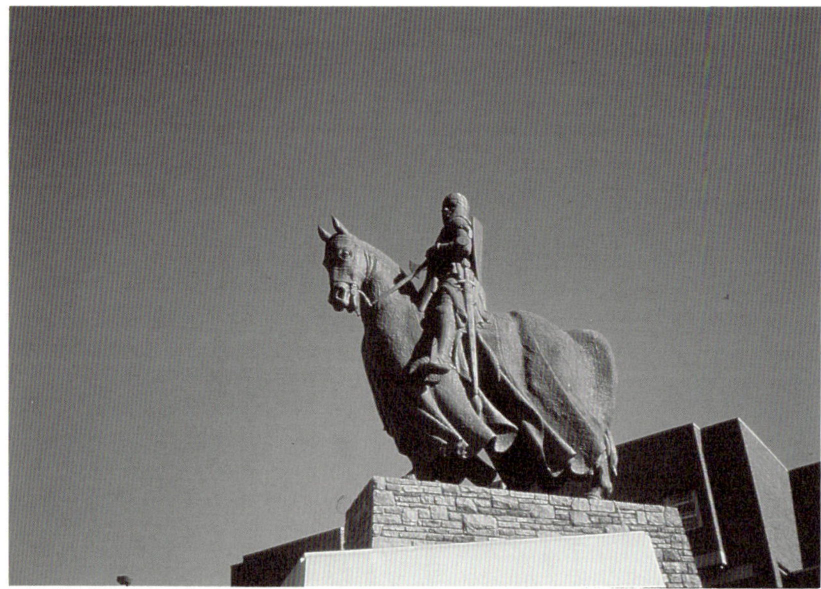

The mounted figure of Robert the Bruce, 14th-century Scottish king, overlooks the city from its vantage point near the Jubilee Auditorium. A gift from the late Eric Harvie, noted Calgary philanthropist, the bronze is one of the most impressive sculptures in the city, standing over 8 metres high.

Harvie commissioned two castings of the statue to commemorate the epic confrontation in which Robert the Bruce of Scotland defeated the English under Edward II and won independence for Scotland. After the two statues were cast, the original die was destroyed. One was unveiled at the site of the Battle of Bannockburn by Queen Elizabeth II in 1964, and its Calgary counterpart was installed in 1967.

There was considerable controversy over the suitability of a statue of a Scottish king on an Alberta hillside, but Harvie said at the unveiling ceremony, "Robert the Bruce has played a large part in the history of all English-speaking peoples."

Location: 1415 - 14th Street N.W., Jubilee Auditorium
Date: 1967

153. Koshetz (1875-1944)

Leo Mol

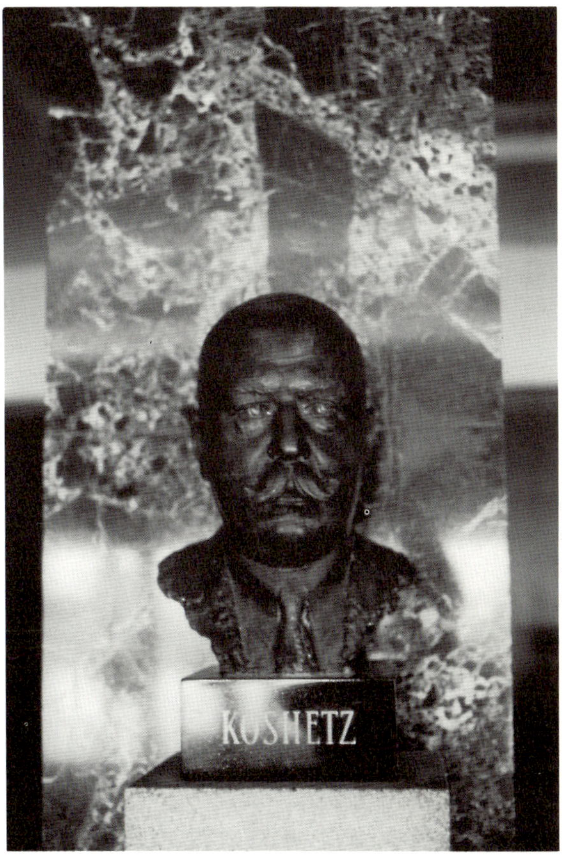

Born in the Kiev region of the Ukraine, Olexandr Koshetz was a noted lecturer in choral arts, as well as a conductor and choirmaster. In addition to opera, symphony and liturgical arrangements, he composed over a thousand pieces of music for choral work.

A concert tour he made through the United States and Canada caused a great upsurge of interest in choral ensembles in both countries.

The bronze bust, which is installed in the lobby of the Jubilee Auditorium, was a gift of the Ukrainian Canadian Committee on the occasion of Calgary's Centennial.

Location: 1415 - 14th Street N.W., Jubilee Auditorium
Date: 1975

154. Steel Wave

Roy Leadbeater

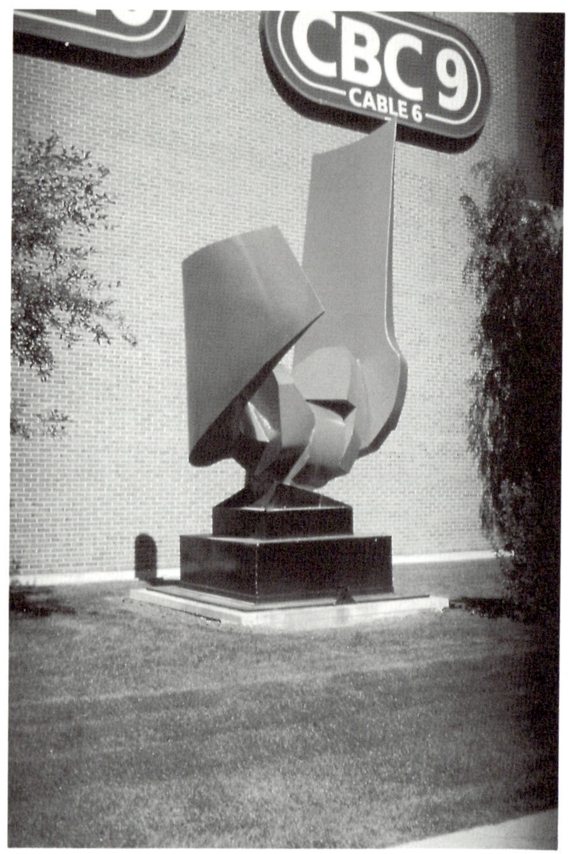

The 5.4-metre high, welded-steel piece standing in front of the CBC Building represents the strength and power of the word.

The abstract wings and the cranklike forms between them refer to media — its ability to carry messages to all parts of the world, and the balance, power and timing of media technology.

Location: 1724 Westmount Boulevard N.W.
Date: 1979

Northeast

155. Deerfoot

John Weaver

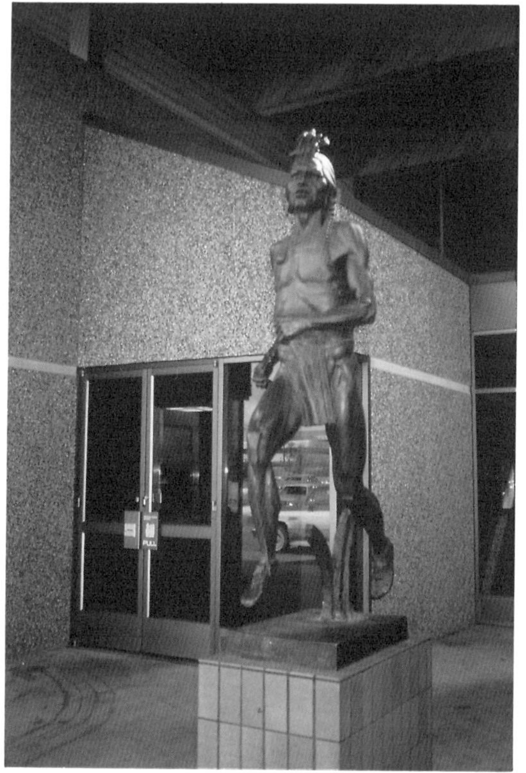

Cast in bronze, this heroic-size bronze statue faces into the north wind. The following is the artist's description of the Alberta foot runner.

"At the end of a long, great tradition of Indian-European foot race competition, came this Blackfoot of Cochrane, Alberta. Like the Seneca Indian, Deerfoot of 1870, this Deerfoot of the early 1900s became a household name for victories. His usual opponents were from the North-West Mounted Police. He had never owned a horse, so he ran wherever he went. The statue shows the fluid power of his developed style. His most notable race was at the opening of Louise Crossing. Deerfoot finished the final 300 yards having lost (or, as some said, deliberately dropped) his loin cloth. Deerfoot had gone on, unabashed, leaving at least one woman in a faint — unable to witness his astonishing victory."

This work was commissioned by Cascade Developments.

Location: 901 - 64th Avenue N.E., Deerfoot Mall
Date: 1982

156. Mannequins

Roy Leadbeater

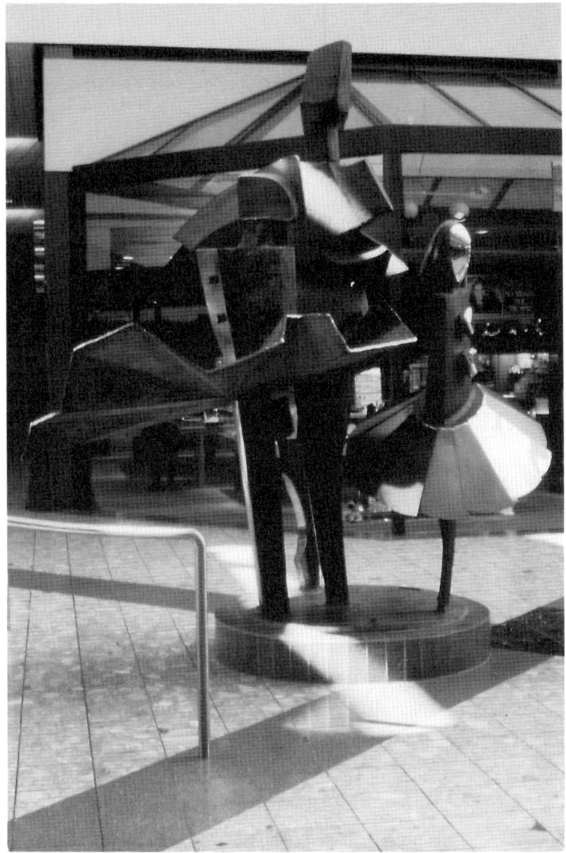

This bronze sculpture-in-the-round is a "light-hearted abstract of a family group featuring a play on clothes," according to the artist.

To get the massive piece into the mall for installation, the 90-kilogram head was removed from one of the figures. It was protected by a foam pad and put on a nearby bench while the rest of the statue was set in place with a huge forklift.

When it was time to install the head, it was missing. It had been stolen as a prank. Fortunately the mall manager remembered a young man speaking on the phone at that time. They were able to track him and his pals down and the head was returned slightly damaged.

It was crated and flown to Edmonton where Leadbeater was able to make the necessary repairs in time for the unveiling.

Location: 901 - 64th Avenue N.E., Deerfoot Mall
Date: 1982

157. Spirit of the Winter Olympics

John Weaver

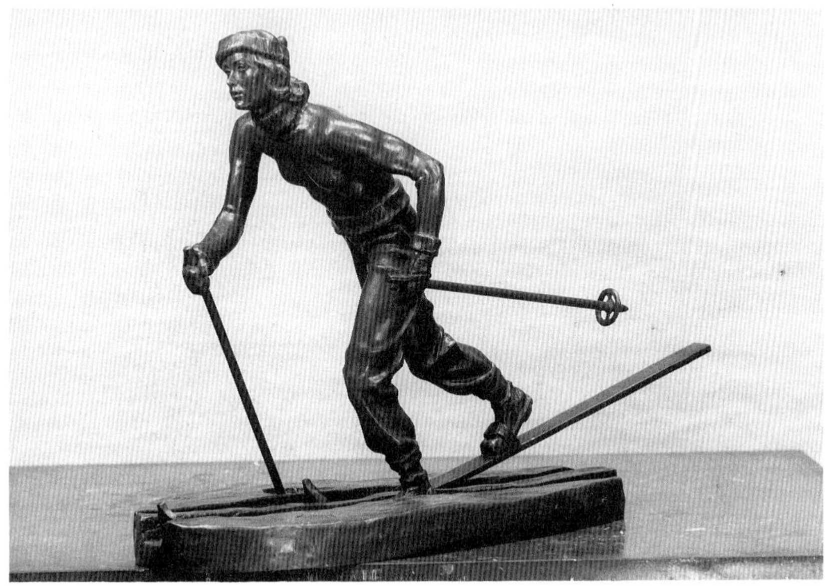

Depicting clothing and equipment used by Olympic competitors of the 1920s, these bronze sculptures represent five Winter Olympic sports: luge, downhill skiing, speed skating, ice hockey and cross-country skiing.

Commissioned by the Calgary Olympic Development Committee as a fund-raiser for the 1988 Olympic Winter Games, the series of sculptures may be found in other Calgary locations (Lavalin Inc. at 909 - 5th Avenue S.W., for example) but were unveiled at Deerfoot Mall. The 500 000 dollars realized from sale of the sculptures was earmarked for the support of amateur athletics.

Location: 901 - 64th Avenue N.E., Deerfoot Mall

Date: 1985

158. The Trader

John Weaver

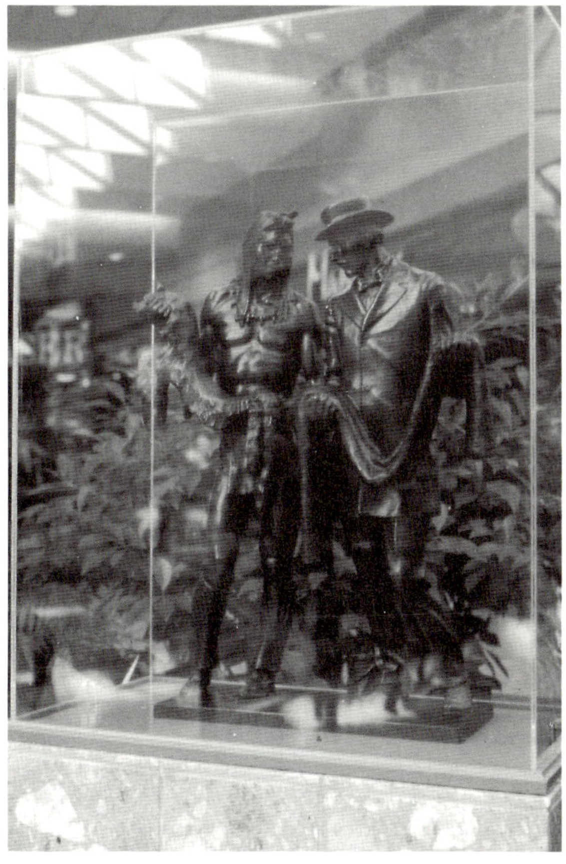

Early white traders have often been accused of taking advantage of the native Indian, but artist John Weaver likes to remind us that the Indians were bartering long before explorers came on the scene.

In this bronze tableau, an Indian is offering an animal skin in trade for a blanket. At the white man's feet is a trading item popular with the natives, a set of three nesting copper tins with lids.

This scale model stands about 2 metres high. A heroic-size sculpture, created from the model, stands on the plaza of the Edmonton Public Library.

Location: 901 - 64th Avenue N.E., Deerfoot Mall
Date: 1982

Miscellaneous

159. Archimedean

Bob Boyce

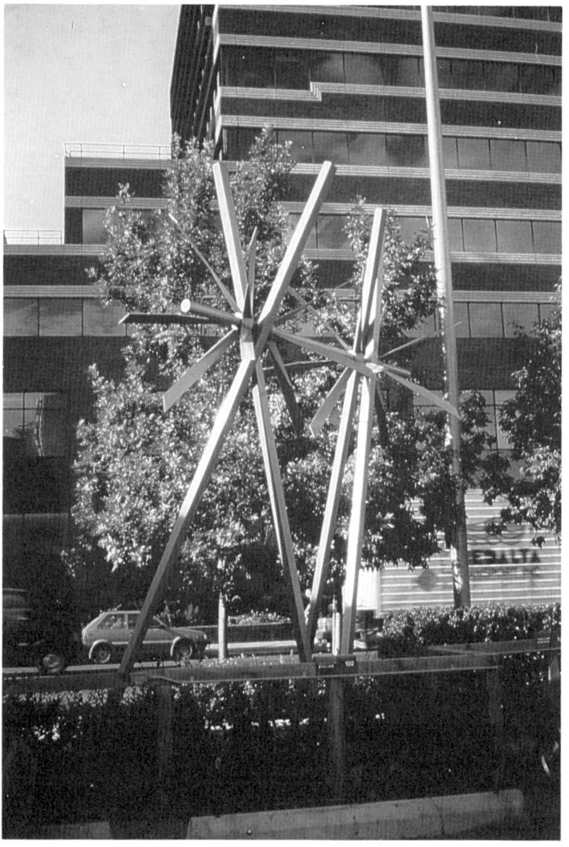

This wind-driven sculpture stands by the offices of Cohos Evamy Architects. The firm has a strong belief that young, emerging artists should be encouraged, and that art should be used in spaces where it can be appreciated and viewed by the public. This was the first corporate commission for Boyce.

The company required a sculpture to complement the landscaping, and decided on a design that emulated palm trees. The piece is also a symbolic compass commemorating the work of Greek mathematician and inventor, Archimedes.

The steel and aluminum sculpture is nearly 6 metres tall, and its aluminum propellers are activated by a stiff breeze.

Location: 902 - 10th Avenue S.W.
Date: 1983

160. Red Cross Mural

James Willer

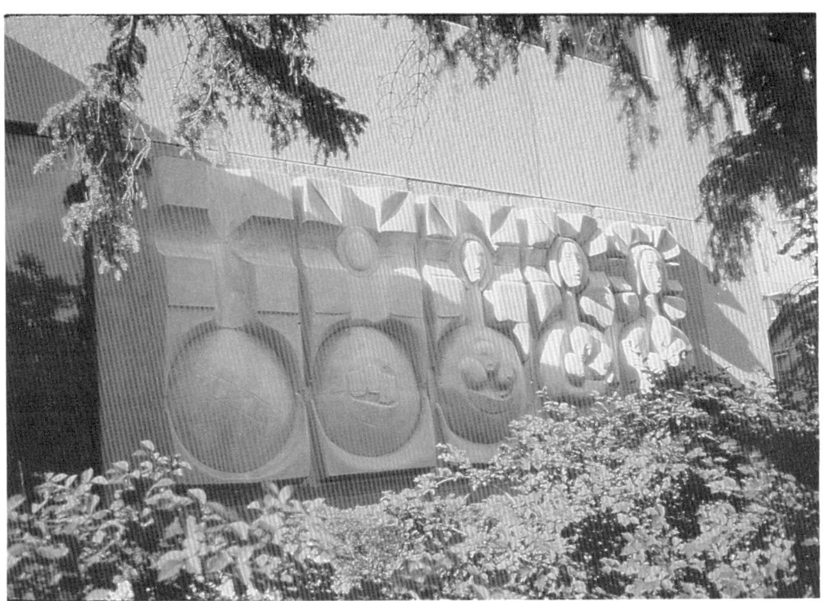

The architects of the new Red Cross Society headquarters in Calgary invited Jim Willer, of British Columbia, to design a mural for the exterior of the building. The artist met with Hank Hilton, supervisor of the project, and recalls that Hilton was "a man who lived and breathed Red Cross, and who had already made a sketch of what he wanted to see on that mural." These suggestions included a cross of five equal squares, the world globe, and figures of all races holding hands.

Willer took the symbols "and Hilton's enthusiasm and unpretentiousness to heart" when he produced his "metamorphosis in five panels."

He explains that, "The geometric Red Cross symbol bursts like a flower into a mother figure. Hank's globe erupts into the three primal races of Earth."

The mural measures nearly 3 by 7 metres and is deeply carved to give shadow and texture to the piece, which is on a north-facing wall.

Location: 737 - 13th Avenue S.W., Red Cross Building
Date: 1978

161. Ashes to Life

Roy Leadbeater

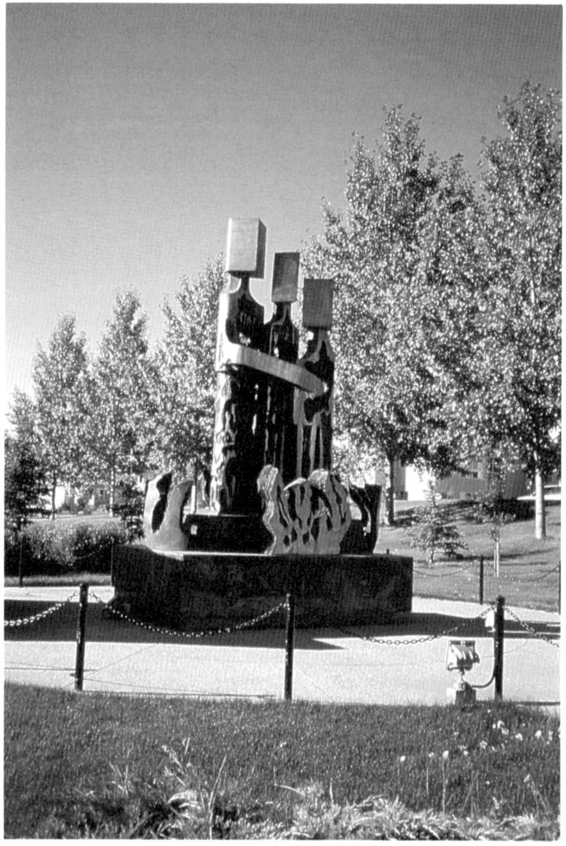

The large bronze sculpture in the courtyard of the Calgary Jewish Centre is designed to show that the spirit of the Jewish people could not be extinguished by the holocaust.

The flames are symbolic of the inferno inflicted upon the Jews of Europe during World War II, with the rough, open areas representing the scars and mutilation of body and mind which took place.

The solidarity of the individual family and the universal family of Jews is symbolized by the protective arm of the tallest figure, while the burnished heads illustrate the contribution made by Jews from every walk of life to the advancement of all people. "Although attempts may be made to break the body and spirit, the creative mind will always triumph." the artist explains.

Location: 1607 - 90th Avenue S.W., Calgary Jewish Centre
Date: 1986

162. Brigadier General Andrew Hamilton Gault (1882-1958)

Don Begg

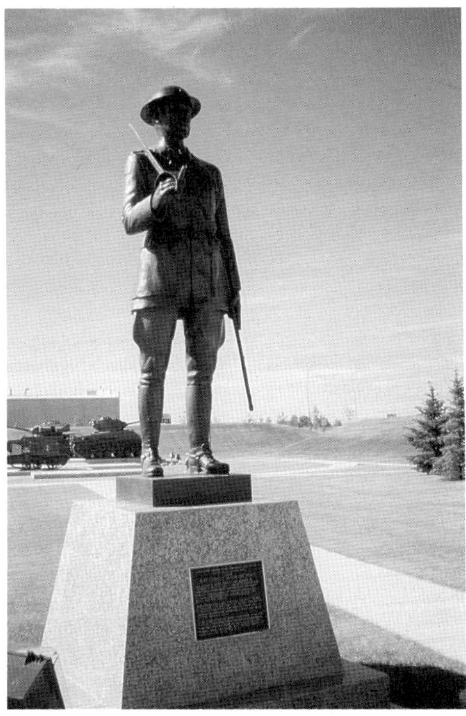

A Canadian, Hamilton Gault served in the South African War. When World War I was imminent, he contributed 100 000 dollars to raise and equip an infantry battalion, which led to the formation of the Princess Patricia's Canadian Light Infantry. Gault was second-in-command, until the loss of a leg ended his active service. The statue depicts him in the uniform he wore as Lieutenant Colonel in command of his regiment when it returned from the Great War in March 1919.

He was recalled to active duty in World War II, serving on staff with the Canadian Army in England. Following the war, he returned to Canada and was appointed honorary colonel, then colonel of his regiment.

Commissioned by the Princess Patricia's Canadian Light Infantry, the statue was unveiled by Her Majesty Queen Elizabeth in 1990. Three castings were made. The first stands at the entrance of the Museum of the Regiments in Calgary, the second is at Canadian Forces Base (CFB) in Wainwright, Alberta, and the third will be placed on Parliament Hill in Ottawa.

Location: Museum of the Regiments, CFB Calgary
Date: 1990

163. Lord Strathcona Driving the Last Spike

Don Begg

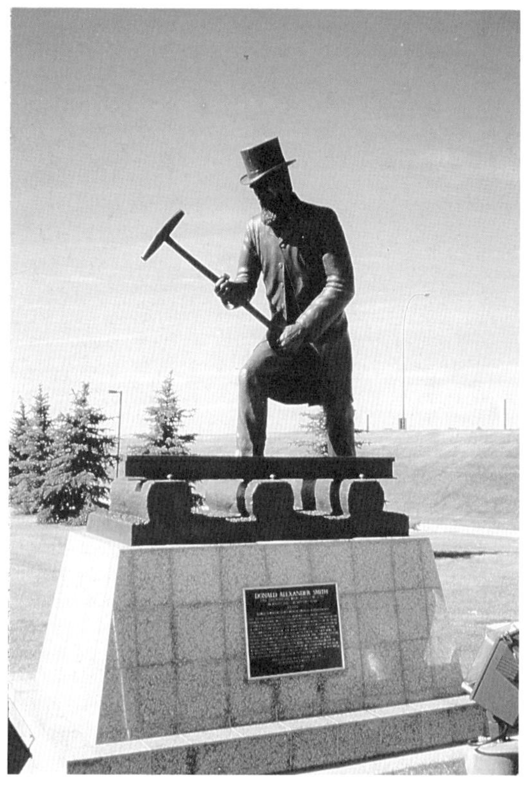

Lord Strathcona, Donald Alexander Smith (1820-1914), was a Scottish fur trader and railroad financier. He came to Canada in 1838 with the Hudson's Bay Company and worked his way up to governor, the company's chief executive position. He went on to attain honors in several fields — as president of the Bank of Montreal, high commissioner for Canada in Great Britain, and chancellor of McGill University.

His financial backing was essential to the successful building of the Canadian Pacific Railway and, in 1885, he drove the last spike, thus linking Canada from Atlantic to Pacific. He named the mountainous site "Craigellachie," for a rugged crag in Morayshire, Scotland, where he grew up.

During the Boer War in South Africa, he maintained Strathcona's Horse, a regiment of over five hundred mounted riflemen. This later became the Lord Strathcona's Horse, a regiment based in Calgary.

Location: Museum of the Regiments, CFB Calgary
Date: 1991

164. Lotus #1

Katie Ohe

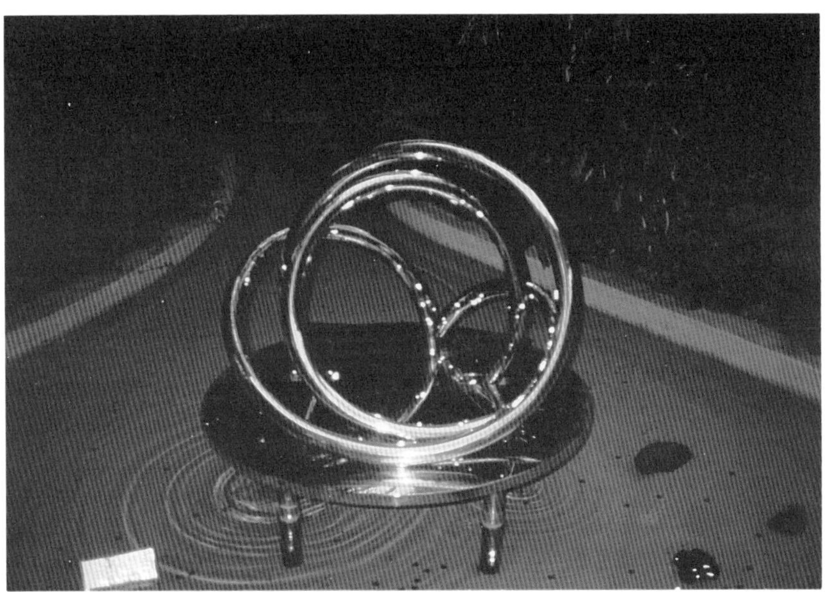

When Marion and Jim Nicoll, noted Calgary artists, moved into the Bethany Care Centre, they gave Ohe *carte blanche* to create a sculpture for the finest space in the facility. "There were no restrictions as to style or type of sculpture," the artist recalls.

As she designed the work, "several seeds for thought emerged." She decided to let this be her first water sculpture, but realized that, as well as enhancing the space provided, the piece should be visually soothing, noiseless and maintenance free. As well, she wanted its movement to be the result of water, not a motor. From these demands, a shape, a meaning, a technique and size developed.

The sculpture's form means many things. The oscillating chrome circles that make up the blossom symbolize the sun, the earth, the beginning and the end, and the wheel of life. The movement of the parts of *Lotus I* suggests the opening and closing of a water lily, which is appropriate to its setting in a pool.

Location: 916 - 18A Street N.W., Bethany Care Centre Arboretum
Date: 1983

165. Out West

Rick Silas

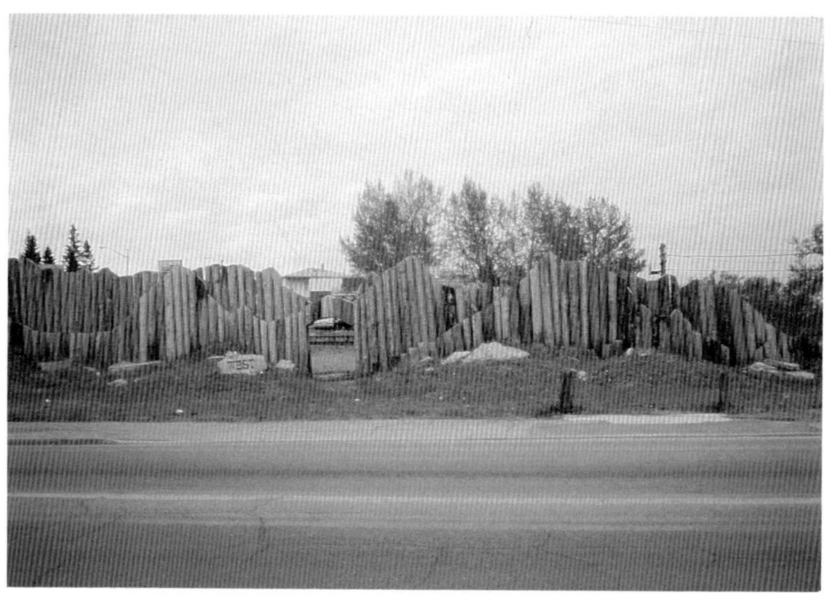

Silas, a sculptor who specializes in wood carving, created the Rocky Mountain skyline silhouette from 200 telephone poles. He has said of the piece, "I came 'out west' about fifteen years ago, and still remember vividly my first impression of the Rockies."

The work, 55 metres long, is a scaled replica of the mountain ranges just west of Calgary, starting at the east end of the lot with Three Sisters and spanning west to Orient Peak. It was commissioned by the Inglewood Community Association in 1988, and is located across from the Deane House on 9th Avenue S.E. Future landscaping plans for the site include a natural garden of native Alberta plants.

Location: 800 Block, 9th Avenue S.E.
Date: 1988

Al-Shaikhly (aka Alan Faith)

(b. 1941)

Al-Shaikhly is the "artistic name" of this self-taught sculptor. Now a full-time artist, he studied engineering in England before coming to Canada.

He was living in Montreal when *Natural Harmonics No. 12* was purchased for the Devonian Gardens, but has lived in Calgary for the past six years.

Mario Armengol

(b. 1909)

Born in Spain, Armengol is a noted sculptor and a recognized painter as well. Now retired, and a British subject, he lives in Cornwall, England.

Armengol summed up his early life in a few words. "Let it suffice to say that a chain of vicissitudes, consequent to the Civil War in Spain, brought me to the U.K. via North Africa and Norway in 1940."

He has completed several other pieces comparable in size to his *Brotherhood of Mankind* but these have been of reinforced plaster, a less durable material than the aluminum used in his Calgary sculpture.

Armengol has also worked as a designer for British industry in many countries, including Canada and Russia. He has exhibited in major cities throughout the world.

Ray Arnatt

(b. 1934)

Born in Nuneham Courtenay, England, Arnatt was educated at the Oxford School of Technology, Art and Commerce, the Oxford School of Art, and the Royal College of Art, where he was a Royal Scholar. He says of his art, "My ideas on binary structuralism form the foundation for my sculpture."

In 1962 he set up a sculpture studio in Berkshire, England, and a research bronze-casting facility to cast his own work. During his time in England, he was senior lecturer at Chelsea School of Art and a visiting artist to many art departments throughout the country. He was also an external assessor for the National Council of Academic Awards.

In 1979 he arranged a year's teaching exchange with the Emily Carr College of Art in Vancouver, then moved from England in 1981 to take up a teaching position at the University of Calgary. At present he is area coordinator for sculpture at the University of Calgary.

He has completed many major public commissions in Great Britain, and has exhibited widely in England and Canada. His most recent commission was in Hong Kong. As well, his work is represented in many private and public collections.

Karoo Ashevak

(1940-1974)

Ashevak was born in Spence Bay, North West Territories, and was considered to be the finest Inuit artist of his time. His works are much sought after by collectors.

He was an unusually expressive and zestful Inuit artist. Rather than beginning with a basic bone or stone and releasing a shape from it, he first visualized a creation and then searched for the appropriate piece of material. Most of his work is in whalebone, with touches of soapstone, caribou antler and ivory, and he derived great pleasure from using a variety of tools to add fine finishing touches to his powerful works.

When he was just thirty-four years old, with a lifework consisting of 250 pieces, Ashevak and his wife Doris died in a fire. At that time his unsold works were put into a trust for their surviving daughter.

Barbara Astman
(b. 1950)

Artist Barbara Astman was born in Rochester, New York, and obtained an associate degree from the Rochester Institute of Technology before moving to Canada to study at the Ontario College of Art in Toronto.

Astman mixes traditional art forms such as drawing, painting, photography and sculpture, and enhances them with current technological developments. She has explored the artistic potential of Xerox color copying, the Polaroid SX-70 camera, linoleum and plastic laminates.

Her work has appeared in over 100 solo and group exhibitions and is in many private and corporate collections. She is on the faculty of the Ontario College of Art and York University.

Jaqueline Badord

Mme. Badord is a French artist whose sculptures can be found in collections around the world.

Brian Baxter
(b. 1952)

Brian Baxter was born in Middleton, Nova Scotia, and received a Bachelor of Design in Visual Communications from Nova Scotia College of Art and Design in Halifax in 1973. In 1977 he travelled west and apprenticed in various glass studios, always pursuing his quest to express appreciation for beauty. His work evolved through art nouveau, art deco and Japanese style to his present urbane, progressive style of graphic design.

Baxter is based in Vancouver, British Columbia.

Gilbert Bayes
(1872-1953)

Bayes was an English artist and began studies at the Royal Academy Schools in 1896. In 1899 he won the gold medal and a travelling scholarship.

Don Begg
(b. 1945)

Begg was born in Calgary and raised on an Alberta cattle ranch. A Cochrane-based sculptor, he has worked in the Western realistic idiom since 1968.

As a student, he had as mentors such noted Western artists as Doug Stephens, Charlie Beil and John Weaver. From them, he learned the intricacies of the lost wax process of bronze casting, and also developed an enthusiasm for sculptures.

He studied at two bronze foundries in California and continued his art education in anatomy and monumental sculpture at the Hoheb Studios of New York City.

For a number of years, he worked as master of Studio West Foundry in Cochrane. Now, along with his wife Shirley Stephens Begg, he is owner of Studio West, the first fine art foundry of its kind in Canada.

Begg's bronzes depicting the history and wildlife of the West are widely collected on four continents, while his monumental sculptures may be seen in Calgary, Edmonton, Wainwright, Cold Lake, Drayton Valley and Wetaskawin, Alberta.

Robin C.H. Bell

(b. 1949)

Robin Charles Hungerford Bell was born in Seaforth, Ontario. Since graduating from the University of Toronto in 1972, he has lived mostly in Italy. He has had exhibitions in Toronto, Paris and throughout Italy. Bell was awarded the Greenshields Foundation Scholarship in 1976.

Douglas Bentham

(b. 1947)

Born in Rosetown, Saskatchewan, Bentham studied at the University of Saskatchewan, Saskatoon, and took part in several of the university's artist workshops at Emma Lake. He has exhibited regularly in Canada since 1969 in both solo and group shows, and his works are found in most Canadian museum collections.

At present, he lives and works near Saskatoon, Saskatchewan.

Germain Bergeron

Bergeron is a Quebec artist, living in Terrebonne. He received his BA from the University of Montreal, and an MA, major in sculpture, from the University of Notre Dame.

In addition to pursuing his own art career, he has been a director of a Montreal gallery and a professor of sculpture at Cégep du Vieux-Montréal.

He has created many massive sculptures — *Don Quichotte* and *Ballerine* are each over 9 metres tall — and his work is collected by a number of Canadian museums and universities. He has been the subject of several films and articles and his works have been a part of over twenty solo and group exhibitions. In 1990 he was honored with a solo retrospective, *thirty years of sculpture* at the Centre d'exposition du Vieux Palais, St-Jérôme.

His work is in metal, and he assembles scraps into human or robot forms, often with tongue-in-cheek humor.

Derek Michael Besant

(b. 1950)

Born in Fort Macleod, Alberta, Derek Besant studied at the University of Calgary where he achieved a BFA, Honors, in 1973, and pursued graduate studies in 1974. He was elected to the Royal Canadian Academy of Arts in 1978.

His work has been widely exhibited nationally and internationally and he is represented in many prestigious collections. Besant's fifteen-storey mural at the Scotia Plaza in downtown Toronto is the largest mural ever produced in Canada.

From 1974 to 1977, he was exhibition designer for the Glenbow Museum in Calgary. He has served as vice-chairman of the National Board for the Print and Drawing Council of Canada, and as head of the drawing department and member of the founding board of governors for the Alberta College of Art (ACA) in Calgary. He is now an instructor at the ACA and on the Board of Trustees of the Calgary Art Gallery Foundation, which is the art committee of the Nickle Arts Museum. He is also on the art committee of the Calgary Centre For the Performing Arts.

Stanley Bleifeld

(b. 1924)

Born in Brooklyn, New York, he received degrees in fine arts and in education from Tingle University, followed by a master's degree and advanced study at the Albert C. Barnes Foundation.

Until he visited Italy in 1960, he was essentially an abstract painter, but he now confines himself almost exclusively to figurative sculpture. He returns to Italy every year for further work.

He has exhibited extensively throughout North America, and his public commissions may be found in many American cities as well as in private collections around the world. The United States Navy Memorial in Washington, D.C., is one example of his major works.

Bleifeld, who is a gifted teacher, currently conducts classes at the Bleifeld Studio Sculpture Group. Forty of his students arranged an exhibition of their work in his honor in New York City in 1990.

Tony Bloom

(b. 1947)

This Canmore artist was born in Tokyo and educated in Tokyo, Paris and Washington, D.C. He studied physics at the University of Maryland before moving to Alberta in the 1970s. Settling in Canmore, he joined the Banff Centre's open studio program in ceramics. Although there was no formal instruction, the program gave him an opportunity to learn from experience, and to network with other participants.

He became a self-taught ceramist and sculptor, and, along with two other artists, founded Stonecrop Studio in Canmore in 1974. He served as chairman of the Crafts Committee on the Arts Festival Board for the Calgary Winter Olympics and was also chairman of the Bow Valley Olympic Arts Committee.

His credits are many in a variety of artistic pursuits — percussionist; dance accompanist; initiator of a number of exhibitions and group shows; and guest artist at Johnson Atelier, New Jersey, casting in bronze.

His work has appeared in many exhibitions and is a part of over two dozen public and private collections throughout Canada. He has received grants, awards and scholarships throughout his career and was the winner of an Alberta Achievement Award in 1988.

Jordi Bonet

(1932-1979)

Jordi Bonet was born in Barcelona, Spain. A fall from a tree when he was seven years old resulted in the loss of his right arm, but this handicap did not prevent him from giving an amateur art show in his parents' home two years later.

Introduced to Spanish treasures at an early age by his art-loving father, Bonet says, "My apprenticeship centred successively around Velazquez, Goya and Picasso." Like Goya, Bonet was fascinated by crowds and much of his early sketching was done of street people.

Moving to Canada in 1954, where he quickly became a noted artist, he developed an interest in ceramics. Between 1960 and 1974, Bonet created over 100 murals and sculptures using a wide variety of materials.

His works are installed in cities from Vancouver to Halifax as well as in many major American centres. His largest work, *The Triptych* (1969) in the Grand Theatre, Quebcc City, is over 100 square metres in size.

Illness forced him to return to drawing in 1973 and he died in Montreal six years later.

Charles Robert Boyce

(b. 1955)

Bob Boyce was born in Coronach, Saskatchewan but has lived in Calgary since 1973. He received his sculpture diploma from the Alberta College of Art in 1977 and continued art studies at the University of Calgary and The Carving Studio in Carrara, Italy. He now lives and works in Calgary and has participated in a number of solo and group exhibitions, and in competitions throughout western Canada.

Catherine Burgess

(b. 1953)

Born in Ponoka, Alberta, this respected Edmonton artist graduated with a BFA from the University of Alberta. She has participated in dozens of solo and group exhibitions and has been the recipient of sixteen awards, grants and fellowships.

For a number of years, she worked exclusively in wood, but since 1981 has concentrated on welded steel pieces. She found that, unlike wood, this medium is incredibly strong and can be joined and cut quickly and easily. For some time she worked mainly with scrap steel but now fabricates all of her own shapes from new material.

She has been a part-time sessional lecturer at the University of Alberta, and a visiting artist at a number of other art schools in Canada. Burgess has also served as a grant juror for Canada Council and Alberta Culture, and as an acquisition juror for the Alberta Art Foundation.

Isla Burns

(b. 1952)

This artist was born in Calcutta, India, and educated in Edinburgh, Scotland. She attended the Edinburgh College of Art and continued her education at the Alberta College of Art, earning a Diploma in Sculpture from 1970 to 1974. She was awarded a Master of Visual Arts degree at the University of Alberta in 1978 and has taught at the U of A, as well as in schools in England and Spain.

Her work is mainly in metals, with steel most frequently chosen for her sculptures. However, she also enjoys the contrast of a variety of types of metals and the unusual effects they achieve — an extension of her interest in the organic world and in organic combinations. She frequently combines "found objects" with sculptured forms to add another dimension to her artworks.

Burns lives in Edmonton where she is a sessional teacher at the University of Alberta. Her work is included in the collections of several universities in Western Canada, the Canada Council Art Bank, and the City of Barcelona Spain, as well as in private collections of several corporations.

Maurice Calka

Calka is a French artist from Aquitaine and was a professor of arts at Beaux Arts, Paris, at the time the mosaic landscape was commissioned for the Aquitaine Tower in Calgary.

Jane Charlotte (formerly Jane Pugh)

(b. 1955)

Charlotte says, "I was always an artist and, fortunately, during my upbringing I was given the opportunity to develop my abilities."

She was born in Calgary and, "as a little person," was taught by Katie Ohe at the Allied Art Centre. She later spent time with Jim Barr and, in New York City, studied with Xavier Gonzalez and Marshal Glazier.

She received a BFA from the University of Calgary in 1978 and a Certificate from the Art Students League of New York in 1989. Her works have been included in over twenty exhibitions and are in private collections in the United States and Canada, and she has been the recipient of a number of awards and scholarships.

Her "struggling artist" experience came during the soul-searching period when she was deciding whether to pursue a career as a full-time artist. It meant leaving a secure position with the Calgary Recreation Department and travelling to New York City to immerse herself in the art world there, a decision she made in 1985 because, as she puts it, "I feel the only antidote to destruction is creation."

Primarily a painter now, she divides her time between New York City and western Canada, spending a period of time each year painting in the Rocky Mountain House area.

Joe Chomistek

(b. 1926)

Living on a farm near Scandia, Alberta, Chomistek does his rock carving with a power grinder, a tool he can handle comfortably from a sitting position. This is important to him, as he was diagnosed with multiple sclerosis in 1971 and is now in a wheelchair.

It was on a visit to Vienna, Austria, in 1973 that he admired the beautiful sculpture in the city and decided to see what he could do in the art field.

"In Edmonton, the Department of Culture suggested I should go to Europe to study," he recalls, "but when I found they still use a hammer and chisel there, I changed my mind. I use a dry grinder and find it much easier and faster."

He prefers to work on calamatic limestone and uses acrylic paint, which he says will penetrate the stone to a depth of 6 millimetres on a warm day. "It's there for a long time," he comments about the durability of the finish on his massive stone carvings.

In addition to his Calgary pieces, his works in Alberta include a large carving of the Eastern Irrigation District (EID) that has been installed at the Bassano Dam, a collection of twenty-six rocks in the EID Historical Park in Scandia, and a carving at St. Joseph's Church in Vauxhall.

Judi Christensen

(See Anubhava Loving Peace)

John Crate and Robert Spaetgens

When they produced the winning design in a students' art competition at the University of Calgary, both men were fourth-year fine arts students. Although Crate was born in the United States and Spaetgens in Saskatchewan, both were raised in Calgary and they had been close friends since earliest school days.

Spaetgens received a Masters of Architecture degree at the University of Manitoba in 1981 and now works in Calgary. Crate graduated in Environmental Design and is thought to be in Ontario.

Stephen Cruise

(b. 1949)

Cruise was born in Montreal, Quebec, and studied at the Ontario College of Art. He went on to co-found and direct A Space Gallery from 1970-74.

In the early 70s, he concentrated on producing film and video pieces, and also began noting occasional dream images in a journal. In Korea and Japan, where he lived from 1976-80, he was able to "achieve total dream content" and has since used these drawings as guides in the production of his surrealistic sculptures.

Robert Davidson

(b. 1946)

A renowned carver, printmaker and jeweller, Haida artist Robert Charles Davidson was born in Hydaburg, Alaska, but grew up in the village of Massett on Haida Gwaii (Queen Charlotte Islands), British Columbia. His father and grandfather, both skilled artists, encouraged him to begin carving in argillite when he was thirteen. By the time he moved to Vancouver to complete his high school, he had become familiar with the medium.

The following year, he began an apprenticeship with master artist Bill Reid, studying Haida engraving and design forms. He enrolled at the Vancouver School of Art.

He is now a successful international artist who combines sensitive innovation with a faithful interpretation of the Haida culture. Although he lives near Vancouver with his wife and family, he pays frequent visits to Haida Gwaii to refresh his spirit.

His carvings, prints and paintings are found in collections around the world, and his unique totem poles are located in Japan, Ireland, Germany, New York, and throughout Canada. Davidson's life and art have been explored in a number of films and publications.

Enzo DiPalma

(b. 1947)

Although Enzo DiPalma was born in Italy, years of residence in Canada influence the themes of his sculptural pieces found in Confederation and Prince's Island park.

Ed Drahanchuk

(b. 1938)

Born in Calgary, Drahanchuk studied at the Alberta College of Art from 1959 to 1963, and was the recipient of nine scholarships and awards during that time.

Following graduation, he began a highly successful career as a ceramist, becoming one of Canada's foremost potters, with work in major collections in Canada and abroad. In 1983 he returned to his first love, painting, and since that time his focus has been on images drawn solely from nature. He now lives on Quadra Island, British Columbia.

He said of his works at the University of Calgary, "A person does not have to see something visual in a mural. He can feel it — the mountains, the openness of the prairies, the gentleness of the wind in the trees."

Walter Drohan

(b. 1932)

Walt Drohan was born in Calgary. He studied at the Alberta College of Art (ACA) and did post-graduate work in ceramics and sculpture at the Cranbrook Academy of Art, Michigan. An instructor at the ACA for many years, he retired as academic dean in 1988.

He has exhibited widely both in Canada and internationally, and his paintings have been shown recently in Toronto, Calgary and Edmonton.

He has acted as juror for both the Canada Council and Alberta Culture, and in 1968 was awarded a senior Canada Council Grant for a year of research in Germany. He was elevated to the Royal Canadian Academy of Arts in 1976.

The sand-cast concrete mural on the exterior of Central Memorial High School in Calgary is another of his works.

Kosso Eloul

(b. 1920)

Born in Russia and raised in Israel, Eloul began his art studies in Tel Aviv in 1938. A year later, he moved to the United States where he studied at the Chicago Art Institute with the innovative architect Frank Lloyd Wright.

His work is architectural in design and he has worked extensively with huge blocks, often in gravity-defying configurations. Variations on the steel block theme in both massive and tabletop size have established his reputation as a minimalist artist.

He has had a longtime involvement with the International Sculpture Conference, and was instrumental in bringing the tenth annual conference to Toronto in 1978.

Eloul's public pieces are installed in many Canadian cities as well as in the United States, Europe, Israel, Japan, China and Mexico. Smaller and maquette-size works are in museums throughout the world.

He is a member of the Royal Academy (1974); Honorary Fellow, Royal Academy of Fine Art, the Hague (1978); and Honorary Member Academia Tiberina, Rome (1962). He lives in Toronto, Ontario.

Edvard Eriksen

(b.1876)

The creator of the *Little Mermaid* was a noted Danish sculptor born in Copenhagen. He studied at the School of Fine Arts in Copenhagen and received a gold medal for his sculpture, *Meditation*. Eriksen also studied with famous artists in Italy.

Many of his fine works may be seen in the Royal Museum in Copenhagen.

Annemarie Schmid Esler

(b. 1937)

This artist's work frequently contains surrealistic elements as well as mundane subjects such as the plates in her *Plate Wall*.

Her early work had a fairy-tale aspect, as she created miniature ceramic beds in ornately decorated porcelain. She has moved from this to a wide variety of expressions of her talent, ranging from an intriguing series containing a cast crow in strange surroundings, to geometric forms combined with steel shelving. She is also an accomplished painter.

Born and educated in Winnipeg (BA) with post graduate work in Munich, Germany, she also attended the Alberta College of Art for four years. She presently resides near Calgary where she is a self-employed artist and part-time lecturer and teacher.

The recipient of several provincial and national awards, Schmid Esler has exhibited in over thirty solo and group exhibitions in Canada, Europe and Japan. Her work can be found in private and corporate collections and in the Glenbow Museum, the Canada Council Art Bank and the Alberta Art Foundation collection.

Sorel Etrog

(b. 1933)

A sculptor, writer, and illustrator, Etrog was born in Jassy, Romania. He remained in Europe during World War II, then studied at the Institute of Painting and Sculpture in Tel Aviv. In 1958 he was awarded a scholarship for study at the Brooklyn Museum Art Institute and, while there, met the late Canadian collector Samuel J. Zacks. The following year, Etrog came to Canada at Zack's invitation and settled in Toronto.

In a preface for an exhibition's catalogue, Marshall McLuhan once said of the artist's abstracts, "Etrog reveals how the contemporary world undergoes a transformation of the old machine and its consumer products into new vital images of primal art and perception."

Among the many public collections which include his sculptures are the Guggenheim Museum in New York, the Tate Gallery in London, the Museum of Tel Aviv, the University of Toronto, and the Hirshhorn in Washington, D.C. He has had dozens of one-artist shows and his pieces have appeared in group shows in the major capitals of the world.

The five large-scale sculptures in Bow Valley Square represent the largest single collection of works by this artist.

In 1988 he represented Canada at the International Sculpture Symposium for the Seoul Summer Olympics and his *Powersoul* now stands in the Olympic Park in Seoul.

Etrog divides his time between Toronto and Florence, Italy, where his sculptures are cast.

In addition to sculpting, he has had success in the fields of designing and illustrating books, in set and costume design, and in film direction and writing. He has also illustrated, choreographed and composed music for a tribute to Samuel Beckett.

Abraham Etungat

(b. 1911)

Etungat was born in Amadjuak, "about a day away from Cape Dorset in a fast boat." In the early days, he lived in an igloo, hunting with kayak and harpoon for seal and walrus, or using dogs, and sleds that he had made himself. He now lives in a comfortable home in Cape Dorset, with his children and grandchildren nearby.

A renowned Inuit artist, he was elected a member of the Royal Canadian Academy of Arts in 1978. His works have been a part of dozens of Inuit art exhibitions and are in galleries across Canada. They are also found in many private collections, including that of the Prince of Wales.

Kathryn Fodchuk

(b. 1960)

Now living in Vancouver, this Ottawa-born artist was educated in Calgary. She studied from 1979 to 1983 at the Alberta College of Art and at the University of Calgary in 1984.

During her second year in art school, she was employed at the Calgary Zoo constructing the Prehistoric Park. The rock work, constructed from steel and concrete, inspired her to change her major from painting to sculpture.

On acquiring the craft of welding, she knew that steel was to be her principal medium. "I find an inner affinity with the material I use. At times the nature of the material implies the next move."

She says of her work, "Through the study of the *I Ching*, primitive art and nature, I have provided myself with a cauldron of information and inspiration . . . above all, I wish my sculpture to speak of the spirit it contains."

Since the completion of Calgary's Prehistoric Park, she has created rock work from Milk River, Alberta, to Vancouver's Aquarium in Stanley Park. At present, she is busy building sets for Vancouver's movie industry and constructing artificial rock for a small company.

David Gilhooly

(b. 1943)

Although born and educated in California, this artist became a Canadian citizen after living in Canada for several years. He taught at both the University of Saskatchewan and York University between 1969 and 1976, and lived in Calgary from 1977 to 1979.

Much of his artwork revolves around a mythical world he has created and named *frogs world*. It depicts frogs in a wide variety of human experiences, and there is even a frog Madonna and Child. These works are in clay, which is sometimes referred to as frog mud.

He has had over thirty solo exhibitions throughout the United States and Canada and has participated in numerous group exhibitions.

In the past few years, Gilhooly has worked mostly in plastic and some bronze, and has also begun printmaking. He says, "I got tired of the snow and now live on a farm in Oregon where I grow fruit and nut trees."

Michael Hayden

(b. 1943)

Born in Vancouver and educated in Toronto, Hayden attended the Ontario College of Art. He is known as a "sculptor in light" and his works usually integrate technology and architecture to create unusual visual effects.

Among his major works are *Arc-in-ciel* (Rainbow) in the Toronto subway, *Trikha (Three)* at the Hyatt Regency Hotel in Buffalo, New York and *Sky's the Limit* in Chicago's O'Hare International Airport. The world's largest permanent light sculpture, the 243-metre long, walk-through *Sky's the Limit* was constructed from approximately 2 kilometres of neon. At least 15 million people a year pass through this unique artwork, which incorporates music composed especially to enhance the experience.

Hayden, who presently resides in Santa Rosa, California, has had over thirty solo exhibitions in Canada, the United States and Europe.

Louis Phillippe Hebert

(1850 - 1917)

Phillippe Hebert was born in St. Sophie d'Halifax, Quebec. In 1869, as a way to get to Rome to study the artworks of Italy, he joined a detachment of Papal Zouaves which was to be stationed in the Holy City. While there he managed to visit a variety of monuments and treasures of ancient and renaissance times.

Returning to Canada in 1871, he studied in Montreal under the great artist Napoleon Bourassa. In recognition of his efforts to make the Canadian past come alive, he was awarded the Confederation Medal in 1894. He was also recognized by the Pope, who honored him with the title of Knight of the Order of Saint Gregory the Great. In 1903 King Edward VII created him Companion of St. Michael and St. George.

Some of his most famous sculptures are those of Lord Elgin and Frontenac in Quebec City and Sir John A. MacDonald, Alexander Mackenzie and Queen Victoria, all in Ottawa.

Hebert is buried in Notre Dame de Neiges Cemetery in Montreal.

Steven Heimbecker

(b. 1959)

Heimbecker was raised on a farm near Biggar, Saskatchewan. From 1977 to 1980, he studied painting and sculpture at the Alberta College of Art, and now works in many media such as electronic time base, sculpture, sound and performance art. Since 1978, he has exhibited in several regional and private group shows in Alberta and Saskatchewan.

He presently lives in Calgary where he is the metal sculpture technician in the art department at the University of Calgary.

Charles Hilton

(b. 1937)

Born in Melville, Saskatchewan, Hilton studied sculpture and ceramics at the University of Manitoba, Winnipeg, where he obtained a Diploma in Fine Art.

In 1967 he moved to Alberta and worked on the railroads for three years. He then moved to Edmonton to establish a ceramic studio, and became one of the city's foremost sculptors.

His sculptures and ceramics have appeared in a number of solo and group shows, and his work is represented in corporate and private collections in Canada and abroad.

At present, he is travelling in Australia, working with the aboriginal artists whose work he admired at the Commonwealth Games sculpture symposium held in Edmonton in 1978.

Malvina Hoffman

(1885-1966)

Malvina Hoffman was deeply influenced by her father Richard Hoffman, a concert pianist. From him, she learned a lifelong appreciation of music but soon realized she wasn't talented enough to be a great musician. Instead, she turned to drawing as an outlet for her creativity.

The American-born artist began with watercolors, then studied oil painting and later experimented with sculpture. She was accepted as a student by Rodin from 1911-14.

The first artist to capture the grace and energy of contemporary dancers in sculpture, she created "La Gavotte" and a twenty-six-panel frieze in honor of Pavlova.

Her greatest accomplishment, commissioned by the Chicago Field Museum, was a series of 101 bronze and 3 marble sculptures begun in 1929 and known as the "Hall of Man" collection. To complete the assignment, she travelled throughout the world creating faces of all cultures and nationalities. She did some of the sculptures in Paris, but the bulk of the work was done on location, with the completed works shipped back to France.

Throughout her life she continued to create masterpieces and, as well, completed three definitive books on sculpture. She died in Manhattan of a heart attack.

James Houston

(b. 1921)

Born in Toronto, Houston studied art at the Toronto Art Gallery and the Ontario College of Art.

It is not surprising that he chose the Aurora Borealis as the theme for his sculpture in the Glenbow Museum, for he is, in effect, an adopted child of the North.

On his first visit to the Arctic, in 1948, he discovered the magnificent Inuit carvings and began his efforts to bring them to the outside world. A versatile artist himself, he learned the art of printmaking in Japan, then taught it to the Inuit. As a result of his work with the northern aboriginal artists, their skills are now recognized throughout the world.

Speaking the Eskimo language fluently, he was the first civil administrator of Baffin Island, a post he held for nine years.

He is also successful in the field of children's literature and is the author of several award-winning books.

Charles D'Orville Pilkington Jackson

(1887 - 1973)

A sculptor in stone, metal, plaster and wood, Charles Jackson was born in Cornwall, England. He was educated at Loretto School (one of his most famous works, *Loretto Boy*, depicts a typical British schoolboy) and later studied at Edinburgh College of Art and in Rome, where he spent a year at the British School on a scholarship award.

His principal works in Great Britain are found on the Scottish National War Memorial, in the Scottish United Services Museum, in the Imperial War Museum, at Bannockburn, and in several major churches. Other statues are found in Hong Kong, Singapore, New York and South Africa.

A collection of Scottish military statuettes is displayed in the Naval and British Museum at Edinburgh Castle. These wooden pieces were designed by Jackson and executed by a team of skilled carvers, of which he was the chief artist.

The Calgary Highlanders were the recipients of unusual silver statuettes created by Jackson. They were presented to the Officers' Mess by Eric Harvie when he was honorary colonel of the regiment.

Robert Jekyll

(b. 1933)

Born in Montreal and trained as a naval officer and aeronautical engineer, Jekyll has a degree in economics from York University. After twenty years in the navy, he decided to turn his hand to something very different. Although he was qualified to find employment in the aerospace industry, he was more attracted to a career in the arts and it was as a serious amateur artist that he travelled in Europe in 1972. In England he met and later studied with Patrick Reyntiens, a leading stained glass artist in that country. This led to work on major commissions with Reyntiens and during this period he studied first-hand the stained glass work of major European artists.

Returning to Canada, now a full-time artist, he set up his Toronto studio in 1974. Over the years he has produced many unique residential, commercial and municipal windows, as well as teaching his craft through Sheridan College's School of Craft and Design. He has also served as president of the Artists in Stained Glass Association and edited its magazine, *The Leadline.*

He recognizes the architectural aspect of his work. "Architectural art is complicated from the standpoint of displaying in galleries. But I question whether the independent (glass) panel, as an art form of its own, works. Is it a sculpture, a painting, or what is it? It is a hybrid at best."

He continues to work in Toronto, where he is presently with the Ontario Crafts Council. He is responsible for all craft programs and for developing new programs for ten design disciplines ". . . all the way from architecture to fashion."

J. Seward Johnson, Jr.

(b. 1930)

Seward Johnson is a man who works for the joy of it. As an heir to the Johnson and Johnson pharmaceutical empire, he is a multimillionaire and has no financial need to succeed in his artistic endeavors.

Born in New York, he attended the University of Maine and Harvard University, and was a dedicated and prolific painter before turning to sculpture in 1968.

He founded the Johnson Atelier, a professional foundry for artists, in 1975 and most of his works are cast there by the lost wax method. He begins with an 46-centimetre model which is enlarged to full size. The painstaking casting process that produces the exact detail of Johnson's work can take up to two years for a single figure.

He has created over 100 life-size sculptures, often depicting two or more figures in a familiar situation. His most dramatic work, a 21-metre-tall giant titled *The Awakening*, was selected for the 1980 International Sculpture Exhibition and is now in Washington, D.C.

His work is recognized worldwide and his statues are found in collections in the United States, western Europe, Australia, Japan and Hong Kong. As well as the three narrative sculptures in Calgary, his works in Canada are found in Edmonton, Vancouver, Toronto and Montreal.

When you visit the Calgary Zoo, look for his amusing bronze of two girls sharing an ice cream cone. *Just a Taste* is found at the entrance to the Children's Zoo.

Garry Jones

(b. 1949)

Born in Edmonton, Garry Jones received an honors degree in fine art from the University of Alberta in 1972. He resides in Edmonton where he works with a wide variety of materials such as bronze, fiberglass, stainless steel and plastic. He is also an accomplished painter and photographer.

Specializing in large-scale suspended sculpture, the artist says, "I see technology as the principal expression of a culture. It must therefore be integrated into an art form that is a true expression of that culture."

Works by Jones are in collections in the Bank of Montreal, Toronto; Alberta Art Foundation, Government House, Edmonton; Alberta House, London, England, and in many private collections. Commissioned installations are in Edmonton, Calgary and Athabasca University.

John Kanerva

(1883-1974)

"I don't carve the figures, I only take away from the wood the material that doesn't belong," said the man who was primarily a wood carver but gained his greatest fame from working in concrete.

Hundreds of his delicately carved wooden animals, both prehistoric and present-day, are scattered around the world. A few still remain in the possession of his son, Jack Kanerva, who lives in Calgary. He explains that his father got his inspiration for the creation of prehistoric figures when he saw the film *The Lost World* in 1930 and was captivated by the unusual creatures.

Born in Finland, where his father was an artist, Kanerva learned to paint theatre backdrops in the United States before emigrating to Canada. In his early years in Alberta, he hand painted automobiles and was later employed as a painter at the Calgary Zoo, where he created several murals. But, regardless of his employment, in his spare time he carved figures with an ordinary pocket knife.

A modest man who received very little monetary reward for his work, he is remembered by Calgarians as "The Father of Dinosaur Park."

Pierre Karlik

(b. 1931)

A well-known Inuit sculptor, Karlik has several works in the Museum of Man in Ottawa and in the Twomey collection, one of the world's largest private collections of Eskimo art. He also created the largest soapstone carving ever made by an Inuit artist in the north — a monumental walrus located in the municipal building of Etobicoke, Ontario.

During his late teens and early twenties, he spent several years in hospital for treatment of polio and tuberculosis. During this time, he learned to speak English and to carve. He returned to the Arctic, moving to Rankin Inlet in order to sell his carvings to men working in the local mine.

Quiet and thoughtful, Karlik loves solitude but has always been active in the community — a member of the hamlet council, the Roman Catholic church and the art co-op.

As a younger man he was a caribou hunter and fur trapper, and fished commercially for arctic char. His familiarity with the wildlife of the north is evident in his sensitive sculptures.

Karlik lives in Rankin Inlet, and his work continues to be a part of major exhibitions of Inuit art throughout Canada.

Gernot Kiefer

(b. 1942)

In 1972 this native of West Germany decided to emigrate to Canada. He was born in Loerrach, near both the Swiss and French borders, an area rich in ancient artifacts. His education included three years of apprenticeship in stone sculpting and a masters degree in fine arts from the University of Freiburg in Breisgau.

After arriving in Canada, he was employed as a carpenter while he adjusted to the new culture and new country. In 1978 he enrolled in the Alberta College of Art and resumed his art career.

Although his specialty is abstract stone sculpture, he also has done extensive work in wood sculpting. His first choice of material for stonework is Rocky Mountain limestone because of its cutting quality and relative availability, but he also works in marble, sandstone and a wide variety of woods.

Samples of Kiefer's work may be found in private or business locations in Calgary, Edmonton and Kelowna, British Columbia.

He lives and has his studio in northeast Calgary.

Paul Kipps

Kipps, a graduate of the University of Western Ontario (1972), is both a practising artist and a teacher of art and art history at the University of Toronto. As well, he instructs in craft and design at Sheridan College in Oakville, Ontario.

He has exhibited at several Toronto galleries and is the recipient of two Canada Council awards.

For more than ten years, he has collaborated with Colette Whiten to create public sculptures.

Ron Kostyniuk

(b. 1941)

Born in Wakaw, Saskatchewan, Kostyniuk was educated at the University of Saskatchewan, graduating with a BA and BEd in biology. He also holds a fine arts degree from the University of Alberta and masters degrees in both science and fine arts from the University of Wisconsin.

Kostyniuk's work reflects the variations in nature's inherent order. He is recognized as one of the foremost North American exponents of the "Structurist" movement, and his interest in biology brings an unusual dimension to the architectural lines in his work.

His work may be found in collections of the Kresge Foundation, Detroit, Michigan; Canada Council Art Bank, Ottawa; Alberta Energy, Edmonton, and in many Canadian universities.

He is presently a professor of fine art at the University of Calgary.

Sir Edwin Landseer
(1802 - 1873)

Born in London, England, the son of the famous engraver John Landseer, Sir Edwin first studied art under his father, then became a student of the Royal Academy Schools at fourteen.

He was made an Artist of the Royal Academy in 1826 and was elected its president in 1865, but declined the honor because of precarious health. He was knighted by Queen Victoria in 1850.

Although best known as an outstanding painter of animals and other wildlife, Landseer was equally successful as a sculptor.

He was a personal friend of the British royal family and was at home in the highest levels of London society. In spite of a rigorous social life, he was a prolific artist. Today his work can be found in such places as the Royal Academy of Arts, University of London, Tate Gallery and Victoria and Albert Museum.

Roy Leadbeater
(b. 1928)

Leadbeater comes from an artistic family; his father was a painter and his grandmother was one of the Wedgwood family. He was born in Derbyshire, England, but raised in a Staffordshire orphanage after he was orphaned at age eight.

By fourteen he was an apprentice electrician and later, while serving in the merchant marine, became a marine engineer. He served with the Palestine Police Force from 1946 to 1948, then returned to sea until coming to Canada in 1953. He lived in Calgary before moving to Edmonton, where he is a power engineer with Alberta Government Services. He became a Canadian citizen in 1975.

Leadbeater sculptures have appeared in many group and one-man shows. In 1978 he gave his first one-artist show in Britain at the Alwin Gallery, London. Four films have been made of his work, including BBC-TV's *Roy Leadbeater's Space Figures.*

Although he attended night classes in drawing at the Birmingham School of Art and also studied drawing as a part-time student at the University of Alberta, he is largely a self-taught artist and has had no formal training in sculpture.

He says of his work, "Art is a way of communicating. Sculpture, for me, is like a language I am learning . . . to express my thoughts and vision. The sculpture provides no answers. It simply asks the question."

Kevan Leycraft
(b. 1955)

Leycraft, born in Fairview, Alberta, has had a lifelong interest in art and design. Even as a preschooler, he enjoyed playing with toys he had invented.

He studied graphics and technology at Southern Alberta Institute of Technology, 1974-75, and business arts at Mount Royal College, 1976-77. In the midst of engineering studies, he designed and received patents on a revolutionary skibob frame, and marketed the skibobs along with a speed-skiing helmet he had designed. Leycraft is an expert skibobber himself, and was declared North American Skibob Champion at a West German competition in 1989.

Because his business is seasonal, he is able to devote a long off-season to his art, which includes everything from massive metal sculptures to fine jewellery.

His works are found in many private and corporate collections.

Anubhava Loving Peace (formerly Judi Christensen)

(b. 1940)

Born in Calgary, Loving Peace studied with Katie Ohe, then obtained a BA in English from the University of Calgary.

Postgraduate work in fine arts followed as she attended the Banff School of Fine Arts and studied with S.W. Hayter at his *Atelier Dix-Sept* in Paris.

Later she lived for twelve years in Barbados where she continued to sculpt, concentrating on large indigenous mahogany works. One of her sculptures completed during this time may be seen in the Barbados airport.

At present, she is located in Louisville, Kentucky, where, she explains, "deep exploration for the spiritual in art has led me toward the path of enlightenment and purification of ego so I may serve art in many forms."

William Mac

(see William McElcheran)

Couer-De-Leon MacCarthy

(d. 1979)

This noted Canadian sculptor was born in England, the son of a British sculptor, Hamilton Plantagenet MacCarthy. The family emigrated to Canada about 1885 and settled first in Toronto, then Ottawa.

MacCarthy studied under his father until 1918, when he established his own studio in Montreal. He received commissions for a number of war memorials, including those in Windsor Station, Montreal, Verdun, Three Rivers and Knowlton, Quebec.

He is also responsible for many of the stone designs on the Parliament Buildings and Peace Tower in Ottawa, and the bust of Queen Victoria above the Speaker's chair in the Senate Chamber.

Shamas Malik

(b. 1965)

Malik was born in Multan, Pakistan, and emigrated to Canada in 1970. He enrolled in the University of Calgary intending to study mechanical engineering. However, after two years he realized there was limited opportunity for creativity in this pursuit and switched to art, with a particular interest in welded steel sculpture. He also studied at the Alberta College of Art, where he completed first-year glassblowing.

He says of his art studies, "It wasn't until I was introduced to sculpture that I understood what people meant by 'going and finding one's self.' Nothing I have ever done in my life, thus far, has obsessed or satisfied me as much as being a sculptor."

In his art he explores how individuals interact with one another and how they interact with the environment. He is also interested in "how we deal with day-to-day urban life in the twentieth century, and how this is similar to or different from the past."

Mark V. Marshall

(1879 - 1912)

Little is known of the personal history of Mark Marshall, but his professional accomplishments are many. He joined the renowned British Royal Doulton Group as an artist-designer in their Lambeth pottery and china studio around 1880. Previously he had worked as a stone carver on Gothic Revival churches, which may explain his taste for impish and grotesque stone carvings. This influence also carried over into many of his smaller works such as paper weights and figurines.

A fellow artist once said of him, "He had the most extra-ordinary ability in carving the wet clay — great architectural details such as grotesque eagles supporting shields; tall vases, some four feet high, with a marvelous wealth of finely designed ornament; jugs with decoration equally ornate in high relief and open work. . . ."

Most of his creations are in the hands of private collectors, but examples can be found in the Royal Doulton Museum in Stoke-on-Trent and in the Victoria and Albert Museum in London.

The Calgary gargoyles, created for the Southam family, were his last commission and were installed shortly after his death.

William McElcheran (also known as William Mac)

(b. 1927)

William Hadd McElcheran was born in Hamilton, Ontario. He studied sculpture, drawing and painting at the Ontario College of Art, and was the recipient of the Lieutenant-Governor's Medal for outstanding achievement.

Following graduation in 1947, he concentrated on designing churches and church furniture for twenty years. During this time, he planned and designed twenty-three churches and university buildings. From 1960-1966 he taught at the Ontario College of Art in Toronto and from 1970-1974 was artist-in-residence at the University of Toronto School of Architecture. He has since become an independent artist, creating secular sculptures in wood, bronze, polyester resin and stone.

He is a member of the Royal Canadian Academy of Arts and his works are found in major private and corporate art collections and in museums and public spaces in Canada, the United States, Italy, Germany and Japan. In 1991 he had his first exhibition in Germany.

Robert Tait McKenzie

(1867-1938)

McKenzie was born in Almonte, Ontario, and entered McGill University in 1885, graduating from medical school. In 1904 he accepted an appointment to head the new physical education department at the University of Pennsylvania. During World War I, he went to England where he served in the Royal Medical Corps and, following the war, initiated programs to rehabilitate disabled veterans.

He was an outstanding athlete in his school years, and his great interest during his medical career was physical fitness and training. Later he became intrigued with sculpture, and used this medium to demonstrate points he made in his anatomy lectures.

He continued to produce fine sculptures throughout his lifetime and was, perhaps, as famous for his art as his medical contributions. He was devoted to the Olympic

Games and attended every one from 1904 until his death in Philadelphia at the age of seventy.

Ben McLeod

(b. 1948)

Born in Aberdeen, Scotland, McLeod is now a resident of Cochrane, Alberta. He studied at the Alberta College of Art in Calgary.

He says of his art, "My work grows through feelings and emotions and becomes a presence in the material world when the energy and magic of a work takes on a life of its own. This happens when a work becomes a whole, not just a conglomeration of this and that. . . . When it's right, it feels right; when it's finished, I know."

Doug Moen

(b. 1945)

Moen was born in Rosetown, Saskatchewan, and attended school in Zealandia and Rosetown. He graduated with an honors degree in fine arts from the University of Saskatchewan, Saskatoon.

At present he lives in Toronto.

Leo Mol

(b. 1915)

The artist who created the bust of Koshetz in the Jubilee Auditorium and the wrestling bear cubs in Century Gardens, was born in the Ukraine and emigrated to Canada in 1948. He has been a prolific and successful sculptor for many years, and is world renowned for his work in portrait sculpture. He has completed commissioned works in Italy, Germany, Holland, the United States, Brazil and many other countries.

Some of his portrait busts are of John Diefenbaker, Dwight Eisenhower, Winston Churchill, and Popes Paul VI, John XXIII and John Paul II. He has also produced many life-size sculptures of other noted personages, and these are in various international locations. In addition he has created over eighty stained glass works.

A resident of Winnipeg, he is past president of the Manitoba Society of Artists, and a member of other art associations. He has received honorary degrees from the University of Winnipeg, the University of Alberta and the University of Manitoba, and was honored with a Centennial Medal in 1967. In 1989 he was made an Officer of the Order of Canada in recognition of his contributions.

Over 100 of his bronze sculptures are on display in the Leo Mol Sculpture Garden in Winnipeg's Assiniboine Park.

George Norris

(b. 1928)

Norris was born in Victoria, British Columbia. When he was six, his family moved to Vancouver where he attended children's art classes. As a teenager he studied painting and drawing in evening classes at the Vancouver School of Art and, after high school, graduated from the Vancouver School of Art, where he was the only full-time sculpture student.

In order to finance postgraduate studies, and then to enable him to continue sculpting, he worked at a variety of laboring jobs — carpenter's helper, mill worker, logger, miner — all of which he considers to be part of his artistic training.

He studied for two years with the renowned sculptor, Ivan Mestrovic, in Syracuse, New York, and still employs the design process learned there.

In 1974 he was elected to the Royal Canadian Academy of Arts (RCA) but says, "I feel my membership in the Sheet Metal Worker's Union was of more significance," and has since resigned from the RCA.

Many Norris works are found in the public art of British Columbia, the most visible and famous being *The Crab*, a stainless steel fountain sculpture in the reflecting pool in front of the Museum/Planetarium in Vancouver.

Prince Monyo Mihailescu Nastural

No information is available for this artist.

Hazel O'Brien

(b. 1927)

"There are so many things I want to do, and I like to do them all at once," says Hazel O'Brien.

Her basement studio in her Calgary home proves this is true. Partly finished sculptures, an easel, sketches, paintings in various stages of completion and bits and pieces of art material all clamor for her attention. Compulsively creative, O'Brien produces a wide variety of artwork.

Born and raised in southern Alberta, she grew up loving the outdoors, and much of her work reflects this affection.

She has studied at the Banff School of Fine Arts, the Chouinard Art Institute in Los Angeles, and the American Academy of Art in Chicago.

Her work for the Calgary Horseman's Hall of Fame, now dismantled and in storage, brought her talent to the attention of the public in 1973. She has since created a number of trophies for Calgary Exhibition and Stampede rodeo events, and completed commissions for many private collectors.

Harry O'Hanlon

(b. 1916)

Born in Edmonton, this artist has had a varied and exciting career. Educated mainly in American boarding schools, he has been a soldier, adventurer, oilman and rancher. Before and after World War II, he travelled extensively, sailing, hiking and treasure hunting along the way.

Returning to Canada in 1949, he began to pursue painting as a hobby, but soon turned to sculpture as a more satisfying medium. He is a self-taught Western artist and has studied Indian life and culture extensively. His work depicts a variety of aspects of their everyday life.

His bronzes are found in collections of Her Majesty Queen Elizabeth II, the Nickle Family Foundation, Alberta Government Museum, Home Oil Company, Glenbow Foundation and many private collectors.

At the 1977 commemoration of the historic signing of Treaty Number Seven, HRH Prince Charles was presented with the O'Hanlon sculpture *Trailing the Buffalo Hunters.* "This isn't going to any museum, it's going to Buckingham Palace," the Prince said when accepting the gift.

O'Hanlon resides on his ranch near Calgary where he continues with his work.

Katie Ohe

(b. 1937)

Many Ohe sculptures are semi-kinetic and her pieces move because, as she says, "The forms are of a shape to provoke touch, and touch induces motion." Her hope is that viewers will touch her work intuitively.

Born Katherine Minna von der Ohe near Peers, Alberta, she is a graduate of the Alberta College of Art's four-year program. In addition she studied for a year with Arthur Lismer, one of the Group of Seven, and for two years at the Sculpture Centre in New York. An informal year of study was spent in London, England, with the aid of a Canada Council grant, and she has spent several summers in Verona, Italy, learning the technique of casting in bronze.

Ohe's works have appeared in numerous solo and group exhibitions and in private and corporate collections.

She teaches at the Alberta College of Art and lives west of Calgary with her husband, Harry Kiyooka, a noted painter and professor of art at the University of Calgary. In 1989 she was presented with the Calgary YWCA's Women of Distinction Award in the arts and culture category. In 1991 she was honored with a twenty-year retrospective show of her works at the Alberta College of Art gallery. "Sculpture is my life . . . my first language" the dedicated teacher and artist said during a lecture to a group of students at this show.

Other Ohe works in Calgary include a cast stone mural on the exterior of St. Michael the Archangel Catholic Church; the carved oak baptismal font, communion table and pulpit in Grace Presbyterian Church; *Child Bearers* at the Calgary Board of Education; and *Earthprobe* in the Esso Resources building at 3535 Research Road Northwest.

Bob Oldrich

(1920 - 1983)

Unlike many Alberta artists, Oldrich learned his craft by apprenticeship rather than formal schooling. He was a native of Czechoslovakia, where he worked in industry.

"I would still honestly consider myself a craftsman, not a sculptor. But the separations between art and craft are irrelevant anyway . . . either you're good or you're lousy," the shaggy-headed, greying artist said in 1977.

As a young rebel, he fled his homeland during the 1951 upheaval. He recalled of this experience, "I crawled for it. The whole dramatic bit. Through mine fields and barbed wire, the lights that move and the dog patrols."

After an initial stint with pick and shovel in Canada, he was soon busy with his artworks, and moved to Calgary in 1958 and taught at the Alberta College of Art for four years.

Concrete and steel were his favorite media, and he was a prolific artist with sculptures and murals in dozens of offices and private homes, as well as in many Calgary schools and churches. He refused to title any of his work. "If you label it, people take it literally," he explained.

Oldrich died in Hawaii as a result of injuries sustained from a fall while hiking.

David Panneok

(b. 1948)

An Inuit carver, Panneok was born in a tent at Lake Harbour, Northwest Territories. He says of his earliest days, "There was no doctor in Lake Harbour at the time — and still no doctor in the settlement. Not long after I was born, the high tide went up to the tent." He grew up in an outpost camp 100 kilometres from Lake Harbour and moved to Iqaluit (Frobisher Bay) in 1957.

In the fall of 1979 and spring of 1980, he studied at the Nova Scotia College of Art and Design, taking fine art courses in silversmithing and sculpture. He picked up thirty credits in two terms at the college and then continued to study in Iqaluit. His courses included "jewellery work, taking fine arts like silversmith with ivory." He still works with soapstone and ivory, silver and gold, and assures his many customers, "I'll not give up that kind of art work. I love it."

Nikolas Pavropoulos

(b. 1909)

Known professionally simply as Nikolas, he is a contemporary Athens artist noted for his heroic sculptures.

George Pratt

(b. 1939)

George Forbes Pratt was born in Minden, Ontario. He spent two years studying the tundra life near Fort Churchill, Manitoba, then worked with Metalsmiths of Toronto, a firm owned by architect Court Noxon, who is a designer of contemporary business furniture.

Although in the 1970s he worked for a time with E.B. Cox, a professional sculptor, he is largely a self-taught artist. Pratt recalls that the first time he saw Cox's work, he knew intuitively he, too, could carve stone.

He now has his own gallery in Vancouver, and recently worked with Canadian aboriginal craftsmen to complete a major commission in Toronto.

Richard Prince

(b. 1949)

This British Columbia artist is a graduate of the University of British Columbia. He has done postgraduate work in fine arts at UBC, and attended the Emma Lake Workshop of the University of Saskatchewan

He is a prolific and versatile artist with a wide range of artistic interests. In general his works are classified as *urban interpretations*. He has produced many "things" with doors that open, parts that move and a purpose that requires imagination. Prince is noted for his urban landscapes, which usually contain an element of unexpected detail luring the viewer to examine them more closely.

He also has shown an interest in the human figure with work in body casting, and has produced a wide range of variations on this theme, often in a surrealistic mode.

Prince has exhibited in many cities in Canada and his work is on display in public and private art galleries across the country. He is associate professor of fine arts at the University of British Columbia.

Jane Pugh

(see Jane Charlotte)

Donald Proch

(b. 1944)

Don Proch was born in Inglis, Manitoba, and raised in a log cabin on his Ukrainian grandparents' farm at Grandview. He was eight years old when his parents moved to Inglis and became owners of the local hotel.

As a youngster, he loved to bicycle to the deserted village of Asessippi and these trips, and his awareness of the relationship between rural and urban life, are reflected in much of his art.

He attended the University of Manitoba, first in the faculty of engineering, later in the school of art, and now lives and sculpts in Winnipeg.

Alan Reynolds

(b. 1947)

Reynolds was born in Edmonton, but raised on NATO army bases in Europe — a "no frills" upbringing. In high school, he trained to be a legal secretary, but found it didn't appeal as a lifetime occupation. After a series of laboring jobs and a short term as publisher of an underground newspaper, he dropped into an art store in Edmonton and came out with painting supplies and an enthusiasm for a "world he could really identify with."

He attended the University of Alberta as a mature student and was given on-campus studio space, an unusual honor for a first-year student. However he soon left the classes, and it was at a workshop given by U.S. sculptor Michael Steiner that Reynolds became committed to art as a career.

Within two years he became the *wunderkind* of Canadian art when his work was included in "Fourteen Canadians, a Critic's Choice" at the Hirshhorm Museum in Washington, D.C.

His sculptures are widely collected by individuals, corporations and governments and his works have been included in national and international group shows as well as many solo shows in Canada. He has acted as visiting artist to a number of Canadian workshops, colleges and universities.

John Massey Rhinn

(1860-1936)

Born in Scotland, J. Massey Rhinn was the pupil of his artist-father, John Rhinn, RSE. He later studied in Paris, then, in 1889, emigrated to the United States where he spent the major part of his life.

He was a member of many art associations, including the Royal Scottish Academy, Edinburgh, and was honored with a National Scholarship in London, a Gold Medal in 1904 at the St. Louis Exposition and many lesser awards.

He is probably most famous for his four bronze statues flanking the entrance to the Carnegie Institute in Pittsburgh, Pennysylvania. The figures, which have been acclaimed by art critics throughout the world, are of Gallileo, Bach, Shakespeare and Michelangelo.

Also among the artist's major works are the equestrian statue of George Washington in Newark, New Jersey; Stephen Girard in Philadelphia; Peter Stuyvesant in

Jersey City; the McKinley Memorial in Niles, Ohio; and several in the Butler Art Institute in Youngstown, Ohio.

Rhinn died in the United States.

John Robinson

No information is available for this artist.

Rich Roenisch

(b. 1944)

Although born and raised in Calgary, Roenisch spent all his spare time as a youngster either on ranches or engaged in rodeo or polo activities. He has a degree in animal husbandry from Washington State University.

Now a noted Western artist, he devotes his life to painting and sculpting the subjects he knows best — the people and animals of the foothills. Using the lost wax process, he is able to produce much detail in his models. His casting is done in Studio West in Cochrane.

The Devonian Foundation has aquired a collection of his bronze works depicting many aspects of the Old West, and the Calgary Stampede commissioned him to do two bronze sculptures as rodeo trophies. As well as sculpting in bronze, he paints and does commercial illustrations.

Roenisch has exhibited his work at the El Dorado Polo Club, the Calgary Stampede Art Show, the Leighton Centre, and the San Antonio Polo Centre, and has received many commissions for public and private sculptures.

Says the artist, "I sell on my own most of the time. I put on my own exhibitions and don't exhibit in galleries very often. My wife and I raise and train polo ponies and, because we travel a lot with them, it has given me a lot of exposure for my sculptures — especially in the United States. A lot of my work goes by word of mouth."

Roenisch lives and works in the Longview area of southwestern Alberta.

Sabatier Of Paris

Sabatier is a French artist. No further information is available for this artist.

Suzanne Sable

(b. 1926)

This artist was born in Paris, France, where she attended the Ecole Supérieure de Peinture et Sculpture for four years. She later opened a ceramics studio and also did oil portraits. During this period she won prizes for both painting and ceramics.

In 1956 Sable moved to the United States to continue her work. She has exhibited her sculptures in New York City and Rochester, New York, and in Monterey, Seaside and Carmel, California. She resides in Monterey, where she also has her studio and exhibits permanently.

Her work may be seen in galleries and private collections in North America and Europe.

Henry Saxe

(b. 1937)

Although his ambition was to be an architect, he realized in high school that his math grades weren't good enough to enable him to pursue this career. Drawing was a course he was consistently good at, so, as Saxe says, "I decided to become an artist when it became apparent that I really couldn't excel at anything else."

He went on to study at L'Ecole des Beaux Arts, Montreal, and to teach fine art at the University of Quebec, Concordia University, Laval University, the University of Ottawa, Queen's University and Mount Allison.

His choice of an art career seems to have been a wise one, as his rewards and awards have been many. He is an Officer of the Order of Canada, and represented Canada at the *Venice Bienale* in 1978, and the *Bienale of Artists under Thirty-five* in Paris in 1968. His works are in regular exhibitions in Toronto and Montreal commercial galleries, and have also been shown at the National Gallery of Canada and in other prestigious galleries across Canada and in New York and Paris.

In 1972 he moved from Montreal to Tamworth, Ontario, away from the politics of art, which he deplores. In the small community he finds "lots of grass to mow or snow to plow depending on the season."

JoAnne Schachtel
(b. 1960)

A 1986 graduate from the University of Calgary's arts program, Schachtel majored in sculpture, starting her own screen-printing business to finance her beginning art work.

Born and educated in Saskatchewan, she has lived near Cochrane for the past eight years with her husband and fellow artist, Ray Arnatt. They have separate, adjacent studios where they pursue their individual expressions of art.

Schachtel prefers to work with organic materials, outdoors if possible. She sees the disintegration of the work as part of the natural process, wherein the material becomes part of nature and emerges again in another form as part of the world's continuing life cycle.

She has exhibited works in several Edmonton and Calgary locations, including the University of Calgary, Muttart Gallery and The Nickle Arts Museum. In June and July of 1991, she exhibited *Primeval Sleep*, life-size figures in natural materials placed into the environment in four downtown Edmonton locations.

Bob Scriver
(b. 1915)

In 1900 Scriver's parents emigrated from Quebec to the United States, and Robert Macfie Scriver was born in Browning, Montana. He still lives and works in his home town.

It was only after spending more than twenty years studying, performing and teaching music that he discovered his gift for sculpture. He decided he would rather be a taxidermist than a musician, and began his new career in 1951 in an old garage in Browning. Before long he was Montana's best-known taxidermist and built a workshop adjacent to the Museum of the Plains Indian in Browning. There, in addition to his taxidermy, he began casting a collection of miniature animals, his first sculptures.

Today the Scriver Studio houses an impressive collection of wildlife in natural habitat displays, along with his sculpture workshop and his foundry. His Western Indian and rodeo sculptures are found in many major collections, including the

Cowboy Hall of Fame in Oklahoma City; the Whitney Gallery of Western Art in Cody, Wyoming; and the World Board of Trade in Kansas City, Missouri. He has been honored with a doctor of arts degree from Carrol College in Helena, Montana.

His *No More Buffalo* collection, a series of fifty-three pieces ranging from .5 metres to nearly 2 metres in size, was on tour for three years. It is now displayed in the Museum of Wildlife and Hall of Bronze in Browning.

A number of his Western bronzes, on loan from the Glenbow Museum, are on display in the departure lounge of the Calgary International Airport. Now seventy-seven years old, Scriver continues to work seven days a week.

Rick Silas
(b.1951)

Born in Montreal, Quebec, but now residing in Calgary, Silas studied painting at John Abbott College for three years. Later, from 1980 to 1982, he majored in sculpture at the Alberta College of Art.

His favorite medium is wood and, besides the examples represented in this book, he created the very visible dog and *Maytag Man* on 9th Avenue S.E. The man was carved from a single log over 4 metres tall and 1 metre in diameter.

Books are one of his favorite subjects, and he has depicted them in many of his carvings.

Krystana Sadowska-Siwinski
(b. 1912)

Krystyna Sadowska-Siwinski was born in Lublan, Poland, and studied at the Warsaw Academy of Fine Arts; the Central School of Arts and Crafts, London, England; and the Grande Chaumiere, Paris.

In 1937 she accepted an assignment from the Polish government to teach handicrafts to Polish immigrants in Brazil. There she met her first husband, the late ceramist Konrad Sadowska. They returned to Poland just before World War II and escaped to England when their country was invaded. After the war they returned to Brazil, where she held solo exhibitions of her paintings, drawings, tapestries and ceramics. One tapestry, *Dream of Canada*, attracted an invitation from the Nova Scotia Ministry of Trade and Industry for them to move to Canada. They worked and taught in Nova Scotia for several years before moving to Toronto, where she lectured in design at the Ontario College of Art for six years. She is now married to Stefan Siwinski, Toronto-based furniture designer.

Her work has appeared in many major international exhibitions and she has received a number of medals and awards for her tapestries, ceramics and batiks.

Steven Smalley

Born in Leicester, England, Smalley has been a Canadian citizen for most of his life.

He is a graduate of the Alberta College of Art's sculpture program (1975), and also attended Okanagan College where he studied fine arts.

Peter Smith
(b. 1943)

Peter Smith was born in South Shields, England, during the World War II blitz. He was raised in Luseland, Saskatchewan, then attended the Alberta College of Art in Calgary. He is now a full-time artist working in Calgary.

Robert Spaetgens
(see John Crate and Robert Spaetgens)

Robert Stowell
(b. 1941)

Born and educated in Calgary, Robert Stowell is a graduate of the Alberta College of Art (1971), majoring in sculpture and painting. He has instructed at the University of Calgary, the Alberta College of Art and the Form and Function Design Academy. He was closely associated with the creation of the Prehistoric Park at the Calgary Zoo, where he was responsible for construction of part of the hoodoo and badlands formations. He also designed and supervised some of the bas-relief murals in the zoo underpass and LRT plaza, as well as the very visible elephant and bird railings on the Memorial Drive overpass to the Calgary Zoo.

The artist has exhibited in many Calgary shows and is the winner of the 1987 David Crowchild competition award. He also has a keen interest in music and, for a short time, was a music teacher. He is presently a member of the Calgary Philharmonic Chorus.

Laszlo Szilvassy
(b. 1925)

From the age of three years, Hungarian-born Szilvassy was determined to be an artist, and later assured that this ambition would become a reality by studying architecture and art at the University of Budapest. He then studied stage design and lighting at the Hungarian State Opera House, before emigrating to England in 1948.

He worked in the ballet world in England (Sadler Wells, Ballet Rambert, London Ballet and Ballet Workshop) as designer, artist and art director. As well, he exhibited drawings, paintings, marbles, silver works and vitreous enamels at various London galleries.

In 1967 he came to Canada, gaining admission as a photographer. He worked as a still photographer in the motion picture industry, including a movie for Disney in the foothills near Calgary. Since 1975 he has completed commissions for many corporate clients, and his paintings, murals and bronzes are also in private collections from Vancouver to Jerusalem.

He now lives in Tweed, Ontario.

James Thomson
(1858 -1924)

The man who gave Calgary its lions was born in Scotland and lived there until he and his wife followed their four grown sons to Calgary. They arrived in the Alberta city not long before World War I.

It was not a happy move for the elder Thomson, who had been a respected craftsman in Scotland. There was little work for a stonemason in Calgary, and he spent most of his working life as a laborer for the City of Calgary.

In addition to the lions on Centre Street Bridge, he created the Indian heads that decorate the Bow River Bridge in Banff, Alberta.

James Thomson died in Calgary on February 24, 1924.

Susan Velder

(b. 1939)

Susanna Thalheimer Velder lived in Calgary from 1970 to 1986. She is a graduate of the Alberta College of Art sculpture program and also attained a diploma in art education from the University of Calgary. She has received a number of awards and has taken part in many solo and group shows. Several large commissions can be found in churches in Saskatchewan and Alberta, and her works are also in corporate and private collections.

She presently lives and works in St. Walburg, Saskatchewan.

Marjorie Walrond

(b. 1932)

This Alberta artist was born in Innisfail and graduated from the Alberta College of Art (1984) and the University of Calgary (1986), where she majored in sculpture and ceramics.

Her works have been included in a number of shows, including Artworks in the Public Domain, Culpepper Ceramic Show, the Leighton Foundation Show, Women in the Arts Showcase, and the Marion Nicoll Gallery Alumni Show at the Alberta College of Art in 1990.

Tom Ward

(1910-1984)

A self-taught artist, Ward came to Alberta from Ontario in 1937, lured west by the Aberhart government's promise of a guaranteed income for all Albertans. He worked at odd jobs until the outbreak of World War II when he enlisted in the Calgary Tanks Unit.

He returned to post-war Calgary and became a civil servant, first in the tax assessment, then in the planning and public information departments at City Hall.

When he retired in 1975, he began a challenging new career with the provincial government as park historian at Fish Creek Provincial Park in south Calgary. As well, his interest in native Indians inspired a new hobby — carving knobby burls from Alberta trees into figures and faces inspired by the Indian legends he loved. Many of these could be found on the walls of the Fish Creek interpretive centre while he was employed there, but they now have been relocated to Devonian Gardens.

John Barney Weaver

(b. 1920)

Born in Anoconda, Montana, the son of a distinguished artist, John Weaver, LLD (honoris causa), graduated from the Art Institute of Chicago and later taught at the Layton School of Art in Milwaukee. He was curator of the Montana Historical Society for five years.

A prolific artist, he has produced numerous busts and dioramas. During a five-year period with the Smithsonian Institute, he produced twenty-seven life-size figures, along with a number of heads and smaller works. He has sculpted several heroic bronze statues, including one of Wayne Gretzky, and of such notables as U.S. first ladies Jacqueline Kennedy and Lady Bird Johnston. Among his best works is a bronze sculpture of Charles M. Russell in Washington, D.C.

He came to Canada in 1966 and founded the John Weaver Sculpture Museum in Edmonton in 1977, where he produced many public artworks.

His sculptures are found in public places in countries throughout the world. In Alberta, they may be found in Calgary, Red Deer, and Edmonton. In addition to the pieces found in this book, he has to his credit two portrait sculptures in Calgary: Grant MacEwan, found in the Grant MacEwan Library in City Hall; and Sam Livingston, at the Sam Livingston Fish Hatchery in east Calgary.

Weaver is now a Canadian citizen and resides in Hope, British Columbia.

Ross Weaver

(b. 1947)

Weaver was born in Calgary and studied sculpture for four years at the Alberta College of Art and the Institute Allende, San Miguel, Mexico. He now lives in Millarville and one of his sculptures, *Crucifixion*, may be found in the churchyard of Christ Church in that community.

Nels Weismose

(1904 - 1972)

Nels Weismose was the son of a finishing carpenter specializing in stairwells. Born in Denmark, Weismose came to Calgary where he established a high-quality furniture shop featuring handcrafted pieces.

He enjoyed wood carving all his life and estimated an average project to take about 100 hours. A recognized artist in his field, his works appear in Sharon Lutheran Church, 210 - 10th Avenue N.E.; Faith Lutheran Church, 1909 - 19th Avenue N.W., and in such faraway places as Anchorage, Alaska, Winnipeg, Edmonton, and the NASA Space Centre in Houston, Texas.

Harold Weiss

(b. 1943)

Weiss, who was raised and educated in Morden, Manitoba, has always been interested in drawing. He studied at the Alberta College of Art for four year as a mature student, taking three years of sculpture and one of ceramics.

Since graduating from ACA, he has been kept busy "raising a family and paying a mortage," and has not been very active in the field of art. However he has produced some ceramic pieces, and one was selected to appear in the *Clay in the Windows Exposition* in Calgary in 1988.

Colette Whiten

(b. 1945)

This sculptor was born in Birmingham, England. She is a graduate of the Ontario College of Art, and was the recipient of the Governor General's Award in 1972. Her work usually embodies the nature of human existence in a wide variety of experiences.

Examples of her artistry are on display in many locations, including the National Art Gallery in Ottawa and the Art Gallery of Ontario, as well as in Calgary. She is a resident of Toronto, Ontario.

Irene F. Whittome
(b. 1942)

Born in Vancouver, the artist studied first at the Vancouver School of Art, then later was a student of Stanley William Hayter at Atelier 17 in Paris.

Since the late 1960s, she has lived and worked in Montreal, where she is a professor at Concordia University and also pursues private artistic projects.

A mixed-media artist, she has received many national and international awards and has held solo exhibitions in Paris, Brussels, London, New York and Tokyo, as well as in numerous Canadian cities. Her work has also been part of group exhibitions throughout the world. It is found in many private and public collections, and is often included in art publications.

Her most recent solo exhibition was *Le Musée des Traces*, which began as the artist's private anthropological collection. Over a period of four years, it grew into the larger, public installation showcased at the Art Gallery of Ontario in 1991. Part of her inspiration for the Calgary work came from this source.

James Willer
(b. 1921)

Jim Willer was born in the borough of Fulham, London, England, and received his art education at the Hornsey School of Art, London; the Winnipeg School of Art; and the Royal Academy, Amsterdam.

Commenting on his forty-year career in art he says, "I received great encouragement from, and owe my two year stay in Europe . . . to Lawren Harris who supported my application for a Canadian Overseas Award to the Netherlands in 1954."

Willer's is a multifaceted talent, and he has received honors for sculpting, painting and literary achievement. His novel *Paramind*, published in 1973, shared first prize in the competition "Canada 2000 A.D." Public and private collections across Canada contain his artworks, and his sculptures and murals may be found in Vancouver, Calgary and Winnipeg. Willer lives in Errington, British Columbia.

Hollis Williford
(b. 1940)

This respected Western artist was born in the hill country of north central Texas. When he was five years old, his dad gave him a penknife, and Williford whittled and carved "little things out of pecans," a humble beginning to a successful career in the arts.

After graduating from high school, he attended three years at the University of Texas in Arlington (arts major and English minor), then worked for a time in the aerospace industry as a technical illustrator and graphic artist while continuing his education as a night student. In 1970 he graduated with a BA from the Art Center College of Design in Los Angeles.

He chose to settle in Loveland, Colorado, near the foothills of the Rockies, but his sculptures, drawings and paintings enjoy national and international exhibitions and sales.

At the 1988 National Academy of Western Art Show, Williford won the "Best of the West" award. Two of his sculptures have been awarded the prestigious *Prix de West* by the Cowboy Hall of Fame, and he is one of only two artists to be so honored.

Alice Winant

(1928 - 1989)

Born in Romania, Winant (nee Czitron) left school at age fourteen and apprenticed to a photographer. She soon owned her own small studio. In 1944 she and members of her family were among 5 000 Jews taken from their homes and herded in cattle cars to Auschwitz.

After surviving the horrors of the holocaust, she spent two years in hospital but never completely regained her health. While in hospital, she discovered her talent for sculpture and her artistic career began.

During her lifetime she created more than 3 000 sculptures, and both art critics and admirers praised her for mirroring gratitude for survival, rather than anguish over suffering.

Her work, mostly in bronze, can be seen in public and private collections worldwide. She exhibited extensively in Canada, the United States, Europe and Japan.

Stanislaw Wyspianski

(1869-1907)

This artist, poet and dramatist was born and died in Krakow, Poland. He studied classical literature and fine arts and, in 1890, received a grant to visit the art cities of western and central Europe. He was a professor at the Krakow Academy of Fine Arts until 1905 and was famous for his paintings and for his visionary and dramatic designs for stained glass windows.

Vilem Zach

(b.1946)

Born in Prague, Czechoslovakia, Zach began sketching and modelling in clay as a child. He studied privately with a respected painter while learning a trade in a culinary school. This latter proved a useful talent when he arrived in Canada, but he was able to give up his chef's job in 1978 and devote full time to his art.

Zach's admiration for the work of Nicholas de Grandmaison is reflected in his portraits of Canada's aboriginal people, many of which were done in his early years in Calgary.

In 1976 his interest began to focus on sculpting, and his work is done almost exclusively in bronze using the lost wax method. He most commonly depicts a larger-than-life Western theme and his works are often of heroic proportions. Each bronze bears a seal mark taken from a ring which belonged to his great grandfather. Frequently he produces a limited number of miniatures of a large sculpture.

Vilem Zach has won many prizes in exhibitions in North America, and his works can be viewed in public locations in Calgary, Banff (Banff Springs Hotel), Lake Louise (Chateau Lake Louise), and Ottawa.

artifact: simple and practical object showing human workmanship

bas-relief: type of sculpture in which the figures project only slightly from the background

bust: sculpture representing the upper part of a human figure, including head, neck and usually part of the shoulders and breast

heroic size: 1 ⅓ life size

kinetic: capable of motion

lost wax technique: process dating from ancient Egypt and Assyria. A negative wax mold is made from a plaster or clay model, then liquid metal is poured into the "lost wax" molds

lumetric: a sculpture with light as a major component

maquette: usually small, preliminary model of a sculpture

mobile: construction or sculpture with parts that can be set in motion by air currents

monumental size: larger than life size

mosaic: inlaid work composed of bits of stone, glass, etc., formed into a pattern or picture

mural: painting or decoration applied to, and made integral with, a wall

obelisk: upright, four-sided pillar that gradually tapers as it rises until it terminates in a pyramid

patina: green film either formed naturally on copper and bronze by long exposure to the elements or added artificially, often by the use of acid

sculpture: artwork produced by carving, modelling or welding

signature sculpture: three-dimensional work of art designed to present a significant element to its chosen site

statue: human or animal figure produced by sculpting, modelling or casting, especially when life size or larger

structurist: a direction dealing with a three-dimensional extension of early cubist principles

tactile: inviting touch

Index

644.89, 134
A.J. Diamond and Partners 140
ACA (see Alberta College of Art)
Agriculture Canada 21
Al-Shaikhly 57, 173
Alberta Art Foundation 24, 25
Alberta College of Art 111, 117, 118, 119, 120, 175, 176, 177, 179, 180, 181, 182, 183, 187, 189, 191, 193, 198, 199, 200, 201
Alberta Family 101
Alberta Government Telephones 9, 10, 12
Alberta Hotel Building 12
Alberta Natural Gas Company 46
Alberta Science Centre 91-94,
Alberta Wheat Pool 54
Amoco Centre 45-48
Andersen, Hans Christian 13
Aquitaine Company 87, 178
Aquitaine Landscape 78
Aquitaine Tower 76-78,
Archimedean 165
Armengol, Mario 22, 173
Arnatt, Ray 24, 197, 173
Art Gallery of Ontario 26, 145, 201, 202
Ashes to Life 167
Ashevak, Karoo 67, 173-174
Astman, Barbara 148, 174
Athlete, The 145,
Aurora Borealis 14
Badord, Jacqueline 76, 174
Balancing Act 39
Bank of Canada 74
Bank of Montreal 70, 106, 186
Bankers Hall 71, 72
Baxter, Brian 86, 147, 174
Bayes, Gilbert 68, 174
Bears, The 37
Bears 102
Beaver and Fallen Tree 40
Begg, Don 40, 85, 168, 169, 174-175
Bell, Robin C. H. 63, 175
Bentham, Doug 17, 122, 175
Bergeron, Germain 142, 175
Besant, Derek 114, 115, 175-176
Bethany Care Centre 170
Bird in Flight 97
Bird of Spring 62
Bleifeld, Stanley 101, 176
Bloodhound and Retriever 66
Bloom, Tony 154, 176
Blowing 136
Boer War Memorial 108
Bonet, Jordi 93, 176-177
Book Totems 109
Boucher, Gaetan 142
Boundary Waters 83
Bow River Bridge, Banff 200
Bow Valley Square 49-52, 181
Boy and Girl Fishing 59
Boy and Swan 69
Boyce, Bob 141, 165, 177
Bread Wall 20
Brigadier General Andrew Hamilton Gault 168
Britamco Club 112
Bronc Twister 105
Bronze Spaceflower 11
Brotherhood of Mankind 22
Brothers of the Wind 146
Buffalo Grass and Tumbleweed 98
Buffalo Trails 81
Builders, The 88
Burgess, Catherine 133, 177
Burns, Isla 25, 135, 177
Calgary and District Dental Association 93
Calgary Board of Education 22, 193
Calgary Catholic Board of Education 29
Calgary Centennial Planetarium (see Alberta Science Centre)
Calgary Centre for Performing Arts 24-28, 175
Calgary Convention Centre 10, 11, 12, 13
Calgary Education Centre 22
Calgary Exhibition and Stampede 85, 104-106, 192, 196
Calgary House 80
Calgary Jaycees 10, 70, 106
Calgary Jewish Centre 167
Calgary Labour Council 91
Calgary Municipal Building (see Municipal Building)
Calgary Olympic Development Committee 162
Calgary Revitalization Zone 42, 81
Calgary Zoo 103, 182, 185, 186, 199
Calka, Maurice 78, 178
Campbell, Dr. William 14
Canada Council 177, 180, 187, 193
Canada Council Art Bank 27; 177; 180, 187
Canadian Hunter Exploration Ltd. 83
Canada Olympic Park 21, 43
Canadian Broadcasting Corporation 158
Carlsburg Arts Foundation 13
Carved Wood Plaques 94
Cascade Developments 160
Cascade Group 85
Cathedral Evening 122
CBC (see Canadian Broadcasting Corporation)
Central Memorial High School 180
Central Park 107, 108

Centre Street Bridge 8, 200
Century Gardens 100-102, 191
Charlotte, Jane 60, 178
Chief David Crowchild Memorial Sculpture 35
Children's Commemorative Obelisk 29
Chomistek Joe 21, 178
Christensen, Judi 152, 178
Citizen of the Century 10
Cityscape 86
Coat of Arms 21
CODA (see Calgary Olympic Development Committee)
Cohos, Evamy Architects 165
Colonel Macleod Chapter IODE, 107, 108
Colonel Walker Mini Park 12
Comcheq Services Inc. 27
Comet 111
Condon, Jimmy 125, 155
Confederation Park 112, 179
Conic Free Form 129
Conversation 53, 151
Copernicus 99
Copper Wall 77
Cork Mural 54
Court House 81
Cracked Pot Fountains 96
Crate, John 128, 179
Cruise, Stephen 131, 179
Cummings, Robert M. 22
Dancer 36
Danish Canadian Club 13
Davidson, Robert 47, 179
Deerfoot 160
Deerfoot Mall 160-163
Devonian Gardens 15, 56-70, 173, 200
Devonian Foundation, The (see Devonian Group)
Devonian Group of Charitable Foundations, The 15, 23, 33, 36, 37, 40, 62, 67, 101, 196
Dinny the Dinosaur 103
DiPalma, Enzo 98, 112, 179
Discobolus III 138
Dive 27
Drahanchuk, Ed 126, 139, 179-180
Drohan Walt 116, 180
Ducks 98
Duet 24
Earthprobe 193
Edgecombe Properties 79
Eloul, Kosso 89, 180
Emergence 119
ENCOR Building 85
Encounter 151
Endless Totem 27
Energy Resources Conservation Board 82
Engineering Institute of Canada Wives Club of Calgary 129
Enigma 114
Eriksen, Edvard 13, 180
Esler, Annemarie Schmid 19, 180-181
Esso Resources 193
Etrog, Sorel 26, 49-52, 181
Etungat, Abraham 62, 181-182
Faculty of Management, University of Calgary 123
Faith, Alan 57, 173
Faith Lutheran Church 201
Family of Horses 38
Firetell 131
First Jewels 65
Flames 45
Flying Dreams 55
Fodchuk, Kathryn 111, 182
Foothills Hospital, Special Services Building 151-154
Friendship 73
Frontiersman - Elephant Hunter 64
Galaxy 74
Garden Terrace 11, 13
Gargoyles 12
Gatekeeper 25
Genesis 152
Geological Survey of Canada 150
Gilhooly, David 20, 182
Glenbow Exterior Murals 16
Glenbow-Alberta Institute 15, 192
Glenbow Museum 14, 15, 35, 64, 106, 175, 181, 184, 198
Government of Canada Building (see Harry Hays Building)
Grace Presbyterian Church 193
Grant MacEwan Library 201
Greyhound Building 12
Greyhound Bus Terminal 12
Guardian 63
Gurevich family 34
Harry Hays Building 17-21
Harvie, Donald 37, 101
Harvie, Eric 15, 56, 59, 92, 156, 185
Hayden, Michael 27, 46, 182-183
Hebert, Louis Phillipe 107, 183
Heimbecker, Steven 137, 183
Herald Building 12
Heroic Entrance 148
Hilton, Charles 73, 183
Hippocrates 155
Hoffman, Malvina 64, 183-184
Homage 115
Houston, James 14, 184
Hudson's Bay Oil and Gas 126
Hunter, John 85
Icarus 75
ICU 104
Inglewood Community Association 70

Inuit Man 67
Jack Singer Concert Hall 24
Jacks 18
Jackson, Charles D'Orville Pilkington 156, 184-185
James Short Park 42
Jekill, Peter 28,
Jekyll, Robert 28, 46, 185
Jensdotter, Hansina 118
Johnson, J. Seward Jr. 33, 100, 185-186
Jones, Garry 44, 186
Joy 34
Jubilee Auditorium 156, 157, 191
Just a Taste 186
Kabuki 49
Kanerva, John 103, 186
Karlik, Pierre 87, 186-187
Kiefer, Gernot 42, 187
Killer Whales 47
Kipps, Paul 71, 140, 187
Koshetz 157
Kostyniuk, Ron 48, 187-188
La Patineur de Vitesse '84; The Speedskater 142
Landscape 86
Landseer, Sir Edwin 66, 188
Leadbeater, Roy 9, 11, 34, 39, 74, 75, 84, 132, 158, 162, 167, 188
Leycraft, Kevan 55, 79, 188-189
Libin family, 34
Library Frieze 31
Library Book, The 32
Life's Journey 123
Light Rain 44
Lions, The 8
Little Mermaid, The 13
Locus VII 133
Lord Strathcona Driving the Last Spike 169
Lord Strathcona's Horse Regiment 107, 169
Lost in Flight 59
Lotus #1 170
Loving Peace, Anubhava 152, 189
MacCarthy, Coeur-de-Leon 108, 189
Mah, Bill 130
Maiden and Four Toads 68
Malik, Shamas 123, 189
Mannequins 161
Map of Canada 21
Maple Seeds 9
Marathon Realty 44
Marshall, Mark V. 12, 190
Martha Cohen Theatre 28
Mating Dance 79
Max Bell Theatre 27
Maxwell Cummings and Sons 22
McElcheran, William 53, 151, 190
McKenzie, Robert 145, 146, 190-191
McLeod, Ben 134, 191
Memories 48
Moen, Doug 138, 191
Mol, Leo 102, 157, 191
Moonstairs 76
Mother and Children 90
Mount Royal College 114, 115, 188
Municipal Building 33-37, 39, 140
Municipal Plaza 38, 39
Museum of the Regiments 168, 169
Mihailescu-Nasturel Prince Monyo, 36, 192
National Bank Building 75
Natural Harmonics No. 12 57
Nickle Arts Museum 132, 176, 197
Nickle, Carl 132
Nicoll, Marion and Jim 170
Nimmons Cairn 110
Nimmons Park 110
Nirvana 137
Norcen Energy Resources 53
Norris, George 124, 191-192
Nova Corporation, The 89, 90
Nova Gate 89
Nova Building 89, 90
O'Brien, Hazel 10, 192
O'Hanlon, Harry 38, 192
Ohe, Katie 96, 110, 127, 129, 150, 170, 193
Oldrich, Bob 16, 31, 54, 91, 193
Olympia and York 46
Olympic Arch 140
Olympic Oval 141-148
Olympic Plaza 23
Olympic Runner 23
Olympics 21, 23, 43, 140, 141-148, 162, 176, 181, 190-191
Others, The 93
Our Land - Our Future; Alberta Farm Family 70, 106
Out West 171
Oxford Development Group 73
Pagoglyphs (Marks on Ice) 147
Pan and the Three Graces 80
PanCanadian Plaza 44
Panneok, David 90, 194
Past, Present and Future 42
Pavropoulos, Nikolas 125, 155, 194
Petro-Canada 43
Petro-Canada Building 43
Pieces of Eight 132
Plate Wall 19
Pleistocene Wedge 117
Pocket Jungle 154
Pod 30
Porte Cochère de Lumière 46
Prairie Collage 98
Prairie Farm Rehabilitation Administration 21
Prairie Progression 98

Pratt, George 88, 194
Prince, Richard 82, 194
Prince's Island Park 96-99
Princess Patricia's Canadian Light Infantry 168
Proch, Don 143, 195
RCA, (see Royal Canadian Academy of Arts)
Rani 135
Red Cross Society 166
Red Cross Mural 166
Reynolds, Alan 136, 195
Rhinn, J. Massey 92, 195-196
Rhythm One 139
Ritual Head 51
Robert the Bruce 15, 156
Robinson, John 59, 196
Rocky Mountain Mining Mask 143
Rockyview Hospital 40
Roenisch, Rich 104, 105, 196
Royal Canadian Academy of Arts (RCA) 175, 180, 181, 190, 192,
Rushman 50
Sabatier of Paris 77, 196
Sable, Suzanne 37, 196
Sadko 49
St. Michael the Archangel Catholic Church 193
SAIT (see Southern Alberta Institute of Technology)
Sam Livingston Fish Hatchery 201
Saxe, Henry 18, 196-197
Schachtel, JoAnne 24, 81, 197
Scriver, Bob 15, 197-198
Sculptured Wall Panel 128
Seibens, W.W. 105
Selkirk House 79
Serpentine 138
Share the Flame 43
Sharon Lutheran Church 201
Sheftel, Leo and Goldie 11, 34
Shell Canada Resources Limited 111
Silas, Rick 32, 109, 171, 198
Sitting Eagle 85
Sadowska-Siwinski, Krystyna 80, 198
Smalley, Steven 30, 198
Smith, Peter 97, 199
So the Bishop Said to the Actress 33
Soapstone Carving 87
Society of Directors of Physical Education in Colleges 145
Sophocles, Plato and Krito 125
Source 52
Southam, family 12, 190
Southern Alberta Institute of Technology (SAIT) 12, 116, 117, 118, 188
Southern, Marg 38
Spaetgens, Robert 128, 199
Spectral Arch, 28
Speedskater, The 144
Spire 141
Spirit of the Winter Olympics 162
Stampede Park 104-106
Steel Wave 158
Steeples 84
Stephen Avenue Mall 53, 62, 67
Story on a Summer's Day 59
Stowell, Robert 35, 199
Sunbird II 26
Sundial 91
Szilvassy, Laszlo 45, 199
Thomson, James L. 199-200
Tompkins Park 109
Trader, The 163
TransCanada PipeLines Ltd. 140
Transition '67 112
Treasury Branch Building 12
Tree of Life 153
Tribute to Land 72
Ukrainian Canadian Committee 157
University of Calgary 12, 60, 121-148, 173, 175, 177, 178, 179, 180, 182, 183, 188, 189, 189, 193, 197, 199, 200
University of Toronto 181, 187, 190
Untitled pieces 17, 60, 116, 118, 120, 124, 126, 130, 150
Velder, Susan 119, 200
Venus at her Bath 58
W.R. Castell Central Library 31
Walker, Colonel James 10
Walrond, Marjorie 117, 200
Ward, Tom 61, 200
Weather Vanes 71
Weaver, John 144, 162, 163, 200-201
Weaver, Ross 153, 201
Weismose, Nels 94, 201
Weiss, Harold 120, 201
Western Canadian Place 86-88
Whiten, Charlotte 71, 140, 201
Whittome, Irene F. 202
Willer, James 166, 202
Williford, Hollis 83, 202
Winant, Alice 65, 203
Winner, The 100
Wolfe, General James 15, 92
Wonderful Energy Machine, The 82
Wood Carvings 61
World War I Memorial 107
Wyspianski, Stanislaw 99, 203
Zach, Vilem 43, 70, 106, 203
Zipper, 127